Programmed Learning Aid for
SOCIAL PROBLEMS

Programmed learning aid for

SOCIAL PROBLEMS

ROBERT L. HORTON
Idaho State University

Coordinating Editor
ROGER H. HERMANSON
Georgia State University

LEARNING SYSTEMS COMPANY

 A division of
RICHARD D. IRWIN, INC.　Homewood, Illinois　60430

Also available through
IRWIN-DORSEY INTERNATIONAL　London, England　WC2H 9NJ
IRWIN-DORSEY LIMITED　Georgetown, Ontario　L7G 4B3

© LEARNING SYSTEMS COMPANY, 1975

All rights reserved. No part of this publication may be reproduced, stored in a retrieval system, or transmitted, in any form or by any means, electronic, mechanical, photocopying, recording, or otherwise, without the prior written permission of the publisher.

ISBN 0-256-01483-3

Printed in the United States of America

1 2 3 4 5 6 7 8 9 0 K 4 3 2 1 0 9 8 7 6 5

PREFACE

Within the last decade a wide variety of textbooks and readers on social problems has been introduced to the academic community. Most of the texts use a single theoretical orientation for the analysis of social problems, and most readers seek to present different radical perspectives about social problems. In this text I have sought to do something different than the others: (1) to present the four major theoretical orientations for the analysis of social problems, specifically, social disorganization, value conflict, personal deviation, and the new emerging perspective of social conflict; (2) to provide a brief but concise description of how different sociological theories and perspectives can be applied to the study of social problems, and (3) to provide substantive information about some of the most critical social problems to allow students to grasp the current issues and thought of sociologists.

Although social problems are taught at the freshman or sophomore level in most colleges, they are not easy subjects to analyze. Most people are confused and easily become frustrated when they attempt to understand and sort out the issues in modern social problems. Today's social problems represent a wide variety of concerns that some things in our society are not as they should be, that inequities and inequalities in society should be changed, and that something should be done to improve the quality of life in society. They represent the confusion over rapid social change, the "future shock" of technological change, and the fear that in our society moral standards and ethics are degenerating.

This text explains how social problems are created by man, and *can* be controlled by man if he is willing to incur the cost. The task is not easy or simple, but it is not beyond the ability of man to take rational action and use technological innovation to remedy most social problems. In most cases, it is agreeing on the decision to take positive and constructive action that is the limiting factor.

This PLAID is designed to present information about the different theoretical perspectives and social problems in capsule form. As such, this text should be useful to:

1. Students in an introductory course in social problems, either as a basic text with supplementary readers or lectures added, or as a supplementary text to balance the content of textbooks that present only a single theoretical perspective.
2. Students who wish to gain background information about current social problems for other courses in the social sciences.
3. Graduate students who have not taken a basic course in social problems, and wish to strengthen their background for other courses in the social sciences.
4. All persons who wish to improve their knowledge of the world in which we live.

The programmed sequence of this PLAID allows each student to progress at his or her own pace, and test themselves without the pressure of the classroom situation. Students should consider the following suggestions for its use:

1. If the text is used as a basic or supplementary text, follow the instructor's organization of the course. After the initial section on the theory and definition of social problems, the chapters may be read independently to coincide with the instructor's organization of the course.
2. Carefully check the test questions at the end of each frame, and if you answered any of the questions incorrectly, reread the appropriate section in the text.
3. Occasionally refer back to the first three chapters of the text to refresh your understanding of the definition of social problems and the different theoretical perspectives. With each review, these concepts tend to assume a new and greater meaning.
4. At the end of each three chapters, complete the section examination at the end of the book to test your general comprehension of the material.
5. Although every attempt has been made to present as much information as possible in each chapter, this brief text cannot possibly cover all dimensions of each social problem. The reader is encouraged to refer to additional sources where more information is desired.

The author expresses deep appreciation to Dr. Paul Horton and Dr. Beverly Benson for their editorial assistance in writing this PLAID.

ROBERT L. HORTON

TOPICAL OUTLINE OF COURSE CONTENT

Alcoholism, 63–64
Alternate life styles, 25
American Dilemma (The), 47–48
Basic sociological concepts, 8–12
Changing level of expectations, 113
Civil rights and liberties, 123–26
Communities, rural and urban, 103–4
Consciousness levels and attitudes, 36–38
Contact, role in reducing prejudice, 45–46
Crime, 67–79
Criminal statistics, 71–73
Demographic transition, theory of, 98–99
Deschooling society, 91
Deviance, 19–20, 60–66, 107
Ecological laws, 111–12
Education, philosophies of, 89–90
Eugenics movement, 99
Gemeinschaft-gesellschaft communities, 104–5
Generation gap, between youth and adults, 34–36
Labeling theory, 19
Learning theory, of deviance, 61–62
Minority-majority group dominance, 49–50
Modern family, 23–25
Observability and anonymity, 107

Organized crime, 69–70
Personal deviation approach to social problems 19–20
Political groups, rightist and leftist, 126–27
Population control, demographic factors, 95–97
Population control theories, 97–100
Poverty, 53–59
Power groups, 120–21
Prejudice and stereotypes, 41–47
Racial groups, 41–42
Religions, 81–88
Sexual deviation, 64–66
Social change, 10
Social conflict approach to social problems, 17–18
Social disorganization approach to social problems, 13–14
Social problems, 1–8
Traditional family, 21–23
Value conflict approach to social problems, 15–16
Vested interest and pressure groups, 116–19
Vicious circle of discrimination, 47–48
Women, changing roles and status, 29–30
Women's liberation movement, 31–33
Youth movement, 38–39

CONTENTS

1. The Theory of Social Problems 1
2. Sociological Concepts 8
3. Conceptual Approaches to Social Problems 13
4. Problems of the Family 21
5. Women in Modern Society 28
6. The Youth Movement 34
7. Minority Groups: Prejudices and Stereotypes 41
8. Minority Groups: Adaptation and Reform 47
9. Poverty 53
10. Social Deviance 60
11. Crime in Society 67
12. Theories and Treatment of Criminality 74
13. Religion 81
14. Education 89
15. Population 95
16. Urban and Rural Communities 103
17. Ecology and the Environment 109
18. Vested Interests and Pressure Groups 116
19. Civil Rights and Civil Liberties 123
Examination 1: Chapters 1–3 131
Examination 2: Chapters 4–6 134
Examination 3: Chapters 7–9 137
Examination 4: Chapters 10–12 139
Examination 5: Chapters 13–15 141
Examination 6: Chapters 16–19 143
Answers to Examinations 146
Glossary/Index 151

chapter 1

THE THEORY OF SOCIAL PROBLEMS

Frame 1[1]

Social problems have plagued man's conscience since the origin of modern civilization. Social problems are products of man's culture, of his relations with other men, and of his personal behavior.

Currently, our nation is divided over civil rights, racial and social inequality, and the treatment of the poor. America is disturbed over ascending crime rates, the growth of drug subcultures, and violence in the streets. People are confused over problems of overpopulation, urban congestion, the growth of the military-industrial complex. Alarm is expressed over change in family values and moral standards. Where do we turn to understand the nature of these problems? Why do they exist? What is the impact of these problems upon the "American way of life"? These questions are the province of the sociology of social problems.

Social problems are products of the collective conscience of man. They represent the shared concern of people that certain conditions in society are not as they should be. Should poverty exist within the richest nation on earth? Many people feel it should not. Should any group or race of people in a democratic nation be denied their right to a decent job, a comfortable home, or an education? Our constitution has repeatedly been interpreted by the courts to imply that equal rights and opportunities should be available to every person. Thus when people become concerned about social inequities in their society, and feel that something should be done to correct them, then inequality becomes a social problem.

The amorphous nature of social problems makes it difficult to specify an exact number of social problems, but one could easily compile a list of over a hundred major social concerns of the American people. The news media serves as an excellent indice of the current status of various social problems and gives an indication of which are the most pressing problems. Any social concern that attracts the attention of many journalists and appears regularly in the news media would qualify as a social problem.

However, just as a series of photographs fails to portray the full essence of a person's life, a listing or description of current social problems does not give us a full understanding of social problems in general. For this, we must learn the nature of social problems themselves.

DEFINITION OF A SOCIAL PROBLEM

Sociologists disagree upon whether social problems should be defined by the public or by the experts. Popular definition holds that a social problem is anything about which there is widespread popular concern. Expert definition designates as a social problem any condition or development which social scientists recognize as disorganizing or disruptive to people or to the society. By popular definition, communist subversion was probably our greatest social problem in the 1950s, while population growth attracted little popular concern; expert opinion would have exactly reversed this order. One sociologist sought to resolve this difficulty by accepting the popular definition of social problems, while identifying as *societal problems* those which the experts recognized as threatening to the society. [Robert A. Nisbet, *The Social Bond* (New York: Alfred A. Knopf, Inc., 1970), 18–19.] His distinction, while logically sound, has not been widely followed. Most social problem textbooks seek to straddle the issue by including "problems" as defined by both definitions.

One widely used textbook defines social problems as *"a condition affecting a significant number of people in ways considered undesirable about which it is felt that something should be done through collective social action."* [Paul B. Horton and Gerald R. Leslie, *The Sociology of Social Problems,* 5th ed. (Englewood Cliffs, N.J.: Prentice-Hall, Inc., 1974), 4.]

Social problems represent complex patterns of social behavior, thus are not easily described. Let us examine each element of the definition more thoroughly.

A condition. Social problems are created by men as they carry out the normal process of living in society, thus they are *social in origin* and not products of nature or of supernatural powers. Man can do nothing about the forces of nature or acts of God. He cannot prevent an earthquake or a hurricane (at least not yet). He can only react to the ravages of natural disasters.

But man can do something about poverty, crime in the streets, and racial inequality. He can build better hospitals, schools, and provide for the aged. Only the conditions that are created by man and that man can change become social problems. Thus social problems are *normal* products of man living in a civilized society.

The conditions that become social problems must also have *some degree of permanency.* A flash of lightning that knocks out electrical service in a community is a temporary inconvenience that is soon forgotten by the few people affected. But repeated "brown-outs" and shortages of natural fuels affecting the activity of millions of people throughout the years creates a permanent inconvenience. Thus, the energy crisis in America becomes a very real social problem.

Affecting a significant number of people. The late C. Wright Mills provides some guidance in selecting between personal troubles and public issues. [C. Wright Mills, *The Sociological Imagination* (New York: Grove Press, Inc., 1959), Chap. 1.] When one man in a city is unemployed, it is his personal problem to find a job; but when an economic recession causes unemployment for thousands of men throughout the nation, unemployment becomes a public issue. Social problems generally extend beyond the local community, state, or region to affect the whole society. Thus a major portion of the society's population must be affected before a social problem is created.

In ways considered undesirable. The objective conditions may exist for a considerable time without being recognized or specified as a social problem. For centuries people in European cities used to dump their chamber pots, garbage, and dead animals in the streets. It is claimed that in some cities the residents had to add upper stories to their houses when the layers of decomposing materials rose above the top of their front doors. From the time of Columbus, venereal diseases swept through European communities, ravaging royalty and paupers alike, but VD has been recognized as a social problem for only the last few decades. Many conditions that have recently been recognized as social problems have existed for centuries. Before a condition can be called a "social problem," people must feel that they can and should do something about that condition; the existence of the condition alone does not assure its recognition as a social problem. Until people add the subjective interpretation that the condition is socially undesirable and that something should be done about the objective condition, the awareness of the social problem does not develop in the minds of the general population.

Social problems do not affect everyone alike in that a condition that is disruptive to one person may be viewed as providing an opportunity for another. Ministers and church leaders look upon the climbing divorce rates of recent decades with dismay, but few divorce lawyers are equally concerned. Indeed, some persons may profit from the undesirable conditions. For example, a high rate of unemployment tends to create a cheaper labor for industrialists, loan agencies thrive, and discount stores prosper. Currently, the stock of companies producing pollution control devices is soaring upward in the stock market (while the stock of polluters sours).

Whether a condition is desirable or not depends upon the current values held by the majority of the population, and these values are subject to change through time. The sale of liquor was legal for centuries, was banned during prohibition, then legalized again within a decade. Abortion reform is currently sweeping the nation, and penalties for the possession of marijuana in many states have been reduced from a felony to a misdemeanor. As the social ethnologist Sumner points out, values are never absolute and are relative to the time and cultural beliefs. [William Graham Sumner, *Folkways* (New York: Dover Publications, Inc., 1940).] Thus, people may define almost any condition as a social problem, or change their values to neutralize the stigma of the social problem.

About which something could be done through collective social action. As the historic killers of children were brought under medical control in the 20th century, polio moved to the front as the major killer and crippler of children. Parents united in an "all-out" campaign against the dreaded disease—children contributed dimes from their allowances, and mothers marched for dollars to finance research upon the dreaded virus. Here we see the combination of the elements which made polio into a national social problem: an awareness of an undesirable condition, a feeling that something could be done (that research would provide a cure, if given adequate funds), and a feeling that if only enough people would support the project, the problem of polio could be solved.

But why has not there been a similar campaign mounted against the common cold, which affects even a greater population every year? The answer lies within the last part of the definition above. Most people accept the current medical opinion that research will not find a cure for the common cold in the foreseeable future, and that even if a national campaign were mounted, it would not be effective. Thus the common cold seems too resistant to solution to be recognized as a social problem.

Indicate whether each of the following statements is true or false by writing "T" or "F" in the space provided.

_____ 1. A social concern must be shared by a wide variety of people before it becomes a social problem.
_____ 2. Only experts can tell what are the real social problems.
_____ 3. Social problems are normal and expected conditions for a complex industrialized society.
_____ 4. Everyone agrees that all social problems are undesirable.

Now turn to Answer frame 1[1] on page 4 to check your answers.

Frame 2[1]

THE ORIGIN OF SOCIAL PROBLEMS

Social problems are products of change in complex societies, particularly large populations of people living in industrial-urbanized societies. Early Cro-Magnon man did not experience social problems because his tribal life was simple in form (though not necessarily easy). He was mainly concerned with gathering enough food for survival, finding a comfortable, warm cave to live in, and protecting himself and his family from the elements of nature. He lived

Answer frame 1[1]

1. True. A major proportion of the population must be disturbed about or affected by the condition before a social problem is created.
2. False. Social problems exist by definition—whatever people collectively define as a problem is a social problem. Students can get a good idea of the most important social problems by reviewing magazines and newspapers.
3. True. Since social problems are inevitable products of complex industrialized societies, they are considered as normal and expected.
4. False. What may be undesirable conditions to one person may be desirable or profitable to another, thus there may be considerable disagreement among people as to the undesirability of the social problem.

If you missed any of the above, reread Frame 1[1] before starting Frame 2[1] on page 3. This same procedure should be used throughout the PLAID.

Frame 2[1] continued

in small groups or tribes that did not require any bureaucratic form of organization or government. He lived as his father did through the generations. Today, however, much more social and technological change occurs within one year than Cro-Magnon man experienced in dozens of generations.

Social problems originate in social and cultural change. *Social change* is change in the *organization* of the society—such as the distribution of population, the specialization of labor, the networks of human relationships, the political and administrative structures and bureaucracies. *Cultural change* is change in the norms, values, knowledge systems, goals, and other aspects of the culture of a society. Among cultural changes, *technological change* is most crucial. While all changes in a society are interrelated and interdependent, technological change is most often the driving force that causes changes in other aspects of the culture and society. Technological change and industrial development produce change in the structure of norms and values, while new emerging norms affect the nature of industrialization and technology. For example, the technological development of the automobile has given greater mobility to youth and thus contributed to the reorganization of the modern family. It also influenced the state of industrial development, and allowed the emergence of suburbia in America. Emerging norms for individualism and personal satisfaction have affected standards for premarital sexual behavior, the educational system, and the development of a new industry of leisure. New attitudes toward work are forcing industry to reconsider its procedures. Each of these areas have developed into major problems in the American society.

As change produces the means which make it possible to correct undesirable social conditions, new social concerns are brought to the attention of the people. For example, in preindustrial society, poverty was taken for granted because there were few means to prevent it. However, modern industrialization has produced the economic means (if the people so desire) to alleviate poverty in the American society. The technological development of the "birth control pill" has created moral confusion while the possibility of effective family planning raises new questions and calls for positive decisions in matters which were formerly beyond effective human control. Thus, many social problems are created through social, technological, or organizational change in society.

THE SELECTION OF SOCIAL PROBLEMS

Why are certain conditions selected as social problems while other equally undesirable conditions are not? As stated above, social problems represent the shared concern of people, and people must feel that something can or should be done about the condition through working together. We see above that if the condition does not attract the attention of a large portion of people, or if they do not feel that the condition can be resolved, it does not become a social problem. Scholars have been writing about overpopulation and ecological destruction for decades, but only recently did these topics become social problems. Thus the selection of current social problems is subjective—depending upon the current social concerns of people. This is why we say that social problems represent *subjective interpretations of objective conditions,* and that an undesirable condition will not necessarily become a social problem unless people select it and define it as such.

Further, a condition that is a major concern of people today may lose its importance to people tomorrow. It is even possible for a social problem to lose its popularity and cease to exist as a shared social concern, even though the objective condition may still persist. Thus *poverty* has been a major topic in social problems textbooks ever since their first appearance, but largely disappeared from the textbooks and from the newspapers and popular magazines about 1940, only to be rediscovered in the mid-1960s. There is nothing absolute or permanent about the current selection of social problems, but all problems are relative and dependent upon the current mind and mood of people in society.

Indicate whether each of the following statements is true or false by writing "T" or "F" in the space provided.

_____ 1. Social problems have always existed, even for primitive man.
_____ 2. The primary cause of social problems is social change.
_____ 3. All objectively undesirable conditions in society always become social problems.
_____ 4. Many social problems are the direct result of technological change in society.

Now turn to Answer frame 2[1] on page 6 to check your answers.

Frame 3[1]

STAGES OF A SOCIAL PROBLEM

Although social problems may seem to appear suddenly, Fuller and Myers, in one of the first theoretical essays on social problems, note that social problems actually evolve through a series of stages of growth. [Richard C. Fuller and Richard R. Myers, "The Natural History of a Social Problem," *American Sociological Review,* June 1941, pp. 321–28.] The first stage is the development of *awareness* in the minds of the people, that certain cherished values are being threatened by a change in social conditions. This awareness is manifested when the problem becomes a topic of frequent discussion and comment, and people feel some social action should be taken to rectify the condition.

Policy determination. After awareness of the social problem is created among the population, people begin to debate possible solutions. Frequently there is considerable divergence of opinion as to the best approach for resolution of the problem; for example, some may feel that the police should stop the drug trade, others may feel that some other government agency should assume the responsibility, still others feel that community organizations should be more active; finally, some feel that no one should do anything!

This divergence of opinion is characteristic of social problems, and arises from the variety of value positions and normative standards held by people from different backgrounds. Actually, some people may not even agree that the condition is a social problem! This divergence of opinion naturally complicates the process of finding any satisfactory resolution for social problems in society.

The undesirable aspects of a social problem may persist indefinitely until a majority of the population expresses a preference for a particular solution, then the *reform* phase begins.

Answer frame 2[1]

1. False. Although primitive man may have had many personal problems, social problems are products of large complex societies.
2. True. Social change in the society creates most social problems.
3. False. Although an objectively undesirable condition *may* become a social problem, most undesirable conditions fail to become social problems. It is the *subjective interpretation* of the objective conditions that defines the social problem.
4. True. Technological change is a major force in creating social problems.

If you missed any of the questions, review Frame 2[1] before starting Frame 3[1] on page 5.

Frame 3[1] continued

Reform actions may be taken by legislative bodies, official agencies, or through community action. The resolution of the social problem may be rapid (as with abortion reform or the polio epidemic) or painfully slow (as with the war on poverty, civil rights, and ecological problems). In either event, the social problem may persist until people of a society decide to take constructive and positive action. Even then, the problem still may *persist* despite their efforts or treatment.

Although Fuller and Myers define three concise steps in the development of the social problem, in reality the stages may overlap or be intermeshed. In large metropolitan areas, the problems of pollution, crime, and urban congestion are more prominent concerns than in sparsely settled areas, thus the importance of the condition may be differently perceived in different areas. In either event, the resolution of most social problems is usually a slow, gradual process that should be measured in time frames of decades rather than months or years.

THE SCIENCE OF SOCIAL PROBLEMS

During the formative years of the growth of sociology as a discipline, many of its early members were humanists, social reformists, and religious zealots who were committed to curing the "ills and evils" of society. Social problems were viewed as pathogenic (diseased) aspects of society that should be treated and cured to produce a healthy society. Thus, the early study of social problems was known as social pathology. Its advocates were often guided (or misguided) by moral judgments that more often reflected a vested interest or sought to impose a particular set of moral values, rather than representing an objective, systematic analysis.

For the past several decades, the trend has been towards the use of the *scientific method* for the analysis of social problems. Basically, the method as applied to the analysis of social problems is to (1) specify the problem; (2) plan the research design; (3) collect relevant data and information; (4) analyze the data; and (5) draw objective conclusions that represent the data. Sociologists have attempted to be *value-free* and *ethically neutral* (seeking scientific truth regardless of whom it pleases or displeases) in their analysis of social problems and attempted to ascertain the correct facts about the problem. Occasionally the facts will lead to an unpopular conclusion, or one that may conflict with conventional morality, but the scientific method has been regarded as the only reliable method to use in understanding the true nature of the social problem.

Once the data are collected and analyzed, the sociologist may form an *hypothesis* about the problem (a tentative conclusion proposed for further testing). After several hypotheses are tested, a *theory* might be developed (a systematic organization of a considerable body of facts and verified hypotheses into an overall interpretation). Theories provide explanations about the nature of the social problem. For example, there are several theories of racial prejudice: the economic competition theory that prejudice arises from economic competition between races; the frustration-aggression theory, that frustration leads to aggressive prejudicial acts; the social neurosis theory, that prejudiced persons are maladjusted; the class-exploitation theory that racism is simply another form of class exploitation, and so on. Theories can then be used to explain the problem when it arises in society.

In recent years, this image of sociology as an objective, value-free scientific discipline, engaged in the systematic, dispassionate study of social problems has been challenged by a group who are known as radical sociologists. These sociologists (in common with radical economists, political scientists, and historians) charge that "objective" social science is actually biased, and that the pretense of ethical neutrality disguises an insidious support of the "establishment" against the poor and the oppressed. Thus the radical sociologists challenge both the possibility and the desirability of ethical neutrality, and call for a sociology that is actively committed to the support of humane social values. Most radical sociologists believe that any effective solution for social problems is impossible under a capitalist-competitive-materialistic society. They feel that a good sociologist must therefore be a revolutionist. Although a relatively small minority among American sociologists, the radical sociologists are an influential body, especially among graduate students and younger sociologists. Their policy recommendations appear in the journal *Social Policy*.

It is quite true that absolute objectivity may be impossible. The definition of social problems inevitably carries some bias. For example, the problem of poverty may be stated, "Why are some people poor?" This implies that the personal shortcomings of the poor may be responsible. If the question is phrased, "How does the system create and perpetuate poverty?" the "blame" is, by implication, shifted from the defects of individuals to the defects of the system. Each definition of the problem carries an implicit bias.

While it is agreed that perfect objectivity may be unattainable, disagreement rages over whether sociologists should seek to be as objective as possible. The more conservative sociologists seek as high a degree of objectivity as humanly possible, and recommend reformist solutions to social problems; radical sociologists advocate value-commitment rather than objectivity, and recommend revolutionary solutions to social problems.

Indicate whether each of the following statements is true or false by writing "T" or "F" in the space provided.

_____ 1. Social problems just bloom into existence without any organized pattern of development.

_____ 2. In its early history, the study of social problems was known as social pathology.

_____ 3. Sociology attempts to be value-free and ethically neutral in its method.

_____ 4. Radical sociologists tend to believe that sociologists should concentrate upon improving humanity rather than reforming society.

Now turn to Answer frame 3[1] on page 8 to check your answers.

Answer frame 3[1]

1. False. Social problems follow a precise pattern in their development (according to Fuller and Myers). The first stage is the development of awareness, followed by policy determination, and then reform.
2. True. Social problems were first thought to represent the "diseased" aspects of society, thus their study was called social pathology.
3. True. This is the major goal of all sociology, although some radical sociologists feel that this goal is unattainable.
4. True. Radical sociologists tend to seek humanistic goals, while conservative sociologists usually concentrate upon reforming society.

If you missed any of the above, reread Frame 3[1] before starting Chapter 2.

chapter 2

SOCIOLOGICAL CONCEPTS

Frame 1[2]

A variety of sociological concepts are used in the study of social problems. Since the reader may be unfamiliar with the particular meaning of each concept in this PLAID, they are briefly described below. [For a complete review of sociological theory and concepts, see *Self Review in Introductory Sociology*, a PLAID by Paul B. Horton and Robert L. Horton (Homewood, Ill.: Learning Systems Co., 1971).]

Every nation possesses a unique culture. A *culture* consists of the complex whole of knowledge, beliefs, morals, norms, laws, customs, and values acquired by the people of a society. It includes any common learned patterns of behavior as well as the cultural artifacts shared by the people. Anything that the people of a nation construct, design, employ, or otherwise use is known as part of their culture. Culture also includes behavior that may be considered not "nice," such as obscenities, vulgarities, crudities, and so on.

A *society* consists of all the people who share a common culture. Within any society people share a common set of cultural norms and values. *Norms* are standards for behavior, or the expected behavior for a given situation. As such, there are thousands of norms in a culture—that men wear trousers instead of dresses, that people drive on the right side of the road, and that one does not use his finger to stir his coffee.

Ideal norms are those which are generally approved in the society. The *behavioral norms* are the actual behaviors or standards followed. Our ideal norms call for students to be studious and honorable; but cutting class, bluffing, and cheating are not uncommon. The ideal norms of most people favor law enforcement and condemn crime, yet in their behavior, almost everyone violates a series of laws each day. Divergence between real and ideal norms is one of the roots of social problems.

William Sumner, one of the first sociologists, observes that there are three types of norms: folkways, mores, and laws. [Sumner, *Folkways*.] *Folkways* (the way of the folk) are customary modes of behavior—such as eating with knives and forks, answering a phone with "hello," and using the right hand for handshakes, and so on. One may violate folkways with no great punishment, yet most people follow folkways most of the time.

Mores are norms that are believed to be vital to the society and thus are rigorously enforced. American mores condemn murder, stealing, and rape, and require child support and payment of honest debts. In simple tribal societies, most people obey the mores because of their need for group acceptance and approval. In complex modern societies, such informal social controls are less effective, and laws have been added as controls. *Laws* are formalized norms, which means that the standards for behavior are formally written, along with specified punishments for their violation.

The norms and values of a culture are organized into institutions. *Institutions* are clusters of related norms and values centering around a major social concern. The most prominent social institutions of our society are the family, education, religion, government, and the economy. Society encourages behavioral conformity to institutional norms by applying negative sanctions to the person who violates the norms. For example, the law may punish people who do not send their children to school or fail to pay their income taxes. For other violations of the mores, one may lose social prestige or respect in the community if he fails to adhere to institutional norms (such as a prominent community leader who cheats on his wife). Institutional norms often change through time, creating confusion as to which norm to follow, and thus cause social problems to develop (such as the current tendency toward more liberal or permissive sexual behavior).

A *subculture* is a set of norms that are somewhat divergent from the norms of the dominant culture, and which are shared by a number of people. The youth of our society share many of the adult norms, but they also have other unique norms that are shared only by other adolescents. People who dwell in ghettos may also have unique sets of norms that often run counter to those held by the larger population. Some subcultures are different from, but are not in opposition to, the dominant culture. Examples would include occupational subcultures (of physicians, circus people, or farmers), religious subcultures (Catholics, Baptists), recreational subcultures (hunting, scuba diving), and many others. But some subcultures are in sharp conflict with the dominant culture (the drug subculture, the radical-activist subculture), and thus are called *countercultures*.

Cultural integration refers to the degree of harmonious interrelatedness of the various norms and values of a culture. The American culture is integrated around the values of work, competition, and success. Family life, education, and religion reinforce these values. The culture of the American Indian of the great plains was integrated around the presence of the buffalo, and when the herds were destroyed by hunters and soldiers, the Indian culture almost disintegrated. Social change affects the degree of cultural integration, and also creates the basis for the emergence of a wider variety of social problems in society.

Social status refers to the rank or position of a person in a group or social system. Each person holds a variety of status positions—age status, occupational status, marital status, and social standing in the community. With each status, there is an appropriate *role*, which is the expected behavior for a person who holds a particular status. *Role behavior* is the actual behavior of a person filling a role (whereas the role is the expected behavior). Social problems develop when the role behavior of many people diverges widely from traditional expectations.

A status may be ascribed or achieved. *Ascribed statuses* are those that are assigned according to factors unalterable by the person—age, sex, or race are common examples. *Achieved statuses* are those which are attained through one's own effort or choice. One must earn the status of criminal, wife, or carpenter; one is not automatically assigned these statuses, but acquires them through his own efforts.

Social class. A social class consists of a group of people who share a similar social status. Social classes arise from the division of labor and specialization of occupation in societies. Wherever there is specialization of labor, some occupations tend to carry more prestige than others, creating a system of stratification. Usually, the greater the knowledge, training, or skill required for the work, or the greater the power it carries, the greater the status and financial rewards that are associated with the position.

Karl Marx (a famous class theorist) noted that people's attitudes and values tend to flow from their class position; blue-collar workers are set apart from white-collar management, while low-income people tend to hold different attitudes, lifestyles, and behavioral patterns than upper-class people. The lower classes tend to bear the brunt of the social problems in society (poverty, poor medical care, substandard housing, and so on) and often are most directly affected by the social problems. Thus social class becomes a major variable in understanding the impact of social problems upon the people in society.

Indicate whether each of the following statements is true or false by writing "T" or "F" in the space provided.

_____ 1. Social problems are created when people fail to follow the ideal norms of a society.

_____ 2. Widespread violation of the mores create social problems.

_____ 3. The greater the degree of cultural integration in a society, the fewer social problems there are likely to be.

_____ 4. Social problems may be created when people's role behavior does not conform to their status position.

Now turn to Answer frame 1[2] on page 12 to check your answers.

Frame 2[2]

Social change. Complex technological societies are characterized by a rapid rate of change, both in the material and social dimensions of the society. The concept of social change is important in the study of social problems because change constantly affects the social organization of society, creating opportunities for social problems to develop.

The three major processes of change are *discovery, invention,* and *diffusion and application.* New discoveries and inventions change the state of technology in society, permitting or requiring an adaptation to a new state of organization. For example, the invention of the electric pump, the septic tank, and the automobile are largely responsible for the growth of the suburb. The invention of the transistor and miniature diodes led to the development of the computer which has had an impact upon virtually every person in modern societies.

The rates of social change are enhanced through the forces of *technology, industrialization,* and *urbanization.* These three forces combine to produce a process of *modernization* in society. Technological change creates new desires and wants for people to fulfill in life (to acquire more modern appliances, greater comforts, and so on), as well as providing the means to improve the social conditions of a society. Medical advancements and improvements in hospital care have eliminated a variety of diseases, and prolonged the average lifespan of persons (but also, in turn, worsening the social problem of overpopulation). Technological change usually improves the standard of living of a population, but also may create other problems (such as pollution, overpopulation, and parking problems).

Industrialization tends to change the material basis of a society, and may also indirectly change the organization of a society. Often a material change may lead to a reorganization of values in a society, creating social problems in the process; the "planned obsolescence" of automobiles and appliances may leave a nation of junkyards, filled with the rusting hulks of cars and refrigerators, as well as keeping most families in the nation perpetually in debt as they strive to purchase newer and nicer models to keep up with the neighbors. Material changes in a society often produce unintended social consequences, which in turn may create social problems.

The process of urbanization causes sweeping reorganization of society. In America, the process of urbanization moved 90 percent of the rural population to metropolitan areas. As the rural people moved, they changed their values as well as their residences and eventually arrived at a more permissive orientation of values for the entire society. In turn, these new standards for permissiveness eventually led to a redefinition of attitudes and values toward divorce, family size, and role of children in the family.

Modernization, although incorporating some of the features of the other forces of change, involves a general redefinition of values toward a more permissive and liberal interpretation. However, the esthetic cost of modernization often discourages its acceptance (particularly among the older population) as it usually means a sacrifice of traditional values.

Each of the above forces of change are interrelated and influence each other in their consequences as they produce the conditions that become social problems. Technology makes industrialization possible, which in turn sets in motion a whole series of social consequences affecting almost every facet of social life. The point to remember is that although the forces of social change often improve the style of life and the standard of living in society, they may also create the social conditions that become social problems.

Cultural lag. The late William F. Ogburn noted that cultures are integrated and interrelated, and change in one aspect of culture produces change in other related parts of the culture. Cultural lag exists when technological changes are implemented more rapidly than social changes, causing social values and attitudes to lag behind technological changes. For example, American automakers produce over 11 million new automobiles each year, but we have hardly begun to solve the problems of urban congestion and mass transit; often people can fly across several states in less time than they can park their car and check in at the airport; and we can send a spaceship to the moon, but cannot persuade people to use their safety belts in their cars.

In another example, it took little less than a decade to conceive, design, and manufacture a working model of the atomic bomb, but today, almost three decades later, there has been little progress in achieving a fail-safe nuclear arms limitation policy. Social change in values of a society often lag decades behind technological change, and the differential between social and technological change produces the basis for social problems to develop.

Personal and social disorganization. Technological and social change disrupts established routines and relationships, requiring new adjustments to be made. Change occurs on a day-to-day basis, and many changes are simple enough that they can be made with little thought and with limited social consequences. But other innovations such as television or computers may bring revolutionary changes to the whole society.

When change undermines established beliefs and patterns, confusion and uncertainty are created as to just what attitudes and values people should hold or how they should behave. Very few societies are perfectly integrated and some cultural contradictions and inconsistencies between real and ideal norms are found in most cultures. A variety of evasions and rationalizations generally protect the individual from becoming upset by these discrepancies. But when social change is rapid and sweeping, these evasions and rationalizations may be inadequate, and persons may become confused and uncertain. For example, is abortion a selfish act of murder, or is it a humane avoidance of the birth

Answer frame 1²

1. True. Failure to follow the ideal norms creates deviance and reduces the extent of social integration in society.
2. True. Mores are norms that are vital to the social organization of the society, thus failure to follow them creates social problems.
3. True. Social problems tend to develop as a product of social disorganization.
4. True. Each status has a proscribed role, and when a major portion of the population fails to fulfill their role expectations, social problems may be created.

If you missed any of the above, restudy Frame 1² before beginning Frame 2² on page 10.

Frame 2² continued

of an unwanted and neglected child? When a person becomes so confused and uncertain that his behavior is erratic and contradictory, he is said to be in a state of *personal disorganization*. When the integration of the society has been disrupted by social change so that old procedures no longer work well, old values are crumbling, and institutions are in conflict with one another, the society is experiencing *social disorganization*. All of the world's societies (except possibly for a few isolated bands of primitives) are today in a continuous process of social disorganization and reorganization.

While people have a tremendous ability to adapt to change, their capacity is not unlimited. Alvin Toffler, in *Future Shock* [New York: Random House, Inc., 1970.], notes that the "accelerative thrust" of change is increasing so rapidly that people are experiencing cultural shock in attempting to adapt to the quickening pace and pressures of modern industrialized society. This tendency is most exemplified by the problems of returning prisoners of the Vietnam War in that during the three to five years of their imprisonment, the extent of change in our society was so great that the POWs suffered severe problems of readjustment upon their return. Korean POWs suffered a divorce rate of over 50 percent, and a highly disproportionate number committed suicide or were admitted to psychiatric hospitals. Recent Vietnam veterans are expected to have similar problems.

Change is so pervasive in modern society that one might only speculate what changes will occur within the lifetime of today's students. Many of our grandparents went from the horse and buggy to the "space buggy" within their lifetime, and since technological change grows at a geometrical rate, the change and corresponding disorganization we will encounter will be much more than our elders experienced. All of these factors tend to enhance the number of social problems today.

Indicate whether each of the following statements is true or false by writing "T" or "F" in the space provided.

_____ 1. Social change occurs at the same pace in simple societies as in complex societies.
_____ 2. Social change causes a reorganization of values in a society.
_____ 3. Primitive societies usually have a high degree of cultural lag.
_____ 4. Almost all societies experience some degree of social disorganization.

Now check your answers by turning to Answer frame 2² on page 14.

chapter 3

CONCEPTUAL APPROACHES TO SOCIAL PROBLEMS

Frame 1[3]

Many people are confused and anxious when they are confronted with the term "concept" and "theory." Actually, the meaning of these terms is quite simple. A concept is simply a perspective which includes certain assumptions and procedures. For example, religion is a concept that embodies a collection of beliefs about supra-empirical powers. Different denominational approaches to religion represent different *conceptions* of God. Thus, in America, Protestantism represents one conceptual approach to God, Judaism a second, and Catholicism a third. People in other cultures in the world hold additional concepts of supra-empirical powers—Buddhism, Hinduism, Pantheism, and the magic of herbs, voodoo dolls, and spirits.

Just as there are a variety of conceptions of supernatural powers, each embodying different perspectives and practices, there are several conceptual approaches to social problems that give us different insights into the nature and origin of those problems. The most prominent approaches (and ones described in this PLAID) are *social disorganization, value conflict, societal conflict,* and *personal deviation.*

Social disorganization. The social disorganization perspective or social problems is one of the older and most widely used conceptual approaches. It emerged in the early 1920s as scientists began to abandon the moral judgment method of social pathology and developed the scientific, objective method of value-free sociology.

Since social disorganization implies the lack of a state of organization, in order to explain social disorganization, it is first necessary to define social organization in society.

Social organization consists of common shared definitions of social goals, as well as the acceptance of the proper means and role behavior to achieve those goals. In a simpler sense, social organization consists of complex sets of norms, roles, and rules for behavior, shared by the people collectively. Certain key norms and values of our society might be support of the family unit, the work ethic, the law, and the rights and freedoms of others. If everyone in a society accepts and conforms to the "proper" or ideal norms for behavior, the degree of social organization will be strong.

However, in reality not all people accept the "proper" norms of society and some occasionally deviate from the norms. This creates *social disorganization* or weaknesses in the structure of norms of society. Here one might use the analogy of the structure of a large building, of which the timbers of the building are complex and mutually supporting. The main timbers of the building consist of norms, values, statuses, and roles. As long as each timber is strong and durable, the structure remains strong; but if one structural element weakens, as when a norm or role is not followed or accepted by the majority of the population, stress is created upon the other elements of the entire structure. These areas of decay or weakness are analogous to

Answer frame 2[2]

1. False. Simple societies have a slow pace of social change, while complex societies have a rapid pace of change.
2. True. A major effect of social change is to cause a reorganization of values in the society.
3. False. Cultural lag is generated when technological change occurs at a more rapid pace than social or value change; thus, primitive societies with little industrialization or technology have little cultural lag.
4. True. Although societies may differ in the extent of social disorganization, it is a characteristic of almost all societies.

If you missed any of the above, restudy Frame 2[2] before starting Chapter 3 on page 13.

Frame 1[3] continued

social disorganization. Under conditions of social disorganization, people are unsure of exactly what norms to follow, or of what values to hold. Examples of current normative conflicts might be whether people should practice birth control, whether abortion is acceptable, or whether to report a friend who is cheating on his income tax. In complex societies, there are numerous instances where the structure of norms or roles is confusing, contradictory, or unclear. This confusion or unclarity may create many social problems.

Although there is always some degree of disorganization in society, each society attempts to maintain its organization through the mechanisms of *social control,* or the enforcement of the folkways, mores, and laws of the basic institutions. However, as described in Chapter 2, institutions are never fully static but are always undergoing a constant process of social change and adaptation. Certain key norms of each institution are constantly being influenced by other institutional norms; the religious norms influence the family, changes in the political institution affect the educational institution, and changes in the state of the economy affect all other institutions.

As institutions change in society, key norms of one institution may come into conflict with norms of other institutions, creating confusion over the proper norms and also creating social disorganization in the process. For the person, social disorganization may create stress, resulting in personal disorganization. In either case, the basis is created for the development of social problems.

The theory of social disorganization, as applied to social problems, presumes a sequence of stages. First, there is a prior state of organization of the norms and rules of society, which are disrupted through the forces of social change. Key norms or rules are brought into conflict or disharmony, producing disorganization, and the conditions which permit the development of a social problem. To remedy the social problem, it is necessary to reconstruct a new state of social organization in society. This may be accomplished by (1) abandoning the old norms or rules that are in conflict (such as the norms against family planning or birth control); (2) redefining the rules so that they are not in conflict (such as the shift from temperance to moderation at the end of the Prohibition Era; or (3) constructing a whole new complex of rules (for instance, the laws created for the control of drugs or pollution).

In using the social disorganization approach, it is important to ask five key questions: (1) What was the prior state of organization (the key norms, values or rules that were functioning effectively before disorganization occurred)? (2) What were the forces or changes that brought the rules into conflict? (3) How were the rules affected? (4) What new norms or rules need to be instituted (or abandoned) to rectify the conflict? and finally (5) What will be the nature of the new revised state of social organization?

Indicate whether each of the following statements is true or false by writing "T" or "F" in the space provided.

_____ 1. All complex societies always have some degree of social disorganization.

_____ 2. Social change is a primary cause of social disorganization in societies.

_____ 3. Once a state of social disorganization is created, a new state of reorganization cannot be established.

_____ 4. The process of social disorganization and reorganization is unnatural in complex industrial societies.

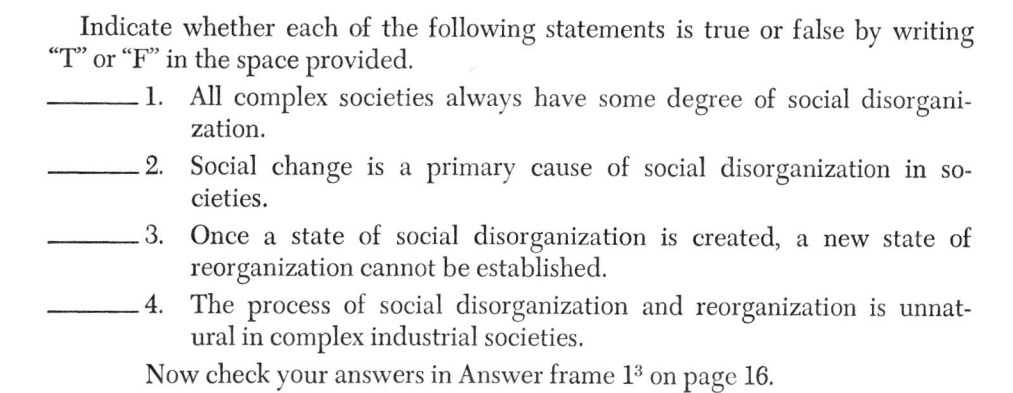

Now check your answers in Answer frame 1³ on page 16.

Frame 2³

Value conflict. It was noted in Chapter 1 that every social problem violates a preferred value judgment—a collective decision that a condition is bad and should be corrected. Thus, social problems are created by value judgments. Also, every solution to a social problem involves value judgments—collective decisions as to what kind of correction is desirable and what means are acceptable. Value conflicts, that is, disagreements in these value judgments, may prevent general acceptance of a condition as a social problem (e.g., is poverty good or bad?), may prevent agreement upon goals (what level of subsistence should be the poverty floor?), and may prevent agreement upon means (individual rehabilitation or income maintenance?).

Complex societies tend to create a proliferation of value positions. Divergence of values flows from the variety of experiences that people have, their different backgrounds, their age and status, and the different interest groups that people may belong to. Whether one is rural or urban in origin, Catholic or Protestant, black or white, early immigrant or recent immigrant, Republican or Democrat, hunter or conservationist, will influence the values he holds.

Although it is necessary for major portions of the population to share similar values in order to maintain the social organization of society, there is still room for a considerable variety of opinions. When groups in society find themselves holding conflicting value positions, the basis for a social problem is created.

However, *not all persons are equally involved in the value conflict;* conditions that constitute a deplorable situation to some people may be desirable to others. The conservationist may wish to limit hunting so that he might have the pleasure of observing wildlife in the wilderness, but the trophy-seeker wishes to kill the best of the species to decorate his den. Both persons will likely be disturbed with the trail biker who heedlessly roars through the wilderness scaring men as well as beasts. The canoeist may wish to preserve the wild rivers, the Corps of Engineers may wish to construct a dam, while the mining executive would like to use the river to dump his waste. The list of examples is endless!

Further, *interest or involvement in the value conflict is not necessarily continuous.* Many self-appointed crusaders, such as the radicals of recent years, violently protest the deplorable state of conditions in society, and they did succeed in bringing several new social problems to national attention. Although they did create awareness (the first stage of a social problem), their interest somehow shifted to other causes when the work of reform began. This is characteristic of social movements or the development of social problems; each stage of the problem attracts the interest and attention of different persons—some people work to create awareness, others develop the policy for reform, and finally others do the work of reform.

Value conflicts produce social problems when one group attempts to impose its will upon another group. Any attack upon the conventional values easily rallys traditional-minded persons

Answer frame 1³

1. True. Some degree of social disorganization always exists in all complex societies, but the extent may vary with different societies.
2. True. Social change is a primary cause of social disorganization in societies, and the greater the rate of social change, generally the greater the degree of social disorganization.
3. False. A new state of reorganization (or social organization) can be accomplished by abandoning old norms, redefining the rules, or constructing a new complex of rules.
4. False. The process of disorganization and reorganization is a natural and expected process of industrial societies.

If you missed any of the above, reread Frame 1³ before starting Frame 2³ on page 15.

Frame 2³ continued

to defend the cause, while the reformers are inspired and guided by a sense of righteous duty in the crusade to improve society.

Value conflicts may also create confusion over the propriety of different value positions, which allows personal deviation to occur. Conflicting values about abortion and the sanctity of life often causes concern for church leaders as Catholic youth deviate from their religious beliefs when they take birth control pills. Other current examples of deviation encouraged by value conflict might include the use of marijuana, participation of premarital sex, and long-haired radicalism among youth.

The resolution of the value conflict usually requires a sacrifice of the value position held by one group or the other. Since values are an important part of each person's identity, an attack upon personal values is often interpreted as an attack upon the person as well; thus value positions are not relinquished easily. Actually, such conflicts are often very bitter and frequently split family members and friends.

Value change in society requires that most of the population change their values, thus any widespread change in value positions usually occurs gradually over a period of years or even decades. In some cases, the value shift might never occur, and the values may remain in conflict through the ages. Poverty is one such example.

In applying the value conflict perspective to the analysis of social problems, the reader might ask the following questions: (1) What are the values that are in conflict? (2) What groups are involved in the conflict, and what is the basis for their beliefs? (3) What value sacrifices would be necessary to resolve the conflict? and (4) What group actions are likely to occur or are necessary to resolve the conflict?

Indicate whether each of the following statements is true or false by writing "T" or "F" in the space provided.

_____ 1. Value conflicts are a major cause of social problems.
_____ 2. Sophisticated complex societies tend to have fewer value conflicts than do simple societies.
_____ 3. Most value conflicts can be resolved without any great sacrifice on the part of either party.
_____ 4. Value conflicts tend to encourage deviant behavior.

Now check your answers by turning to Answer frame 2³ on page 18.

Frame 3[3]

Social conflict. The social conflict school of thought is closely related to the value conflict perspective, and in fact, it found much of its origin within the early conflict theorists—Karl Marx, Albion Small, Robert Park, and others. The revival of conflict theory is so recent that there is not complete agreement among sociologists as to exactly how the school of thought should be classified as it relates to the study of social problems—some would place it under the value-conflict perspective, others feel it is sufficiently different to constitute a separate conceptual approach.

The application of conflict theory to social problems was introduced during the period of radicalism in the 1960s. During this period almost every metropolitan area became inflamed with racial protest. Civil riot became the order for the year in Watts, Chicago, Detroit, Newark, and Washington, D.C. Later in the decade (the late 1960s), campus riots and the anti-war movement brought new young crusaders to the cause of protecting civil liberties and challenging laws perceived to be inequitable. These events encouraged the application of the conflict model to account for the violent state of society.

The extent of the conflict, and the basic causes behind its development encouraged some theorists to suggest that the origin and nature of race riots and war protests went beyond the social problems that could be accounted for in terms of value conflict. Rather, their cause arose from antagonistic power struggles within society. Earlier value conflict theory had assumed a static-state of order, harmony and stability in society, and social problems were thought to be created when the harmony and order was temporarily disturbed. The pre-existing social organization of society was maintained or restored by a change in values or by sacrificing certain of the values that were in conflict.

Recent conflict theorists, however, postulated that the natural state of order of society was one of continuous and regular change, creating a state of controlled conflict. [Ralf Dahrendorf, "Toward a Theory of Social Conflict," *Journal of Conflict Resolution,* 2 (1958): 170–83.] To the conflict theorist, the structure of society was constantly changing, creating conflicting interest groups in society. The basis of the conflict was a struggle for power or scarce resources. (*Power* is defined sociologically as *the ability to enforce one's will upon others.*)

Examples of such power conflicts that have become social problems include the black-white struggle for equality, the problem of the poor struggling to survive in an affluent society, the women's liberation movement, radicalism, the people versus big government and the military-industrial complex, and so on. The essence of these social problems from the conflict perspective, is the battle between those who currently hold power and those who seek power. Ideally, the social problem is resolved when the "underdog" group assumes the new position of power or acquires the resources desired. But this also creates a new underdog—the defeated majority! Thus, the conflict of power positions becomes the normal and enduring state of organization in society.

Both the value conflict theorist and the social conflict theorist seek the same end in society—an improved state of social organization—but they would use different means to achieve the end. The value conflict theorist would change and reorganize the values of a society as a solution to social problems, but the social conflict theorist would restructure the power balance or reallocate the resources of society to resolve the social condition.

Functions of conflict. Much of the strength and application of conflict theory arises from the positive functions served by conflict. First, Lewis Coser (a prominent conflict theorist) notes that conflict sometimes helps to establish unity and cohesion in groups. [Lewis Coser, *The Functions of Social Conflict* (New York: The Free Press, 1956).] For example, in World War II, the American people who had been divided by the depression of the 1930s, united as a nation to plant victory gardens, buy war bonds, and produce war materials. Campus radicals have long recognized that the best way to increase membership and support for their cause is to force campus police into overreacting to a confrontation, encouraging the students to

Answer frame 2³

1. True. A value judgment is a feeling held by an individual or a group, about whether a condition is good or bad. Thus conflicts in judgment create the basis for the growth of social problems.
2. False. Complex societies tend to create a proliferation of different value positions, and thus *increase* the potential for value conflicts.
3. False. People often have a large emotional investment in their value positions, and are deeply hurt when their values are challenged or sacrificed.
4. True. Conflicts over value positions often create confusion as to the appropriate value position, thus people may become deviant out of uncertainty of the proper values.

If you missed any of the above, restudy Frame 2³ before starting Frame 3³ on page 17.

Frame 3³ continued

rally in support of the cause of their "oppressed" fellow students. However, this tactic also unites college administrators and adults against the youthful protestors!

Second, controlled conflict is a means of resolving tension between antagonists. If competing groups can resolve their differences in group discussions or compromises, greater and more damaging conflict may be averted. Forced labor negotiations, or court hearings to resolve conflicts are some examples.

Third, conflict is a means of creating change in society. In this age of industrialization, outdated norms that are incompatible with modern society frequently must be changed and new normative orders established.

Finally, conflict helps to assign power positions among people and groups. America is one of the most barren lands for revolution because the minorities are allowed to protest and be heard, and the public makes a free choice to listen or reject the protesting group. Revolutions are most likely to occur in authoritarian or totalitarian countries, where safety-valve protests are repressed until they explode into an insurgence.

From the social conflict perspective, the following questions would be asked about the social problem. (1) What are the groups in conflict? (2) What is the nature of their goals or differences? (3) What are the actions of the groups as they maneuver to gain position or power? and (4) What will be the effects of the new power balance upon the society?

Indicate whether each of the following statements is true or false by writing "T" or "F" in the space provided.

_____ 1. The social conflict perspective is one of the oldest perspectives used in the examination of social problems.
_____ 2. All sociologists agree that the social conflict perspective is the most useful perspective from which to examine social problems.
_____ 3. Most social conflict theorists believe that a state of "controlled conflict" is the natural state of order for modern societies.
_____ 4. Conflict is always disruptive and damaging to a society.

Now check your answers in Answer frame 3³ on page 20.

Frame 4[3]

Personal deviation. A final prominent conceptual approach for the analysis of social problems is that of deviance or personal deviation. This method is perhaps more social-psychological in nature than sociological, in that it focuses more upon groups of people committing deviant acts than upon the structure or organization of society which produces social problems. From this perspective, social problems are created when a large or major portion of the population follow a deviant pattern of behavior.

It is important to note that a considerable number of people must follow the deviant pattern before it can become a social problem. Each of us at one time or another commits a deviant act, but this does not mean that each of us are social problems. As C. Wright Mills states (see Chapter 1) a person who is an alcoholic has a personal problem to contend with, but when major proportions of the population possess the same affliction (alcoholism among housewives, drug addiction among doctors), it suggests that there are certain common social forces at work for that particular segment of the population that encourages persons to follow deviant patterns.

Further, some theorists would suggest (Becker and Schur) that the condition as a social problem existed less with the deviant persons themselves, than with the larger majority of the population who are affected and disturbed by the deviant behavior. For example, the hippies or "long-haired" radicals are rarely disturbed about themselves as a social problem (they are doing what they define as right for them), but it is the non-hippie adult majority who are disturbed about the hippie's behavior. Thus, from the personal deviation perspective, we tend to look for (1) the social forces that encourage the deviant behavior; (2) how the larger population comes to label and view the behavior as deviant; and (3) the characteristics of the deviant patterns themselves.

Social forces creating deviance. There are a variety of social forces that cause people to become deviant. Structural deviance occurs when a person of one ascribed status attempts to achieve another, inconsistent status (when a woman runs for president, or a white minister joins a black civil rights protest), or when a particular status is not fulfilled (a doctor who performs illegal abortions, or a policeman "on the take"), or when the expected status is not achieved (a woman who does not wish to have children). In these cases, the deviants fail to fulfill the role expectations of their status.

In other cases, conformity to the norms of one group can cause deviance from the norms of another group. The member of the John Birch Society who finds that he must join a union to get the job he wants, or a Roman Catholic priest who marries, cannot maintain his allegiance to both groups at once. Thus he must deviate from one group or the other.

Finally, are the situational or circumstantial causes of deviance where one wishes to follow the proper norms, but because of the immediate circumstances, dares not to. Here we might include the welfare mother who must "lie a little" to get school clothes for her children, or the prominent citizen who "hits and runs" because he was drinking and so on. Situational deviance is seldom intended or repeated, thus sociologists are rarely concerned with it.

Labeling deviance. Howard Becker in his book, *The Outsiders* [New York: The Free Press, 1963.] and Alan Schur [*Labeling Deviant Behavior* (New York: Harper & Row, Inc., 1971).] describe the process whereby the larger majority of people come to define the rules by which an individual is defined as deviant. As all young people are aware, some rules that used to be enforced in the past may no longer be enforced, and some behaviors that used to be permitted are now vigorously condemned. The nature of rules in a society change, and what is viewed as being deviant today may not be tomorrow. For example, long-haired college graduates of a decade ago would be assured of not getting a job offer even from the city sanitation department, but now they may get a job almost anywhere.

Thus, as Becker would argue, it is the established majority who defines the norms and rules for the society (which are open to change with

Answer frame 3³

1. False. The social conflict perspective is quite recent in its development, and not all sociologists agree on its validity.
2. False. Although many sociologists are optimistic as to its future, the social conflict perspective is new and relatively untested in its ability to account for social problems.
3. True. Social conflict theorists feel that social change occurs regularly in modern societies, creating a state of controlled conflict.
4. False. Conflict is not always damaging to a society; at times it is a means of implementing positive change and social reform.

If you missed any of the above, restudy Frame 3³ before starting Frame 4³ on page 19.

Frame 4³ continued

time), and it is in reference to these rules that a person is judged as deviant. Deviance from this perspective, is less a quality of the specific act than a product of the social reaction to the act; in other words, the deviant is one who has been so labeled.

Forms of deviance. Deviance may result from an *inability to follow the generally accepted norms*, such as mental illness, alcohol, or drug addiction, or an inner psychological compulsion to commit the deviant act. In these cases, the causes of deviance are biological, psychological, or physiological in nature and beyond the ability of the person to control the act. Whatever the causes, the deviant behavior has advanced to the stage where the mechanisms of social control are no longer applicable or effective and the person may need institutionalization or special treatment to overcome the deviant patterns.

A second type of deviant behavior involves a *failure to accept the generally preferred norms*. In these cases, the person was socialized to the proper norms but follows deviant norms. In these cases, the deviant usually has internalized a moral sense of right and wrong, but, finding the deviant pattern more rewarding, has rejected the societal norms in preference for the deviant pattern. Usually the deviant in this case has undergone a process of mental manipulation and rationalization, in which the values of the conforming majority are defined as inconsistent, hypocritical, or just stupid, thus justifying the deviant behavior (Jaywalking laws are only for little old ladies who can't move fast enough; What's the difference between you taking a tranquilizer and me smoking pot? . . . They both are the same! That store rips off people anyway, so I was just equalizing my purchase . . .).

A third type of deviant behavior is *subcultural deviance*, where one is completely immersed into a subculture that is deviant itself. Claude Brown, in *Manchild in the Promised Land* [New York: The New American Library, 1965).], vividly illustrates the life of a child born and raised in the ghetto where crime, petty theft, and deviance is a way of life. Under those situations, stealing may be a means for survival, drugs may be a form of recreation, and membership in gangs may be a form of self-protection.

A variety of deviant subcultures have evolved on the American scene; the drug subculture, the radical establishment, motorcycle clubs, super-militant reactionary societies, and so on. Members of these groups are following the socially approved means (conforming to group norms), but tend to reject the socially approved goals in belonging to a deviant subculture.

From the personal deviation perspective, the following questions might be asked: (1) What are the characteristics of the deviants and their behavior? (2) How did society come to define or label the behavior as deviant? (3) What is the reaction of the established majority to the behavior? and (4) What are the alternatives available to the deviant for dealing with the social problem?

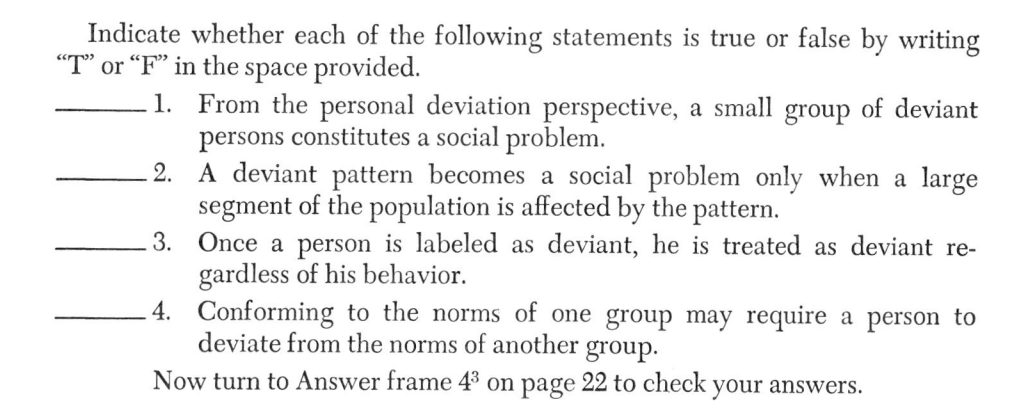

Indicate whether each of the following statements is true or false by writing "T" or "F" in the space provided.

_____ 1. From the personal deviation perspective, a small group of deviant persons constitutes a social problem.

_____ 2. A deviant pattern becomes a social problem only when a large segment of the population is affected by the pattern.

_____ 3. Once a person is labeled as deviant, he is treated as deviant regardless of his behavior.

_____ 4. Conforming to the norms of one group may require a person to deviate from the norms of another group.

Now turn to Answer frame 4[3] on page 22 to check your answers.

chapter 4

PROBLEMS OF THE FAMILY

Frame 1[4]

Everybody worries about the family. Traditionalists lament the rise in divorce rates, parents and school counselors express alarm over increases in venereal disease, illigitimacy, and the sexual permissiveness of youth. Some women's liberationists consign the traditional family to the dustbin of history, and seek to accelerate those social changes which some others decry. Why are these changes occurring? Is the family institution decaying in American society? Is marriage being stripped of its sanctity and meaning? To understand the nature of family problems as social problems, it is helpful to examine the nature of the marriage and family institutions and the history of their development in American society.

THE MARRIAGE AND FAMILY INSTITUTIONS

The family is an institution in society that embodies a complex set of norms, values, statuses, and roles. Marriage and the family are universal institutions found in all societies; thus they are generally considered to be cultural prerequisites for society to exist. Some of the more institutionalized norms and values of "marriage American style" favor monogamy, forbid marital infidelity, and idealize the happiness and security to be found in married life. Marriage is the ultimate rite of passage in our society, and symbolizes the attainment of adulthood, maturity, and stability in life.

The idealized institutionalized norms and

Answer frame 4[3]

1. False. The deviance must be widespread throughout the society before it becomes a social problem.
2. True. A significant number of people must be affected before the deviant pattern becomes a social problem.
3. True. Once the label is successfully applied, people then tend to treat the person as deviant, regardless of his behavior.
4. True. Different groups often have conflicting norms, and conformity to the norms of one group may require the person to deviate from the norms of another group.

If you missed any of the above, restudy Frame 4[3] before working Examination 1 on page 131. Then start Chapter 4 on page 21.

Frame 1[4] continued

values for the family in America favor family unity and stability, procreation, and the establishment of a comfortable home (usually with a comfortable mortgage), complete with children, pets, and a fireplace. The family is frequently viewed as the ultimate repository of the most virtuous elements of social life and personal satisfaction.

But institutions change, and the key to understanding family problems today is to be found within the change in form and function of the marriage and family institutions in society, or more specifically, in the contrast between the early preindustrial frontier family and the industrialized-urbanized family of today.

The traditional family. When most people think of problems of the modern family, they are usually comparing today's family to some idealized traditional version, perhaps as portrayed in the Norman Rockwell paintings that adorn yesteryear's *Saturday Evening Post*. In these portraits, the family was always represented as a tight-knit group of mother-father-children and frequently grandparents, living under one roof, a little bit poor perhaps, but nonetheless enjoying the happiness and pleasures of sharing life together. The traditional family might be described as *large* and *extended* (several children and relatives living together), living on a farm or in a small community, with each member of the family contributing to the family welfare.

And this was the case for most of the families of early America. The early frontier family was *isolated* and thus had to rely upon the talents of its own members for entertainment, education, and survival. All activities were *family-centered* and the weekly or monthly shopping trips to the neighboring community might involve several days of preparation to gather for sale the produce that each family member had made, the income of which would be spent upon mutual family necessities. Thus, the degree of family integration in early American society was strong because each member contributed toward the welfare of all.

Every member of the family was important in rural America. Children helped with farm chores and household tasks; grandparents gave both their time and experience in light work around the farmstead, babysitting, and providing a lifetime of advice on how to survive in a rugged world. The experiences and skills of the elders provided a major part of the children's education. The opinions of the elders were respected as they provided a community of learning for which there were no textbooks or schools. These characteristics are common in agrarian societies and still exist in preindustrial countries today.

There was undisputed *patriarchal authority* in the traditional family in that the husband or father ruled the family while all other members conceded to his direction. Small groups function most efficiently when there is a clearly defined structure of authority, and in the frontier society, the man of the household usually assumed the central role as head of the family. He likely was also the most educated person in the family, as at that time it was generally considered that a woman's place was in the home and if someone had to journey to town to transact business, it was usually the husband. Women were allowed few privileges in the 1700s—they could not vote, divorce their husbands, or control their own property after marriage. When they married, it was permanent and they had little recourse except to accept the situation, happy or not.

Marriage was a necessity for both men and women in a frontier society. A man needed a wife to keep his home while he tended the farm, and a woman needed a husband to provide for her needs. Economic forces tied the marriage together, and made divorce impractical. Except for marriage, there were very few employment opportunities for women at that time, and thus a wife was tied economically to her husband out of necessity. Affection or love in marriage was frequently considered to be a luxury if it occurred, and the presence of love was less important than maintaining the family unit.

Often a wife was chosen more on the basis of her health and potential for survival in a primitive environment than for her beauty; although beauty was pleasant, it did not improve one's ability to keep house and bear children.

Children were an asset as they were both a source of labor and social security. The birth of each son meant an additional 10 or 20 acres could be farmed, while daughters would eventually produce grandchildren who would care for parents as they grew older.

Thus, each preindustrial family was almost a small micro-society that provided for the welfare of all its members. But most importantly for the understanding of social problems of the family, there was a strong emphasis upon *familism,* or emphasis upon the family as a unit rather than upon individualism. From here we change our focus to the modern industrialized-urbanized family of today.

Indicate whether each of the following statements is true or false by writing "T" or "F" in the space provided.

_____ 1. All societies have some form of marriage and family.

_____ 2. In the traditional family in America, economic necessity forced people to marry.

_____ 3. In the frontier family, children were a form of social security for aging parents.

_____ 4. Most social problems of the family are a product of moral decay in the society.

Now turn to Answer frame 1[4] on page 24 to check your answers.

Frame 2[4]

The modern family. Of the many forces of social change, two major processes had the greatest impact upon the family institution—industrialization and urbanization. The growth of industrialization in the early 1800s created a demand for labor and industrialists vigorously recruited laborers from the open fields of rural America. The serenity of the farm failed to compete with the glittering excitement of prosperous cities, and industrialists lured the young and strong of rural areas with expectations of high wages and prospects of a steady income. This started a rural to urban migration that was to endure for the next 100 years.

City life, however, placed different demands upon the transplanted rural family, requiring a reorganization of family structure and function. Among the first changes to occur was a *reshaping of the structure of family authority* and the status of male members. In the farm family the father was always present and available to make decisions, apply discipline, and give direction to family members. He received and controlled all of the family's money in-

Answer frame 1[4]

1. True. Although the form of marriage and family may vary with different societies, all societies have the marriage and family institutions.
2. True. In the frontier society, there were few jobs for women, thus marriage was a primary occupation for women and an economic necessity for men.
3. True. Children were expected to care for and support their parents in their later years, and large families helped to share the burden.
4. False. Most social problems are created by changing needs and value changes in the marriage and family institutions.

If you missed any of the above, reread Frame 1[4] before starting Frame 2[4] on page 23.

Frame 2[4] continued

come. However, in the city, the father usually worked away from the home, requiring the wife to assume many of the responsibilities of home management and discipline of the children. The change in the wife's role has grown so much that today the monthly household budget may easily exceed the yearly farm income of 18th century farmers, and also require management decisions that would bewilder yesteryear farmers. Furthermore, in the city the wife and children began to earn and cash paychecks of their own, undermining the husband's power base as comptroller of family income. The end result of the above changes in family structure was to encourage a redefinition of the status of women, from a subservient position in the rural preindustrial family to a *more nearly equal status* in today's industrialized society.

Children have become an expensive luxury in the modern family. Whereas in the past children contributed to the family welfare through their labor around the farmstead, today there is little useful work that children can do. Thus, the average family size has decreased as children no longer serve the economic function they once did. Today's family values are more *child-centered*, favoring individual development rather than the personal sacrifice of yesteryear. This tendency contrasts sharply with the family-centered orientation of the preindustrial family.

Grandparents and elders have been demoted in status in today's family. Whereas elders were an important source of information for survival in a frontier world, they had little knowledge of how to survive in an industrialized bureaucratic society. The grandparents' contribution to the modern family is frequently limited to simple and mundane tasks that yield little in feelings of personal importance or status in the outside world. Thus for all too many persons, retirement is a degrading process that provides little happiness or satisfaction.

Redefinition of male-female roles. In the early frontier family, male and female roles were clearly defined; the wife cared for the house and children, and the husband supervised the farm and made family decisions. In comparison to today, the structure of family roles and statuses used to be relatively simple.

Modernization, however, has changed the traditional structure of statuses and roles of family members. A century ago a man's stature was judged by his ability to handle a horse, the number of acres he could plow in a day, and the condition of his barns and fences. But what are the modern-day equivalents for a man to establish his stature within the family today? Increasingly, the criteria become that of his bureaucratic management skill, his technical competence, and his suave social manner.

Women have also been confronted with problems of role adjustment. The female college graduate of today may be able to program a computer, serve as a securities analyst, or prepare a nationwide advertising campaign—but her kitchen competence may be limited to thawing a TV dinner. Increasingly one meets career women who are holding occupational positions of greater responsibility than their husbands. The problem is "how do men and women adjust or maintain their sexual identity in a nontraditional world?"

In the past, one's identity was proscribed by his or her status. Today, however, people are increasingly faced with the problem of developing their identity from a nonsexual occupational reference. Thus, in today's urbanized society we see the modern husband assisting with household tasks that traditionally only women might perform, while women assume management roles that were the traditional province of men. These changes have resulted in new definitions of masculinity and feminity, creating additional problems of adjustment to the new roles. From this the conflict over women's rights, as well as conflict over financial and social equality, have become current social problems of the American society.

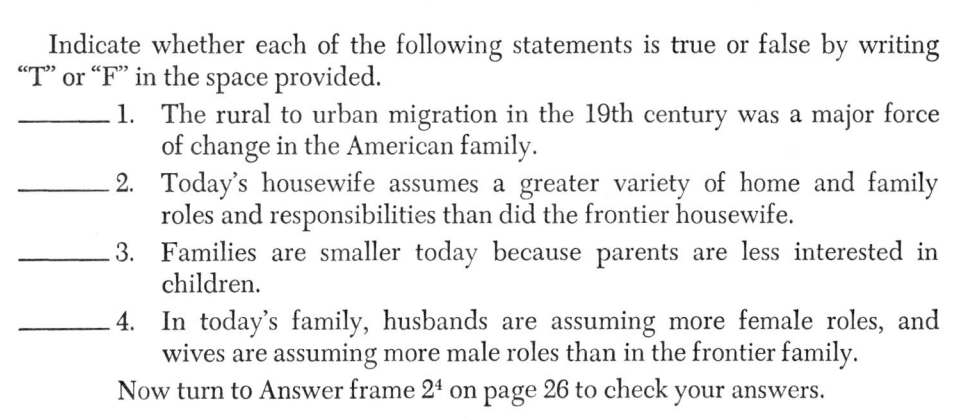

Indicate whether each of the following statements is true or false by writing "T" or "F" in the space provided.

_____ 1. The rural to urban migration in the 19th century was a major force of change in the American family.

_____ 2. Today's housewife assumes a greater variety of home and family roles and responsibilities than did the frontier housewife.

_____ 3. Families are smaller today because parents are less interested in children.

_____ 4. In today's family, husbands are assuming more female roles, and wives are assuming more male roles than in the frontier family.

Now turn to Answer frame 2⁴ on page 26 to check your answers.

Frame 3⁴

Alternatives to marriage. The customs of marriage are changing, and increasingly young couples today are demanding more affection and a higher degree of satisfaction and personal development from marriage. No longer are women searching for the simple pattern of finding a husband, raising children, and being immersed in small mountains of dirty diapers and dishes.

Many young people today are living together, as couples or in communes, in what is sometimes incorrectly called "trial marriage." This term is incorrect because trial marriage implies a serious commitment to marry if all goes well, and most of the young people who are living together today have not made any such commitment. Instead, most of them have made only the temporary agreement to live together as long as they wish. There is evidence that most of these pairings either break up or graduate into a legal marriage in a few years. But the large number of young people who express disbelief in the desirability of marriage is a relatively new development. Not that attacks upon marriage as an institution are at all new—they are as old as written history. What is new is the sharing of these attitudes among a major faction of the young generation.

Nor are any of the proposed alternatives to marriage at all new. Living together in twos, threes, groups, and communes has been tried numerous times throughout history. To date, these forms of marriage have "worked" only in relatively simple, stable, unspecialized, societies. Whether any of the current alternatives can "work" in a changing, individualized, highly differentiated society remains to be seen. Nevertheless, the impact of changed attitudes can be observed. The marriage license listing in the newspapers often show half the licenses issued to couples giving the same address, and whereas yesterday's mothers may most often have worried lest their daughters lose their virginity, today's mothers may be more likely to worry lest their daughters forget their birth control pills!

Divorce. The change in divorce rates is an indirect product of industrialization. Divorce rates in early frontier families were very low (approximately 1 in 36 marriages) as there were few opportunities aside from marriage for a woman to find employment to support herself or

Answer frame 2[4]

1. True. The rural to urban migration changed both the roles of family members and the lifestyles, causing a large scale reorganization of family structure and function.
2. True. Modernization and urbanization has forced today's housewife to be adept at managing a small business (the home) and be skilled in social entertaining in addition to being mother, wife, and housekeeper.
3. False. Industrialization has made large families obsolete, but now the emphasis is placed on the quality of a child's life, rather than on the quantity of children.
4. True. Traditional family roles have been drastically changed by industrialization. Men now pride themselves for their culinary skills, while women have been developing professional and organizational skills.

If you missed any of the above, restudy Frame 2[4] before starting Frame 3[4] on page 25.

Frame 3[4] continued

her children. Divorce in the 1800s was not only socially undesirable, but (for any but the very wealthy) also economically disasterous for both the wife and family as it inevitably led to economic hardship. Thus early American social values condemned marital dissolution in any form, and it became highly dishonorable for a man to leave his wife and children or for a wife to desert her husband.

However, the emergence of economic affluence and equal employment opportunities for women allows financial and social independence for women, neutralizing the economic stigma of divorce or separation as well as reducing the pressures for a woman to find a husband. Economic prosperity in America has been accompanied with a change in personal values, favoring individualism, personal development, and happiness, particularly within the context of marriage. The economic bonds that once tied a couple together in frontier times have weakened and been replaced with ties of affection and happiness with one's mate.

Thus it can be seen that climbing divorce rates do not necessarily represent any decay in public morality, but rather reflect the emergence of new social values of individualism and personal satisfaction.

Frontier marriage was primarily a working relationship and secondarily (if at all) a romantic adventure. Today the order is reversed. Our high standards for marital success, demanding a high level of mutual companionship and affection, are therefore a direct cause of our high divorce rate.

The rapidly climbing divorce rates of recent decades has led many people to predict that the rate of marital disorganization is leading to an increasing disorganization in society and a corresponding decline in public morality. Although there is no question that divorce is disorganizing to the individual family unit, still statistics show that over 90 percent of divorcees remarry within five years. Thus, although divorce is disrupting to the individuals at the time, the rate of remarriage is actually reinstituting a new state of order and organization in society. More people are marrying today than ever before, and more couples are desiring to have children (although fewer children per family unit). These facts lead Reiss to predict that the marriage and family institutions are stronger than they were in the past. [Ira L. Reiss, *The Family System in America* (New York: Holt, Rinehart and Winston, Inc., 1971), pp. 187–95.]

The abortion controversy. Abortion has been known and practiced in various societies for thousands of years. In Europe and the United States, abortion during early pregnancy was a private matter until quite recently. The Catholic Church had no binding prohibition against early abortion until 1918 (except for a short period under Gregory XIV in the 16th century). [R. J. Huser, "Abortion, III (Canon Law)," *The New Catholic Encyclopedia,* I (1967), p. 29.] Beginning in the 1830s the states of the United

States began passing laws prohibiting all abortions except when the life of the mother was threatened by the pregnancy. The pressure for this legislation arose from the fact that *all* surgery was exceedingly dangerous and fatal about one third of the time. Thus the object was to save the lives of women.

This purpose is lost today, as a hospital abortion is one of the least hazardous of surgical procedures, even less dangerous than childbirth. But abortion is one of the most hotly contested of public issues. Opponents of legalized abortion maintain that any act of abortion is an act of murder and taking the life of a human being. Supporters argue that an early embryo is not a human being, that the world is overpopulated, and that bringing a child into the world should be an act of conscious choice, and not an accidental consequence of human passion or weakness.

Moral arguments can be constructed on both sides: For proponents of abortion the "right to life" is the child's "right to be wanted and loved"; while for others the morality of "anticipatory murder" is the morality of "compulsory childbirth." The crucial question is, "When does a human embryo acquire a soul and become a human being?" If "life" begins at the moment of conception, then abortion is murder; if "life" does not begin until some later moment, then abortion is a matter for the exercise of human judgment. Historically, neither the church nor the state has viewed the embryo as a human being. A miscarriage in early pregnancy is not followed by a death announcement, death certificate, funeral, burial, or listing in the family Bible—any of the acts which normally follow the death of a human being. But this fact has been little noted in the abortion controversy.

The United States Supreme Court in 1973 ruled that states may not interfere in early abortion. Opponents are now seeking to reverse this decision through a constitutional amendment, and the bitter controversy seems destined to continue. The value conflict over the desirability of abortion continues to remain a social problem of the American society.

Indicate whether each of the following statements is true or false by writing "T" or "F" in the space provided.

_____ 1. Your author expects that the present form of marriage will soon go out of style.

_____ 2. The increasing divorce rate of the last few decades is a clear reflection of the decline in morality of today's society.

_____ 3. Research clearly shows that family disorganization is disrupting our society.

_____ 4. Abortion has always been illegal throughout history.

Now check your answers by turning to Answer frame 3[4] on page 28.

Answer frame 3[4]

1. False. Although there is a renewed interest in experimenting with alternate marriage forms, it is unlikely that the monogamous marriage will be changed.
2. False. The increase in the divorce rate is more a reflection of the latent effects of industrialization than an indication of any change in morality. Divorcees soon remarry, suggesting that people are not disillusioned with marriage, just their first choice in marriage.
3. False. To the contrary, although there are disorganizing elements in the modern family, most researchers feel that the rate of marriage and remarriage is a reorganizing force in society.
4. False. In the United States, it has only been illegal since 1918.

If you missed any of the above, review Frame 3[4] before starting Chapter 5.

chapter 5

WOMEN IN MODERN SOCIETY

Frame 1[5]

The venerable Henry Higgins in *My Fair Lady* will always be remembered for his question "Why can't a woman be more like a man?" and authors Lerner and Lowe leave the suggestion that Henry Higgins' motivation to marry Elisa Dolittle was inspired by the quality of person that he had made of her.

At most times and places in history women have had little choice over the control of their destiny or themselves, and for the most part they became what men allowed or required them to be. Although it is fashionable to attribute women's lowly status to male chauvinism, this is not the complete explanation. Pregnancy and childbirth have always tied women to the home and the sexual division of labor generally assigned to women those tasks which could be combined with childbearing and baby tending. Although very practical, this had the effect of giving most of the monotonous, repetitive tasks to women and most of the exciting adventurous tasks to men.

Historically, women's status has varied somewhat according to her function. In hunting societies men did the hunting; in agricultural societies, women often did most of the croptending, and their status tended to rise along with the increased importance of their work role. Yet the status gains were limited. Women's status has been supportive and secondary to that of men in nearly every society in history.

The development of new technology for birth control and child care has undermined the physiological and economic necessity that women remain forever tied to the cradle. The industrial revolution so altered the nature of work that the traditional sexual divisions of labor were no longer justified. The discoveries of natural and social science have destroyed the ideological basis for rigid sexual division of labor or for subordinate female roles. These forces have combined to provide the underpinning for most rapid change in traditional sex roles and sex-linked behavior.

The women's liberation movement in America is one of the more recent social movements, and the changing definitions and perceptions of female roles and status is creating a new social problem on the American scene.

Changing roles and status. The problem of sex roles in America can be conceptualized within the context of changing perceptions and definitions of female status and roles in society. Almost from the point of birth, each sex is socialized into its expected future roles; if the baby is male, he is given simple blue clothing and soon a toy truck or play tools. In short, these are items that inspire instrumental acts, such as construction, building, management, and organizational skills. As he matures, the male child is taught to "take it like a man" when he cries, to plan for a profession, and to seek out instrumental tasks such as competition in sports, and to be the leader of his group.

A female child, on the other hand, is decorated in cute frilly clothes, given pictures and puzzles to occupy her time, and a collection of dolls with which she can play "mother." As she matures, she is taught that whenever she competes with boys, she should not win; she is taught to perform in music and dance, but not to compose; and to copy great men in history in form and style, but not to create new patterns. Finally, she is taught to spend hours in learning how to decorate herself with cosmetics and to dress to be attractive to men for marriage, which is alleged to be her ultimate goal in life. In short, female children are taught to perform *expressive* or supportive roles in life, while male children are taught to perform *instrumental* or constructive roles in life. Instrumental roles carry more power and privilege and give men a definite advantage over women in the American society, while the supportive nature of female roles tends to lock women into a subordinate or subservient position in life.

The fundamental differential in power and privilege in sex roles flows from a long tradition based upon the structure and organization of agricultural or tribal societies where men were usually on hand to make the major decisions for the family and to perform the instrumental roles. However, with the development of industrialization, their jobs took men away from the home and women had to perform more instrumental functions within the family. This gave women a new position of power and the modern American family gradually began to shift from a patriarchal rule (father rule) to equalitarian rule (equal power in decision making). Industrialization also required a large pool of trained labor, thus industrialists sought out females to maintain the production lines and do the office work. Women were sent to schools to learn basic skills to fulfill such positions, and also to acquire the refinements necessary to make them attractive wives to professional minded husbands. Employment outside the home gave women a new source of wealth and independence from men. Some women attended colleges and universities and were educated to equalitarian and individualistic values. The convergence of these factors (new wealth and independence, increased education, and the assumption of more instrumental roles within the family), along with the emergence of new values for human rights and individualism in the American society that occurred during the 1960s, created the basis for the emergence of the women's liberation movement of the 1970s. The working woman has now become so common that her role has been institutionalized in the American society, and it is quite unlikely that women will ever return to the subservient role position they have held in the past. Further, the strong shift in values in the American society toward individualism and civil rights will reinforce the emerging movement. Thus it is likely that the women's liberation movement will grow in strength and prominence in the future.

Indicate whether each of the following statements is true or false by writing "T" or "F" in the space provided.

_____ 1. Women are kept in a subordinate status position purely because men are chauvinistic.

_____ 2. The industrial revolution is a primary cause of the change in females' roles and status.

_____ 3. True sexual equality will not occur until female children are socialized to new sex roles.

_____ 4. Instrumental roles are rather powerless roles in the American society.

Now turn to Answer frame 1[5] on page 32 to check your answers.

Frame 2[5]

To Freud's perplexed query, "What *do* women want," there are a variety of answers within the women's liberation movement.

1. *Economic equality* is a minimum goal, to which most people today give at least lip service. This goal includes equal pay for equal work, equal access to and equal recruitment procedures for all jobs (except where inherent sex differences are clearly relevant to job performance, as with actors or sopranos), equal promotions, and so on.

2. *Legal equality* would remove many special limitations upon women as property-owners, loan applicants, and so on. (This would also remove many special protections, such as the wife's right to economic support from her husband.)

3. *Social equality* would end the many indications of subordinate status which are annoying to many women. Loss of maiden name, generic use of masculine gender pronouns, and disapproval of unaccompanied women in bars are examples of many subtle reinforcers of women's subordinate status.

4. *Androgynous sex roles* would go far beyond these relatively moderate proposals, and would eliminate all sex role differences except those absolutely required by biology. With androgynous sex roles, women would still bear and possibly nurse babies, but all other child care duties would be the equal responsibility of both parents. Individual couples might divide child care and income producing responsibilities according to personal preference, but there would be no socially expected assignment of child care to the wife and income producing to the husband. Part-time and split-time jobs would be equally available to both sexes without salary or promotional penalty. Androgynous sex roles would eliminate, insofar as is biologically possible, all sex differences in role behavior, and presumably, in personality as well.

Supporters of women's liberation are divided upon goals. The more moderate supporters view the demand for androgyny as unwarranted, divisive, and inexpedient; the more radical members view the moderates as cowards. As with all social movements, women's liberation is riven with factionalism and dissent.

Are androgynous sex roles desirable? In all known societies, sexual role ascription has been a part of the organization of the society. Performance of any role is known to be most successful when role preparation for precisely known tasks can begin early in life, so that one can develop the attitudes and desires which make the role satisfying and rewarding. Can children be socialized to fill androgynous sex roles successfully and happily? Since there is no historical evidence upon which to judge, perhaps only a trial will tell us.

Indicate whether each of the following statements is true or false by writing "T" or "F" in the space provided.

_____ 1. Basically, women are quite clear in the goals they seek from the women's liberation movement.

_____ 2. For women to gain economic, legal, and social equality, they would have to sacrifice some of the traditional privileges they have received.

_____ 3. If sex roles became truly androgynous, women would not have any roles left to perform in life.

Now turn to Answer frame 2[5] on page 32 to check your answers.

Frame 3[5]

All social movements consist of a convergence of persons and groups, each seeking something slightly different. The diversity in composition of the subgroups and the differences in goals often make it difficult for people outside the movement to understand just what is happening in the social movement.

Although the most volatile segment of the women's liberation movement consists of students and white, middle-class, college-educated women, the broader membership consists of a wide variety of different female groups. These groups give varying degrees of support for the movement, and to understand the movement it is necessary to classify the different factions among women today.

Particularly in the past, and even the largest proportion of women today, are socialized to accept and enjoy the role of mother and *contented housewife*. These women find their primary purpose in life and personal fulfillment through the achievements of their husband and children. They often take pleasure from their housekeeping and cooking, participating in community organizations and school activities, and in caring for their family. In short, they enjoy their position and are satisfied with the rewards that come their way. They are in some cases confused about the women's liberation movement and do not understand the goals of more radical females. Contented housewives are unlikely to join or support any movement for change in the roles of women. The "consciousness-raising" sessions intended to make women aware of their injustices, are rarely effective with contented housewives.

The frustrated housewives on the other hand, are usually those who are disappointed in marriage and find housecleaning and babytending to be boring and unfulfilling. They expected more from marriage or life than they got, and after several years of trying to find fulfillment through conventional means, they may turn to the social movement as a means of escaping from their present station in life. Such members often lack intellectual comprehension of the movement, but they often make up for this lack through idealistic commitment and frenetic activity. Frustrated housewives provide a large body of potential members for the women's liberation movement and are usually responsive to the movement's purposes and actions.

Satisfied working women are often working to fill a stage of life—until they get married, until they have children, or after the children have grown up and are working until retirement. They are often employed in menial or low-paying positions as clerks, waitresses, or secretaries, and rarely plan to make a career of their employment. Since these women are working by choice and are reasonably satisfied with their position, they are unlikely candidates for the women's liberation movement.

The confined working woman works out of necessity to support her home or children. She often resents having to work, finds little satisfaction with her job, and would escape from her present position if she could. These persons

Answer frame 1[5]

1. False. Although male chauvinism is a partial explanation, the subordinate status of women is also attributed to the roles they perform and the status of those roles.
2. True. Industrialization has provided technological means for removing women from the housekeeper and mother status, enabling them to assume new roles.
3. True. Currently female children are still socialized to traditional female roles (motherhood, housekeeper, and nurse). True equality would rquire that both male and female children be socialized to instrumental roles.
4. False. Instrumental roles involve responsibility, power, and privilege, thus are more powerful roles than expressive roles.

If you missed any of the above, restudy Frame 1[5] before starting Frame 2[5] on page 30.

Answer frame 2[5]

1. False. Although most women agree that they desire economic, legal, and social equality, beyond that, there is little consensus.
2. True. However, most liberated women feel that the gain would be much greater than the loss.
3. False. Women would still have roles, only there would be no sex distinction associated with the roles.

If you missed any of the above, reread Frame 2[5] before starting Frame 3[5] on page 31.

Frame 3[5] continued

often join the movement out of desperation and hope to achieve something different in life.

The *semi-professional* woman is one who has trained for an intermediate-status female occupation (nurse, teacher, or office manager) and finds fulfillment in her work. There are usually opportunities to achieve a reasonable degree of success and recognition in such occupations. The semiprofessional woman is usually quite devoted to her work and feels she is making a contribution to the community. The semiprofessional woman may be somewhat sympathetic to the women's movement, but rarely gives much commitment or effort. Like the working-class women, the semiprofessionals often support the job equality parts of the women's liberation movement, without much interest in the rest.

The *liberated professional* is often highly educated and intelligent, and has taken considerable effort to acquire the necessary training for her position. However, she often has chosen a profession that is dominated by males, and fails to receive professional recognition or opportunity for advancement. Thus professional women often become embittered and frustrated and turn to the movement with the hope of achieving the opportunity they feel they deserve. Such persons often compose the intellectual heart of the social movement, and seek institutional change within the society.

The *queen bee professional* is often a woman who has worked her way up through the system the hard way through exceptional effort and ability. She has finally made it to the top through considerable effort and sacrifice, and often resents the youthful liberationists who try to topple the system that has finally rewarded the queen bee with position and security. The queen bee has learned to compete as a man in a man's world, and to use rather aggressive and masculine tactics. Queen bee professionals rarely have any sympathy for younger professional women who try to use the civil rights leverage to attain a position the easy way. Thus, they are often outspoken opponents of the liberation movement and may vigorously resist any change in the system.

Racial minority females often feel the same frustrations as other women but reject the movement for quite different reasons. Their discrimination is twofold: They are discriminated against as women; but to a much greater degree they are discriminated against as minority persons. Thus, female minorities (except for liberated professionals) are occasionally prone to see the movement as only another means of potential oppression, and are likely to see its supporters as a collection of sexually or emotionally frustrated middle-class housewives who do not appreciate what they have attained in life. To poor black or Chicana women, heading a one-parent household, the pampered, dependent housewife role is one that many would love to try.

Different minority women tend to view the women's liberation movement in a different light. Indian and Chicana females may actually resist any changes in the status quo and reject any achievements of the movement, because they have a privileged (although somewhat subordinate) position in their heritage and are accorded considerable respect in their families. Thus, some minority females may not feel oppressed as women and see little from which to be liberated.

Although the vast majority of women in America are marginal members or supporters of the liberation movement, most women are receptive to its achievements. The movement is set on a course of direction and action that is not likely to be neutralized in the near future. Before too long, if not already, we will see a new emerging social problem for men in the American society, that of the respecification and redefinition of male roles as men adapt and adjust to the changing female roles. This area of change in the American society is only beginning.

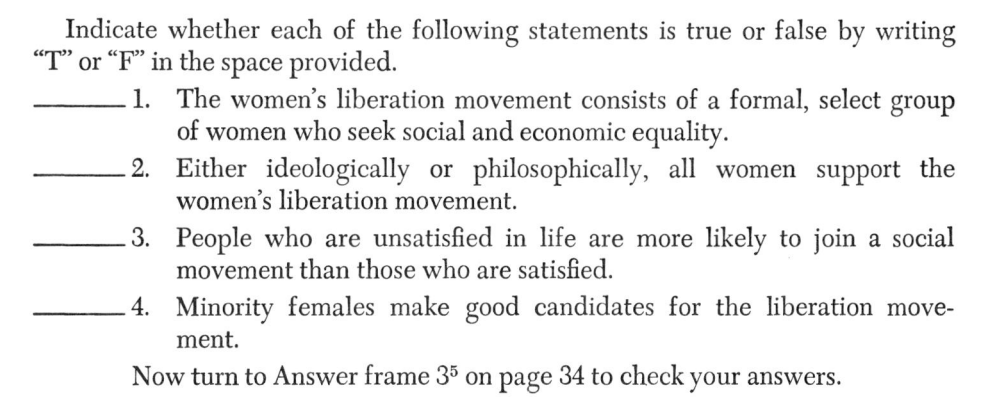

Indicate whether each of the following statements is true or false by writing "T" or "F" in the space provided.

_____ 1. The women's liberation movement consists of a formal, select group of women who seek social and economic equality.

_____ 2. Either ideologically or philosophically, all women support the women's liberation movement.

_____ 3. People who are unsatisfied in life are more likely to join a social movement than those who are satisfied.

_____ 4. Minority females make good candidates for the liberation movement.

Now turn to Answer frame 3[5] on page 34 to check your answers.

Answer frame 3[5]

1. False. The women's liberation movement is a broad social movement with women from a wide variety of backgrounds and ideologies participating.
2. False. Major segments of the female population do not agree with the goals and purposes of the movement, especially contented housewives and those who have found role fulfillment in their job or position.
3. True. Satisfied and contented persons make poor radicals.
4. False. Generally not. Minority females often feel that they have to achieve racial equality before they can hope to achieve sexual equality.

If you missed any of the above, reread Frame 3[5] before beginning Chapter 6.

chapter 6

THE YOUTH MOVEMENT

Frame 1[6]

Throughout history, youth have been portrayed in a negative light and have been viewed as a persistent "social problem" by the adult society. For many adults, Socrates' description of youth as being irresponsible, irrational, and irascible, is as true today as it was in 400 B.C.

Youth, adolescents, and college students today have become best known through student protests in the history of our nation. Although experienced some of the most extreme youth protest in the history of our nation. Although youth protest is not exactly a new phenomena to the American scene, recent protests were of an origin unique in our history and reflect new societal concerns which did not previously exist. The sociology of youth provides some insights into the emergence and growth of this social problem by examining the social changes that are occurring among youth today. [See *The Generation Gap*, a PLAID by Clifford E. Bryan and Robert L. Horton (Homewood, Ill.: Learning Systems Co., 1974).]

Youth-adult differences. The modern dress styles and divergent behavioral patterns tend to make today's youth particularly open to stereotyping (depicting a type of person based on characteristics that are commonly believed but factually inaccurate). The popular press, mass media, and conservative adults often tend to portray youth as radical, inconsiderate, unkempt, and socially undesirable semi-human beings. While for some this image is well earned and perhaps deserved, the stereotype falls far short of representing the majority of today's youth.

Although differences between adults and youth may be characterized in a variety of ways, some of the major differences are (1) age-related in education and experience, and (2) differences in status position and role expectations.

Education and experience. America's youth are blessed with an abundance of life experiences and educational opportunities. Through exposure to countless television programs and movies, today's toddler is more familiar with the launchings at Cape Kennedy (Canaveral) and the intricacies of guerrilla warfare than the literature of Grimm's Fairy Tales or Alice in Wonderland. By age ten, most children have vacationed across the nation, flown in jets, and are more likely to be interested in hipsters and dragsters than building castles in sandboxes.

In this age of affluence in the American society the few years of childhood are packed with more different experiences than grandparents had encountered in a lifetime. The "accelerated rate of life experiences" tends to numb youth to the simple pleasures that their parents might treasure (few youth get very excited about family hymn singing or picnics). Increasingly, parents and children find they have less and less in common in their interest and lifestyles, creating the much touted "generation gap" in American society, as well as causing parents to wonder what is happening to the younger generation which no longer follows traditional values and behavior.

The success of the modern educational system has also contributed to generational differences. Today's fifth grader is exposed to modern math, phonetic reading, and courses in science that far exceed the educational experiences of many parents. Thus, at almost any stage beyond the kindergarten level, children find that their learning in selected areas has exceeded that of their parents. This makes it difficult for children to respect their parents' knowledge and experiences (even though the parents' may be considerably broader).

By the time that the child has entered college, the differences have been so magnified that students sometimes find that there is little common ground for communication with the parents. College courses are designed to give a wide breadth of coverage on a multitude of subjects, and few parents have the time or energy left after a day of work at the office or caring for children to read philosophical treatises or polemical essays on current world events. Thus, when the college student returns home for vacations (after having devoted several months to the study and analysis of esoteric subjects), he finds that his parents are ill-informed and still mired in traditional or archaic attitudes toward education, philosophy, or world events. Thus, differences in education and experience often create barriers of communication and understanding that might never be bridged between the generations.

Role expectations. It seems almost an immutable law that elders will perceive the younger generation in a negative light, but also as immutable is the process whereby the "foot loose and fancy free" youth is transformed into the socially responsible adult pillar of the community. Some insight into this process can be gained by examining the cycle of development of generations in society.

It has long been recognized that a person's attitudes and behavior are a function of the role and status held by that person. Margaret Mead once observed that the adolescent period is a relatively non-status position in American society, and that a separate period of adolescence is characteristic of westernized societies and does not exist in the majority of cultures in the world. In the majority of other cultures, a child is immediately transferred to adulthood whenever he reaches a particular age or ability (proving one's hunting skills or the ability to bear children), and accorded all rights, privileges, and responsibilities of adulthood upon the initiation ceremony.

However, in America, adolescents are neither viewed as children (in which they are not expected to be responsible or mature) nor as fully adult (they must ask permission to go on a date and be home by 10:00 p.m.). A multitude of role expectations are held for adolescents, many of which are contradictory in nature—they can borrow the car and date (adult roles), but only if they clean their room first (child roles). Confusion over role expectations creates indecision, uncertainty, and frustration as the adolescent attempts to decide which role expectation is to be applied in a particular situation. Rebellion and insolence are diminished in families when parents define clear role expectations for their children.

Role socialization. However, in spite of differences in environments, range of experiences, and different lifestyles, for the most part children are socialized into the same adult roles as their parents were. This is both logical and simple that adults are the major role models for children and the whole of the child's educational and play experience is structured toward the anticipated performance of adult roles (boys are given trucks and tools to play with, and little girls are given dolls and homemaking utensils). Thus it is no surprise that Gallup polls report that over 50 percent of today's youth follow the same political lines, religious philosophies, and similar spending patterns as those of their parents.

This point is often overlooked by politicians and moralists. The 18-year-old vote was expected by political conservatives to wreak havoc among the 1972 presidential election, but in fact, the conservative youth vote only provided a greater margin of victory for Republican Richard M. Nixon. Moralists often predict that if the age of drinking is lowered, the highways will be filled with teenaged drunks, but states that have changed the legal age have failed to report most of the expected adverse effects.

Even the moral standards of youth do not appear to be as divergent from adult standards as many persons might think. Reiss, in an analysis of students' moral standards observes that the students' initial standards are those that are provided by their parents. Although a person's moral standards are open to change with experience in life, parents still provide the initial standards for their children. [*Family System*, p. 151–79.]

Since adults provide the major role models for youth to follow, and play a major role in role socialization, it is no surprise that there is a high degree of similarity in parent-child attitudes and behavior, more in fact than most people recognize or expect.

Indicate whether each of the following statements is true or false by writing "T" or "F" in the space provided.

_____ 1. Today's youth tend to burn through life experiences faster than their parents.

_____ 2. The differential between youth and adult experiences creates a "generation gap."

_____ 3. The status of the adolescent is clearly defined in the American society.

_____ 4. Typically, youth in America have rebelled against the political ideologies and religious beliefs of their parents.

Now turn to Answer frame 1[6] on page 38 to check your answers.

Frame 2[6]

The influence of society. The description above is not to suggest that there are no important differences between youth and adults—it would be naive to suggest that there were not. However, a sociological analysis would suggest that the origin of the differences is less a factor of youthful properties themselves than a result of change in the nature and organization of society itself. Social change is occurring at such a pace that each generation almost faces a new world and new nature of social order. Elders often find that the experiences of yesteryear are inapplicable to the modern world, and fail to attract much interest from the younger generation. Charles Reich has characterized this change in terms of consciousness levels, and suggests that today's youth are entering a new state of mind, that of Consciousness III. [Charles A. Reich, *The Greening of America* (New York: Random House, Inc., 1970).]

Reich characterizes the three stages of consciousness in terms of the following: Consciousness I consisted of the 18th century traditional outlook of the American farmer, the small businessman, and the worker who was trying to get ahead in the battle for survival in life. People during this period were home and family oriented, and their life philosophies were guided by a few simple fundamental principles of living. In short, life was simple and hard.

The period of Consciousness II developed, Reich says, with the emergence of industrialization and technology in America when we changed from a rural, traditional society into a massive complex of belching smokestacks and endless production lines. Consciousness II reflected the corporate ideology where men found their identity in the corporation for which they worked, and man and machine were so intricately wedded together that one could not determine where the machine ended and man began. This was the suburban society where each man's dream was to have his own little bungalow, with a fireplace and a tree, a wife and four kids, and a new car every few years. The suburbanite's life was ruled by the 8:00 a.m. to 5:00 p.m. regimen; each man existed to work, and work was the sum total of his existence. Families internalized the morals of the community as their own morality, and their whole perspective was guided toward "that next promotion up the ladder."

Consciousness III, however, was proposed by Reich to be a new state of mind and perspective of youth that provided an "inner guidance" for values and behavior. Although its heritage was born in the suburbia consciousness of the earlier generation, Consciousness III rejected the regimented and highly structured work and life patterns of the earlier generations. It called for individuals to seek out their own identity and purpose in life, then to structure their life so as to find personal fulfillment. Consciousness III accepted the promises of the emerging technological society (affluence for everyone; no hunger, illness, or hardship), and sought to orient technology and production toward humanistic needs. It valued individualism (do your own thing as long as it does not hurt anyone else), personal fulfillment (maximize all creative abilities and life opportunities), and personal satisfaction (the credit ethic of enjoy it today as there may be no tomorrow). However, Consciousness III saw inherent threats within the social organization of society that might prevent the fulfillment of the potential of the new technological society (such as impositions upon the rights of personal privacy, inequality of opportunity based upon institutionalized discrimination, and the corporate mentality embodied within the assertion that what is good for General Motors is good for the nation). Youth in Consciousness III feared the governmental and institutional logic and reasoning that brought us Vietnam, Watergate, and poverty in the midst of affluence. Thus, youth, having the freedom and luxury of time, energy, and idealism, strove to carry the banner forward to the new state of mind. They were encouraged by their eminent leaders—President Kennedy called for youth to "ask not what your country can do for you, but what you can do for your country," and President Johnson raised the hope of the nation in attempting to create the Great Society.

Thus youth in the 1960s were inspired to push hard to create the new society that was promised by technological-industrialism. Youth also, however, were impatient, and being reared in an "instant-oriented" society (instant coffee, instant creation, and instant ecstasy) many became discouraged when they failed to achieve instant reform after a decade of effort.

Answer frame 1[6]

1. True. By the time youth graduate from college, they have already experienced a greater variety of experiences than most of their grandparents have.
2. True. The differential between youth and adult experiences creates little common ground between youth and adults, creating a generation gap.
3. False. In the American society, the adolescent status is rather undefined; adolescents are neither treated consistently as children or adult.
4. False. Actually most youth use their parents as role models, and accept their parents' beliefs as their own initial beliefs.

If you missed any of the above, reread Frame 1[6] before starting Frame 2[6] on page 36.

Frame 2[6] continued

Indicate whether each of the following statements is true or false by writing "T" or "F" in the space provided.

_____ 1. Many parent-youth differences are created by social change.
_____ 2. Yesteryear's youth never experienced the feelings of Reich's Consciousness I and II.
_____ 3. Reich characterized Consciousness III as a youth oriented attitudinal and value system, more than an adult system.
_____ 4. It is Consciousness III that has made youth immoral, and gave rise to laziness and apathy among youth.

Now turn to Answer frame 2[6] on page 40 to check your answers.

Frame 3[6]

The future. Although the future always carries some degree of uncertainty, there are certain sociological factors that will tend to influence the future of the youth scene in America, the foremost among these factors is (1) population, and (2) the possible development of a new social class of youth.

A theory recently proposed by Daniel P. Moynihan (a Harvard sociologist and former advisor to President Nixon) suggests that the radicalism and rebellion of the 1960s can in large part be attributed to the rapid increase in the proportion of youth in the population. Demographers note that the post–World War II baby boom produced a 52 percent increase in the youth population, which was some five times the average rate of growth for earlier decades. The 1960s saw almost 14 million young people graduating from high school and entering colleges. These youth were isolated on college campuses, were drafted into the Army, or were attracted to close-knit hippie subcommunities in metropolitan cities. The high degree of spatial concentration of youth produced a large reservoir of emotionally enlightened and intellectually motivated people whose energy could easily be mobilized against the social inequality and inadequacies of the American society. The lingering Vietnam War, continuing racial and social inequality, and the relative ineffectiveness of the Johnsonian "Great Society" programs both angered and activated many of these young people to seek widespread societal reform. Super-energized youth sought out the idealism of the college atmosphere, and, as suggested by Richard Flacks [Richard Flacks, *Youth and Social Change* (Chicago: Markham Publishing Co., 1971).], they flocked to form an intellectually oriented youth subculture. As a result, anti-war protests, campus revolts, and riots in the streets became the order of the decade in communities all across America.

With the beginning of the 1970s, however, several changes occurred which neutralized the youth movement in America. Institutional reforms defused the social issues over the draft and the Vietnam War; a mini-recession reduced the level of social expectations and invited conservatism and restraint; and President Nixon's passive approach to social issues dampened enthusiasm for radicalism in society. Further, many of yesteryears' radicals had passed the tragic age of 30 and found it hard to sell their ideology and image to a new crop of youth who were only in the primary grades when the burning age of radicalism began. So, from boredom, from frustration, or from a pathetic sense of failure, the radical leaders of yesterday retreated into oblivion.

Demographers now predict that the huge population surge of youth has passed, and their proportion in the society will remain somewhat steady in the 1970s and actually decline in the 1980s. Although youth as a social category in the population will likely remain (as they have built a liberal tradition and ideology), Moynihan predicts that they will not assume the pervasive power that they have gathered in the past. If Moynihan is right, youth will remain a significant force in the American society, but never the controlling force they have enjoyed in the past.

The youth movement of the 1960s created a new age of radicalism, and perhaps a new social class of youthful intelligentsia. Now we are returning to a period of apathy and estrangement among young people today; college campuses are quiet again and college professors who in an earlier decade were sought out for their radical ideologies now may feel fortunate if they can get a student to comment on almost any subject in class. The youth movement has gone another full cycle, and now perhaps will sleep in the peacefulness and humanism of Consciousness III until a new cause and state of activism emerges.

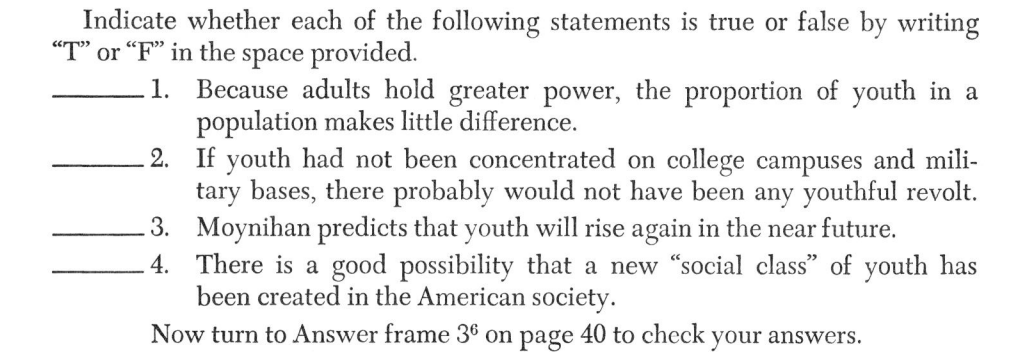

Indicate whether each of the following statements is true or false by writing "T" or "F" in the space provided.

_____ 1. Because adults hold greater power, the proportion of youth in a population makes little difference.
_____ 2. If youth had not been concentrated on college campuses and military bases, there probably would not have been any youthful revolt.
_____ 3. Moynihan predicts that youth will rise again in the near future.
_____ 4. There is a good possibility that a new "social class" of youth has been created in the American society.

Now turn to Answer frame 3[6] on page 40 to check your answers.

Answer frame 2[6]

1. True. With social change, youth have different experiences than their parents, creating a generation gap of sorts.
2. False. Reich's Consciousness I and II were attitudinal and value states of the society in early America, and youth were indoctrinated into these attitudes the same as their parents were.
3. True. Consciousness III stressed values favoring permissiveness, individualism, and the "hang loose and stay cool" ethic, all of which are more youth oriented than adult oriented.
4. False. Consciousness III was a humanitarian ethic, that stressed honesty and dedication in life.

If you missed any of the above, reread Frame 2[6] before starting Frame 3[6] on page 38.

Answer frame 3[6]

1. False. Size of population is potential power, and the large increase in the youth population gave them a vastly increased power base.
2. True. The vastly increased concentration of youth into small spatial areas intensifies the possibilities for interaction and group action.
3. False. On the contrary. Moynihan predicts that youth will not have the power that they held in the past few years, although they still will remain a significant segment of the American society.
4. True. Although youth in America have not assumed all aspects of a social class, there is an emerging youthful intelligentsia, along with specialized patterns for consumption, and accompanying lifestyle.

If you missed any of the above, reread Frame 3[6] before working Examination 2 on page 134. Then begin Chapter 7 on page 41.

chapter 7

MINORITY GROUPS: PREJUDICES AND STEREOTYPES

Frame 1[7]

There is a variety of minority groups in the American society; with a little thought the reader could easily list a dozen or more. The blacks, Indians, and Chicanos are the most publicized groups, but the list could also include the aged, youth, women, the poor, Catholics, Jews, Mormons, Chinese, foreigners, the handicapped, and almost any other identifiable category of people with unique physical, social, or ethnic characteristics.

Several different definitions may be used to specify a minority group—the size of the group relative to the larger population; the possession of unique, distinguishable features such as skin color, speech patterns, or religious beliefs; a social definition of the group as "different"; or the power or status of the group relative to the larger groups in society. The latter definition is often preferred by sociologists because sometimes groups which are numerically the majority in a society may still be in a minority position of power, wealth, or prestige (such as women in the United States, blacks in Rhodesia, and colonialized populations throughout the world).

Strictly speaking, racial problems involve a conflict between two racial groups, but the substance of the problem is usually depicted more accurately as a conflict between opposing power groups in the society—the dominant majority and the minority. Since other minority groups (the poor, handicapped, and women) in the American society share a similar status and power position as the racial groups, this author feels that it is more appropriate to assume a wider perspective and discuss racial problems as a form of minority group problems.

Racial groups. Racial groups are usually distinguished from other minority groups on the basis of anatomical similarities in body shape, skin color, hair texture, and facial features. Most commonly, racial groups are classified into the Caucasoid (white), Mongoloid (oriental), and Negroid (black). Although people often assume that the different races are of different genetic origins, most physical anthropologists and anatomists agree that all races descended from the same genetic ancestors. Many physical characteristics that have become known as "racial features" appear to be less a product of different genetic origins than a product of a long period of anatomical specialization that occurred when the different groups adapted to the climate and environment where they settled. Many supposed racial characteristics such as musical or physical abilities, or food preferences are a product of climatic and cultural adaptation rather than genetic inheritance. As of yet, there are no reliably proven differences among the "races" in intelligence, physical ability, or social behavior; research shows that aside from such features as height and body build (which were developed through anatomical specialization), and the influence of diet (which may limit physical or mental development), each race and ethnic group appears to show approximately the same distribution of physical and mental abilities as the others. Any behavior or ability differences that are observed appear to be either a product of climate, diet, or cultural learning, or of stereotypes artificially ascribed by the larger society.

Social distance. Although Will Rogers became famous for the statement, "I never met a man I didn't like," few persons are as accepting as Rogers. For the most part, people do not like all racial, religious, or ethnic groups equally, and find some groups more acceptable than others. People tend to like those persons who are most like themselves, and the greater the difference from their own social type, the greater the social distance or degree of acceptability of the group.

The concept of social distance was devised by Emory Bogardus, as he noticed that some ethnic or religious groups were assimilated more rapidly than others, and that the rate of assimilation appeared to be associated with the degree of similarity of the minority group to the majority group. [Emory S. Bogardus, "Racial Reactions by Regions," *Sociology and Social Research,* 43 March–April 1959): 286–90.] Bogardus devised a scale to measure social distance by asking people of the majority group if they would allow a person from the group to "move to America," "to move to the neighborhood," "to move next door," or to "marry into the family." He found that Americans could relate rapidly with the English and Northern Europeans because of the high degree of cultural similarity and speech patterns. In contrast, the cultural patterns and physical features of the Iranians, Turkish, or Chinese set them apart and hindered their assimilation. Thus, the social distance between groups is affected by cultural differences, religious and political ideologies, and the similarity of race, color, or physical features.

Indicate whether each of the following statements is true or false by writing "T" or "F" in the space provided.

_____ 1. All racial characteristics are genetically determined.

_____ 2. A minority group is always smaller in population than a majority group.

_____ 3. Some races are just naturally born with more intelligence and abilities than others.

_____ 4. Social distance refers to the geographical separation of races in a society.

Now turn to Answer frame 1[7] on page 44 to check your answers.

Frame 2[7]

Stereotypes and prejudices. It is almost an immutable tendency for groups to develop stereotypes of each other, and on the basis of stereotypes, to develop prejudices which in turn can serve as a basis for discrimination. The tendency to stereotype (to ascribe social or behavioral characteristics to a group without factual basis—"all blacks have a natural sense of rhythm and love to eat watermelon") is present in all groups, dominant and minority (witness the black power assertion that "all whites are racists"). Stereotypes are generated by the tendency to differentiate between the "in-group" (the group in which you are a member) and the "out-group" (which is all others not included in the in-group). In-group membership tends to create a sense of belongingness and loyalty and facilitates the development of an individual's identity. In our modern society, whites stereotype blacks as lazy and shiftless, blacks stereotype whites as exploitative and unworthy of trust, and both groups characterize Indians and Chicanos as people who live like animals; Protestants criticize the Catholics for their allegiance to the Pope, Jews for being lecherous money-grabbers, while both groups reject Mormons for having a modern day saint; Republicans stereotype Democrats; urbanites make fun of the "country hicks"; and even Boy Scouts have been known to take a few swipes at 4-H members. In short, all tend to stereotype the other groups.

A *stereotype* is a gross exaggeration of certain perceived characteristics of some members of a group. Then this caricature is applied to all members of the group. Nonflattering stereotypes spread because they meet the need to demean others whom we dislike or oppose. Thus the stereotype prohibitionist was a sour scarecrow-like killjoy wearing out-of-date clothing. Flattering stereotypes also develop (the wise, kindly country doctor), but more often the stereotyping process is derogatory. Stereotypes thus provide a justification for dislikes and prejudices. A *prejudice* is a judgment of a person according to some presumed group characteristics, instead of by his individual qualities. It is thus a *pre-judgment,* which is made without knowing anything about a person except his group identity. Although prejudices may be positive when they inspire patriotism or in-group loyalties, they are most often pronounced in a negative sense against another group. Through labeling another group as undesirable or disreputable, people may then hate or discriminate against the group without violating their own conscience. And prejudice is a two-way street. Majority prejudice against minorities is equalled by minority prejudice against the majority or against other minorities. "Nigger" and "honkie" are equally prejudicial.

Although prejudices are usually directed toward a group of persons, they are not a product of that group itself, but rather attitudes based upon stereotypes applied to the group. Thus the focus for the study of prejudices is not the group to which the prejudice is directed, but rather the person holding or applying the prejudice. By examining the prejudiced person, we can learn of the nature of prejudice itself, regardless of the group to which it is applied.

In examining the nature of the prejudice, we see first that *prejudices are learned*. Little children when playing tend to accept all other children as equal, and rarely notice whether the playmate is Catholic or Protestant, or black or white, at least not until an older person points out the difference and indicates that the trait is undesirable. Once children are taught what differences to look for and how they are supposed to feel about them, they will be able to act in a prejudicial manner. Thus, people learn their prejudices from their parents, friends, and the people they socialize with.

Prejudice is learned through contact with other people, not from the groups to which it is directed. In fact, the *less* contact the person has with the minority group, the more prejudiced he may be! This conclusion arose from research on antisemitism, which found that school children who had little contact with Jewish people (in this case a small farming community in North Dakota where no Jews lived) were more antisemitic than school children in metropolitan communities with a significant Jewish population. Where there is little or no contact with a minority group, people are likely to accept prejudiced stereotypes as truth, since there is little chance to evaluate the stereotypes themselves. Contact with the minority group allows people an opportunity to examine popular stereotypes and arrive at a more realistic conception of the minority group.

Prejudices are assigned to the group and not individuals. Prejudiced people are often prone to deny their prejudices by pronouncing "I'm not prejudiced, why I even have a friend who is . . ." Meanwhile, the same person may likely protest the invasion of blacks, hippies, and other "undesirables" into the neighborhood, insist upon segregation in the schools, and complain about the requirements of the Fair Employment Practices Law. Many "Sunday liberals" (who praise all people on Sunday, then discriminate on Monday) may come to know and like a minority person on a personal basis ("He's a good one and not like the others"), but still reject the group on a collective basis.

Prejudices are largely unconscious and exist because they are satisfying. Few people are aware of their prejudices—if anything, the degree of prejudice is almost directly related to the intensity with which they deny that they are prejudiced. All persons are prejudiced against some group to some extent, but the most prejudiced are those who do not even realize that

Answer frame 1[7]

1. False. The vast majority of so-called "racial characteristics" are a product of environmental adaptation or are erroneously ascribed to the group.
2. False. Minority groups may be defined in a number of ways; they may be smaller in number, weaker in power, or simply in a disadvantaged position in the social structure of society.
3. False. There are no scientifically proven differences in intelligence or ability among the different races.
4. False. Social distance refers to the social "acceptability" of different racial or cultural groups, regardless of their geographical location.

If you missed any of the above, reread Frame 1[7] before starting Frame 2[7] on page 42.

Frame 2[7] continued

they are. Instead, they perceive their prejudices as *facts* which any reasonable man should recognize as such. Prejudices can be very satisfying at times, as they yield a sense of superiority over the other group and enable people to elevate their own status as they look down upon the minority group.

Prejudices can be created or dissolved and are often encouraged in the name of nationalism and patriotism. However, national prejudices are prone to shift according to the expediency of foreign policy. Since the turn of the century, Americans have had to learn to hate Germans during World War I, to like them after 1919, to hate them again during World War II, and to like them after 1945, then to split the group, liking West Germans and hating those Germans who happened to get caught in East Germany when the Iron Curtain was raised. In another example, Russians were allies during World War II, were cold war enemies under Eisenhower and Nixon, remained enemies under Kennedy and Johnson, then became friends again under the same president who bitterly attacked them when he was vice president in the 1950s. The same shifts in our attitudes have occurred regarding China, Japan, Cuba, the Arabian nations, and Far Eastern nations. National prejudices can become tools of international relations and policy, and governments frequently turn them on and off as the need arises.

Indicate whether each of the following statements is true or false by writing "T" or "F" in the space provided.

_____ 1. Most highly prejudiced people are not aware that they are prejudiced.
_____ 2. Everyone holds some prejudices.
_____ 3. In order to understand prejudices, we study the group that people are prejudiced against.
_____ 4. All prejudices are bad.

Now turn to Answer frame 2[7] on page 46 to check your answers.

Frame 3[7]

The prejudiced personality. Prejudices may assume many forms, and every person holds some prejudice against one group or another. However, some persons tend to be more widely prejudiced than others, and this pattern has been sufficiently established through research that scientists have concluded that a type of "prejudiced personality" does exist. For example, highly prejudiced persons tend to be somewhat insecure in their status, authoritarian with others, aggressive and overly concerned with power and "toughness," highly egocentric and relatively uncreative, often have problems in dealing with their anxieties, and hold rigid conventional moral standards for themselves and others.

The unprejudiced persons, on the other hand, tend to be more passive and secure in their status, are more permissive and tolerant, and rarely seek dominance over others. They generally are more flexible and self-reliant, are more humanitarian and equalitarian in perspective, and accept minorities on a personal basis rather than a group basis.

While there are many individual exceptions, educated persons tend to hold fewer prejudices than the less educated. It is uncertain whether this is because education makes one more tolerant and objective in their perceptions, or because education brings one into association with other people who are less prejudiced.

Techniques for reducing prejudice. Numerous techniques have been proposed for changing the levels of prejudice that people hold. Religious leaders have proposed that a return to religion should make men more humanistic. However, Sunday morning still remains the most segregated hour of the week in most churches. There is some evidence that conventionally religious people are *more* prejudiced than the less religious. Churches may have been as often an obstacle as an aid to racial tolerance.

An improved system of education has also been proposed as a means of reducing levels of prejudice. Although education may tend to make people more objective in accepting stereotypes, a century of mass education in America has done little to bring the races together. In fact, the public schools in many northern cities are more segregated today than they were 50 years ago! Thus we can only conclude that although education may be effective for a few persons, it has thus far been a rather impotent force in changing levels of prejudice in the society.

Since excessive prejudices are often viewed as a psychological abnormality, it has been proposed that prejudiced persons simply be given mass psychotherapy as a solution. Psychotherapy would work on an individual basis, but prejudices are so widely held among the population that almost all persons would have to be psychoanalyzed! This goal may be desirable, but hardly feasible with 225 million people in America.

The role of contact. Research has shown that prejudices are often the strongest in regions that have the least contact with the minority group. Prejudices are also directed toward the group rather than persons, so having one black family in a white community will not likely affect white attitudes toward blacks in general. Segregation, which has the effect of keeping groups separate, actually tends to increase the social distance between the groups and enhances the development of prejudices rather than lessen their development.

Research by Lazarsfeld shows that people in segregated neighborhoods are more highly prejudiced than those in integrated neighborhoods, and when the neighborhoods are forced to integrate, the levels of prejudice held by both groups actually declined with time. He reports that in an Eastern city, prejudices among whites decreased almost fivefold within five years after blacks moved into the neighborhood. [Paul Lazarsfeld, *To Secure These Rights* (Washington, D.C.: Government Printing Office, 1947), p. 85.]

However, the problem is hardly as simple as transplanting some blacks into white neighborhoods, or vice versa. The theory of social distance states that people tend to like those who are like themselves (who are of similar status, position, income, and lifestyles), but are more distant toward those who are different in status. When people of similar status and lifestyle move into a neighborhood, they are soon accepted whether they are white, black, red, or yellow. Effective integration can only be achieved among people who are relatively equal in status.

The same elements function in all social settings whether it be in housing, on the job, in the schools, or in the military. Contact with equals tends to enhance acceptance of the minority group and reduce prejudice levels, while contact with unequals tends to increase social distance and prejudices. Thus, positive equal-status contact is one means of reducing levels of prejudice throughout the whole society. The

Answer frame 2[7]

1. True. Prejudices are largely unconscious, and prejudiced persons are rarely aware that they are prejudiced.
2. True. In-group loyalties inspire the development of prejudices, thus every person who is a member of a group will hold prejudices against the out-group.
3. False. Prejudices are pre-judgments made by others about the group, and not a characteristic of the group, thus we study the person holding the prejudice, not the group to which it is directed.
4. False. Some prejudices are desirable in a society as they tend to reinforce group identity and a sense of belonging (such as nationalism and religious beliefs).

If you missed any of the above, reread Frame 2[7] before starting Frame 3[7] on page 44.

Frame 3[7] continued

functional nature of the contact is also important. Cooperative, mutual-aid contacts reduce prejudice, while competitive or exploitative contacts increase prejudices.

Superordinate goals. A classic study conducted by Mazafer Sherif demonstrates another means of reducing prejudice levels—through creating superordinate goals. [John H. Roher and Muzafer Sherif, eds., "A Preliminary Experimental Study of Inter-Group Relations," in *Social Psychology at the Crossroads* (New York: Harper and Brothers, Publishers, 1951) pp. 388–424.] Superordinate goals are overarching group goals that supersede personal goals, and are crucial to the survival of the group (such as protecting the nation during war, rebuilding the community after a natural disaster, or even uniting to fight a disease epidemic or another social problem). Sherif noted while working at a summer boys' camp that when the boys competed against each other in camp sports (pursuing individual goals), prejudices against the competing group were enhanced. But, when a catastrophe threatened the survival of the camp, all the boys united and worked together with no expression of prejudice in order to save the camp. This confirms the research findings of the effect of cooperative, equal-status contacts in reducing prejudices. Even after the catastrophe had passed, both groups maintained closer friendships as long as they were united into one common group.

Prejudices tend to grow when the groups are divided or separated, but tend to moderate when the groups are united by a common goal. Group organizers are quite familiar with this tendency and often use the principle to unify or destroy groups. National leaders have even been known to declare "national emergencies" to unify the population in an energy crisis or recession. A closer relationship among all people is an unexpected consequence of such actions.

The class-conflict theory of racism. A substantial number of scholars, many of them Marxists, believe that psychological, symbolic, and learning theories miss the point. They believe that race prejudice and race exploitation are rooted in class exploitation, of which racism is but one expression. Some scholars (for example, Robert Blauner, *Racial Oppression in America*) use the colonialism model, viewing racial discrimination in America (and elsewhere) as the exploitation of a colonial people who happen to be here, not in a foreign country. These scholars believe that attempts to end race inequality are futile until class exploitation and inequality is ended.

This analysis draws upon the established fact that competition (for money, power, housing, and so on) and exploitation *do* create prejudice and discrimination. Modern theories of race superiority were invented during the colonial era to provide a moral justification for colonial exploitation. Undoubtedly, the exploitative factor is important in explaining racism.

But is it the *only* important factor? Prejudice and discrimination sometimes arise among groups which are not in any competitive or exploitative relationship to each other. Nor have Marxist-inspired revolutions ended racism in the countries which have experienced them. Racism is too many-faceted a phenomena to be attributed to a single dominant cause.

Indicate whether each of the following statements is true or false by writing "T" or "F" in the space provided.

_____ 1. It is clear that education causes a reduction prejudice.
_____ 2. Prejudice levels would decline if only people would be more religious.
_____ 3. Superordinate goals can often draw people together and reduce prejudices.
_____ 4. It is clear that prejudices are a product of class exploitation and discrimination.

Now turn to Answer frame 3[7] on page 48 to check your answers.

chapter 8

MINORITY GROUPS: ADAPTATION AND REFORM

Frame 1[8]

Vicious circle of discrimination. Gunnar Myrdal, a Swedish sociologist who conducted a wide ranging study of American racial relations in the 1950s, observed that discrimination against minorities tends to have a compounding effect in that subtle forms of discrimination in one area in society (such as in employment) tends to compound the problem of acquiring status in other areas (such as housing and education). [Gunnar Myrdal, *The American Dilemma* (New York: Harper & Row, 1962).] Living in a slum neighborhood tends to limit the educational opportunities for children, which works to limit employment opportunities, which in turn eventually locks the family into a slum neighborhood.

The "American dilemma," as Myrdal saw it, was how to break the vicious circle of racial discrimination in which most minorities were confined. He concluded that it would have to

Answer frame 3[7]

1. False. Although education may reduce prejudices for some persons, it has not been effective on a large scale.
2. False. Although most religions profess the virtues of humanity, religious persons are as prejudiced as nonreligious persons, perhaps actually more so.
3. True. When people have to work together and need each other to complete the goal, prejudices are ignored in preference for the goal.
4. False. Although class exploitation may enhance some prejudices, other factors are of equal or greater importance.

If you missed any of the above, review Frame 3[7] before starting Chapter 8 on page 47.

Frame 1[8] continued

be the middle and upper social classes in America who would have to take the initiative and make the greatest effort to break the cycle, because it was mainly these social classes that held the power in society and the means to implement reform. Thus from Myrdal's perspective, reform in racial relations in America would not occur until it was approached as a problem of the whole society, and not just a problem of the minorities themselves.

Minorities and social class. It is a long-established fact within sociology that a person's social class tends to influence his style of life and the attitudes he holds. Many of the characteristics ascribed to racial or ethnic minorities are more a product of the social class standing of the ascribers than a characteristic of the racial or ethnic group itself. The social class position of minorities is most significantly affected by their opportunities for employment, their low position of social power, and their attitudes and style of life.

Employment. Research clearly shows that there is a strong tendency for minorities to be placed into the lower status positions in employment. The rate of unemployment among blacks is almost twice the rate for comparable whites, and the rate among Indians is often some six to eight times the white rate. Even when employed in comparable jobs, we find that blacks, women, and the handicapped have received far less pay for the same work, and have also been less likely to be promoted in rank or position than white males. Limited opportunities in employment also tend to overlap into other areas, affecting the opportunity to acquire decent housing, education, or improvement of general living conditions.

Social power. Minorities remain disadvantaged because they lack social power. Most of the social, economic, and political power in America is held by the middle and upper social classes, and because of discrimination in employment, education, and life opportunities, the minorities remain clustered toward the lower base of power in society. For the most part, it is the middle and upper-class white male congressmen who establish policies for public assistance and welfare, and is largely the middle-class administrators who supervise the governmental agencies that provide opportunity and assistance to lower class persons. White, middle, and upper-class males also control the sources of credit, financing, and allocation of community services in the American society. Thus, lower-class persons and minorities are often subject to the whims and wishes of the middle- and upper-class bureaucrats and rarely can exert any control over their position in life or in the social structure of society.

Attitudes. Middle-class persons are often prone to criticize lower-class minorities for their lackadaisical attitudes toward education and work, and for their subhuman living patterns. They often proclaim that the poor have little interest in improving their position in life, but this too is usually a class phenomena. It takes money and job security to improve one's station in life, and an upper-class family with $50,000 income can more easily afford to seek and acquire the better things in life. They can value education for their children because they can afford to finance the years of extended study required for higher education; they can appreciate quality in merchandise and life, because their income is far more than sufficient to provide the basic necessities for life; and they can value deferred gratification (investing time or money today to achieve a greater and more satisfying return tomorrow) since their income allows saving.

On the other hand, a poor family with $4,000 annual income or less must spend almost all their income to simply stay alive. They cannot afford a college education for their children, so there is little use in encouraging the children to hope; they cannot afford quality in merchandise because at their price range there is little choice; they cannot invest today for a brighter tomorrow because it takes all the money they have to simply survive today. Even when the poor do get a small bonus, they often rush to spend it immediately because if they wait until tomorrow their creditors may demand it. The sporadic and seasonal nature of their employment tends to encourage the lower class and poor to be fatalistic about job opportunities and suspicious about contractual obligations that would allow them to gain job security and promotion. People of the same social class, whether they be blacks, Puerto Ricans, whites, or any other minority, tend to hold approximately the same attitudes toward education, employment, and style of life regardless of their minority affiliation. Thus, many of the traits ascribed to minorities are actually a class phenomena rather than a racial or ethnic characteristic.

Indicate whether each of the following statements is true or false by writing "T" or "F" in the space provided.

_____ 1. In many respects, the race problem is mainly a class problem.

_____ 2. The "American dilemma" is a question of how minorities are going to change their status in society.

_____ 3. Primarily, a person's attitudes and predominant lifestyle is determined by his social class position.

_____ 4. Discrimination in one area (such as employment) tends to cause discrimination in other areas.

Now turn to Answer frame 1[8] on page 50 to check your answers.

Frame 2[8]

Modes of adjustment to dominance. There are several attitudes of adjustment that minority groups may assume in relation to the majority group—they may simply accept their minority status and be dominated by the majority, they may attempt to join the majority group and be absorbed into it, or they may attempt to establish a separate base of power and coexist as equals with the other groups. The most common modes of adjustment are conceptualized below.

Accommodation consists of a minority group accepting a position subservient to the dominant group and behaving so as to fulfill the expectations and roles that the majority group holds for them. The minority group remains relatively powerless in the society and a reasonable degree of harmony and order is maintained between the groups. Both majority and minority groups often come to view the order as just and proper, and any effort to change the system may be met with considerable resistance from either group. The process of accommodation is most conspicuously demonstrated in some colonialized nations of Africa, where for many decades, white rule over blacks was accepted as proper and legitimate by both groups.

Acculturation is a process whereby the minority group abandons their past cultural heritage and adopts the dominant group's culture. The minority group accepts the new culture as proper and legitimate and as preferable to their earlier heritage. People who move to a new

Answer frame 1⁸

1. True. Social class and racial discrimination are closely linked, and the resolution of minority group problems will also require a changing of their class position.
2. False. The "American dilemma" is a question of how the middle class is going to *allow* minorities the opportunity to change their status.
3. True. Social class position is more important than minority status in determining attitudes and lifestyle. When minorities change social class position, they tend to adopt the attitudes and lifestyle of the new class position.
4. True. Occupational discrimination tends to prevent minorities from having good housing or educational opportunities.

If you missed any of the above, reread Frame 1⁸ before starting Frame 2⁸ on page 49.

Frame 2⁸ continued

land often acquire almost a missionary zeal in their quest to consume and learn the new language, customs, and lifestyles and become superpatriots and defenders of their new land.

Integration consists of a blending of cultures so as to create a new homogeneous culture. Desirable elements of the different cultural groups are integrated to produce the new culture, and in principle all groups become equal in power, position, and prestige. Integration may be considered to have been accomplished when there no longer remains any awareness of group differences in status, power, opportunity, or income.

A wide variety of English and Northern European ethnic and religious groups have been integrated into the American culture. Racial groups, however, tend to be integrated less rapidly than ethnic groups because of their greater social distance from the majority group.

Pluralism consists of a collection of different racial, religious, or social groups coexisting side by side with equal power, prestige, and social acceptability, but each group remains separate in its particular ethnic or religious beliefs and customs. There are two forms of pluralism most often described in minority-majority group relations—cultural pluralism, and structural pluralism.

Cultural pluralism generally refers to a collection of different cultural or ethnic groups coexisting together, with each group retaining its own distinctive elements of its cultural heritage (its religious beliefs, traditional customs, and food preferences).

During the early half of the 20th century, America's population consisted of an amalgam of different ethnic and nationality groups, and cultural pluralism was easily recognized. Every major city had its Polish, Italian, or its Chinese section, complete with their own distinctive shops, churches, and celebrations. However, with time most of the ethnic communities have dissolved and only a few remote rural ethnic communities and the Chinatowns remain yet today.

Structural pluralism on the other hand is usually used to denote a collection of different racial, religious, or political groups that hold approximately equal political power, social acceptability, and prestige in society, but who still remain different in their beliefs and lifestyles. The different groups may live in the same neighborhoods, work in the same factories, and go to the same schools, yet remain completely separate in their visiting patterns and friendship associations. America is considered to have religious pluralism (Catholics, Protestants, and Jews coexist in relative harmony), political pluralism (there is little difference in power between the Republicans and Democrats), and may be moving toward racial pluralism as minority groups acquire more power in the society.

Retreatism and *isolationism* usually involves the gradual physical withdrawal of a minority group from the larger society. The minority group attempts to survive completely apart from the dominant group and forfeits an interest in maintaining any patterns of association.

Retreatism rarely occurs in industrialized societies as few groups are self-sufficient enough to survive alone. The groups which have attempted to achieve some degree of retreatism in the American society might include some Indian tribes, a few small religious groups (the Amish and Mennonites), and perhaps some isolated pockets of Appalachian mountain folk.

It may take several decades for a minority group to establish itself relative to the majority group in society, but eventually the group must assume one of the above forms of adaptation. As a general tendency, cultural or ethnic groups have moved toward acculturation and integration in the American society, while racial and religious groups have gradually moved toward a form of structural pluralism as the preferred mode of adaptation.

Militant nationalism. This is a relatively recent minority movement in American society, combining some elements of pluralism and retreatism. The "black power" movement and the black nationalist demand for black control of all aspects of life in the black community are examples.

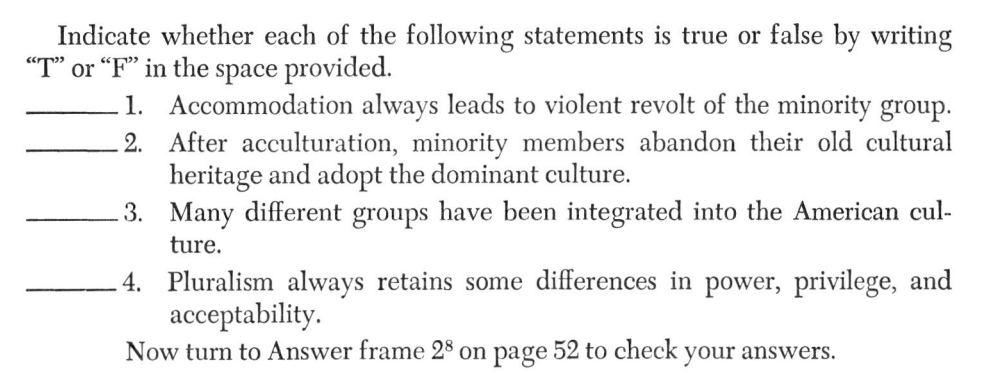

Indicate whether each of the following statements is true or false by writing "T" or "F" in the space provided.

_____ 1. Accommodation always leads to violent revolt of the minority group.

_____ 2. After acculturation, minority members abandon their old cultural heritage and adopt the dominant culture.

_____ 3. Many different groups have been integrated into the American culture.

_____ 4. Pluralism always retains some differences in power, privilege, and acceptability.

Now turn to Answer frame 2[8] on page 52 to check your answers.

Frame 3[8]

Present status and future. The plight of minorities in America has always been a smoldering issue for altruistic liberals, and it is easy for civil rights leaders and social activists to become impatient with the snail-like pace of progress in minority relations. Sensitive people, once they realize an inequity or social injustice exists, quickly develop a consuming desire to correct the situation immediately, and easily become frustrated when they see little progress with time.

However, social change rarely occurs rapidly and is most appropriately measured in time frames of decades rather than years or months. When one examines the change that has occurred since the turn of the century, he will note that considerable progress has been made in integrating ethnic and religious minorities into the American society. Although racial groups still remain highly segregated in many regions (particularly among the blacks in northern cities, Puerto Ricans along the eastern seaboard, and Mexican-Americans and Indians in the western states), a wide variety of other religious and ethnic groups have been totally assimilated into the larger culture. To most Americans today, it makes little difference if one is Catholic or Jew, Polish or Italian, or even if they came from a land that practiced polygamy and lived in igloos. What is most surprising to some scholars is that so much assimilation has occurred in the American society, and when one considers the possibilities for conflict, that so little conflict has occurred!

However, the above is not to suggest that America's minority problem no longer exists or that it is close to being fully resolved. For the most part, the groups that have been assimilated into the American culture are those with the least social distance in religious and ethnic beliefs. Minority groups that are separated by the color bar are far from being inte-

Answer frame 2⁸

1. False. There is usually a reasonably stable order of relationships with accommodation.
2. True. And often they adopt the new culture with almost a missionary zeal.
3. True. Particularly English and Northern European ethnic and religious groups have been integrated into the American culture.
4. False. Pluralism means that there is *equal* power, prestige, and social acceptability.

If you missed any of the above, reread Frame 2⁸ before starting Frame 3⁸ on page 51.

Frame 3⁸ continued

grated into the American society, and this discrepancy manifests itself in a wide variety of discriminatory practices in education, housing, and employment opportunities. Religious or ethnic minorities tend to be assimilated more rapidly than racial minorities, largely because of the color bar, and racial integration will probably take considerably longer to occur than with other groups.

Structural or attitudinal change. The most prominent forces of change in racial relations to date have been structural in nature—for example, open-housing legislation has opened up America's suburbs to financially secure members of racial minorities so that they can finally purchase decent housing. Fair Employment Practices Laws have outlawed discrimination in employment and allowed upward mobility for some minority persons. Increased aid in education has opened opportunities for career training that were nonexistent a decade ago. Although structural changes have only begun to operate to change racial relations, they at least have opened the door and with time will function to affect attitudinal change. As described above, stereotypes tend to dissolve when minorities begin to interact with the majority group as equals, thus structural change in educational and employment opportunities will eventually lead to attitudinal change toward a more equalitarian attitude in racial relations.

Integration or pluralism. During the early part of this century, most of the European immigrants sought cultural pluralism as the ideal in their assimilation into the American culture. Cultural pluralism was largely achieved by the time the second generation of immigrants had matured, and by the time the third generation was born, most immigrants were thoroughly integrated into the American culture. Many people assumed that racial minorities would hold the same ideals and follow the same pattern. However, they failed to give sufficient consideration to the differences between ethnic minorities (who were similar enough to be assimilated rapidly), and racial minorities (who were separated by the color bar).

Early in the civil rights movement many black leaders did espouse the ideals of integration, but as whites later realized, the black leaders were really hoping to achieve the occupational and social equality that integration would provide, rather than seeking social integration of the black and white cultures. During the 1950s, Martin Luther King moved to the forefront of the civil rights movement and sought to achieve equality for blacks within the conventional structure of the American society by encouraging each black American to work painstakingly up the ladder of success until all men could work together as equals. However, blacks soon found that by conforming to white expectations for education and employment, they were sacrificing much of their black heritage. Thus, during the 1960s blacks' goals gradually shifted, seeking a form of structural pluralism whereby they could have educational, occupational, and social equality, yet still retain their rich black heritage. The black power movement exemplified the new goals of blacks, and many black leaders today hold this perspective.

The other racial minorities also appear to be moving toward structural pluralism—the American Indian movement has called for "Indian power," Mexican-Americans proclaimed "La Raza Unita," and grass roots movements across the nation have come forth to proclaim minority rights. The forces of structural change have immutably been set into motion, and with time, change will occur. However, it will take as much as several decades before discriminatory practices and racial prejudices disappear, if, indeed, they ever do. This is by no means a certainty.

Indicate whether each of the following statements is true or false by writing "T" or "F" in the space provided.
_____ 1. The assimilation of minority groups should be measured in time frames of decades.
_____ 2. The rate of assimilation of a minority group is directly dependent upon the social distance of the group.
_____ 3. Racial groups are assimilated more rapidly than religious and ethnic groups.
_____ 4. Attitudinal change is required in a society before any structural change can occur.

Now turn to Answer frame 3[8] on page 54 to check your answers.

chapter 9

POVERTY

Frame 1[9]

It almost seems that each generation must discover the existence of poverty anew. Although the plight of the poor is changeless, public interest in poverty seems to change in cycles of roughly two decades in length. The birth of the last cycle of interest was heralded by Michael Harrington's book *The Other America* in 1962; the interest was nourished by Harry Caudill's *Night Comes to the Cumberlands* in 1963; then peaked during the latter years of President Johnson's "Great Society" program. Since then a shift in governmental policy to reduce federal spending programs, a mini-recession, and rampant inflation have dampened interest and public awareness of the plight of the poor in America. Perhaps now we must await the growth of a new generation to rediscover the social problems of poverty and to renew public interest in the plight of the disadvantaged. [For a more complete examination of poverty in America, see *Basic Facts on Poverty* a PLAID by Lawrence M. Winebrenner (Homewood, Ill.: Learning Systems Co., 1974).]

Answer frame 3⁹

1. True. Social change occurs slowly, and is most appropriately measured by decades.
2. True. The greater the social distance, the slower the rate of assimilation.
3. False. Religious and ethnic groups are assimilated more rapidly than racial groups.
4. False. Structural change can force a change in attitude. Thus, changes in the structure of society (passing a new law), can sometimes cause a change in attitudes toward a minority group.

If you missed any of the above, reread Frame 3⁸ before beginning Chapter 9 on page 53.

Frame 1⁹ continued

THE INVISIBLE POOR

Much of the lack of public awareness of the poor is due to their relative invisibility in society. Typically the poor live out of sight of the larger population: in slums that most commuters manage to bypass, in houses that look abandoned, and even in old railroad freight cars that are more suitable for livestock than people, in junked cars, or simply camped along a stream where they might appear to be a casual group of shoddy tourists. Children without shoes do not go to school or church, mothers without a decent dress do not go downtown shopping, and the infirm stay alone when there is no one to take them anywhere.

Even when the affluent drive through poor neighborhoods they rarely understand the plight of the poor; they are often shocked by the collection of vintage autos scattered around a home, without noting that the cars might serve as an extra bedroom, or a source of spare parts to keep one semi-operable auto running. The affluent are prone to note that shacks with holes in the roof still sprout a TV antenna, without thinking that the TV might serve as a babysitter when the mother works or may be the only source of escape from otherwise dreary surroundings. The poor largely stay out of sight, out of mind, and out of the conscience of the larger population. Thus, the poor in many ways are an invisible social problem.

DEFINITIONS OF POVERTY

It has been said that America has the "richest poor people on earth," for America's welfare poor are more affluent than perhaps three fourths of the Americans who fought the American Revolution, and are probably more affluent than three fourths of the world's people today. But this is irrelevant, for the poor family in Chicago does not compare itself with the poor of Calcutta, but with the rest of the American people. Poverty is *relative*, not absolute. Poverty is the dividing line below which it is considered that no human being should be expected to live. Poverty is, therefore, not an objective fact; it is a value judgment.

The poverty line changes as society becomes more affluent. There are relatively few Americans today who have no place to sleep, no shoes to wear, or who go to bed hungry (in fact, obesity is more common among the poor than among the more affluent), but many Americans are poorly housed, poorly dressed, and ill-nourished. The usual definitions of poverty are of two types—those based upon *fixed levels* of income, and those based upon the *relative need* of a family.

Fixed income definitions are based upon estimates of the annual income a family needs to survive, and may range considerably in amount according to the method and rationale used for defining the minimum level for subsistence. Different definitions of poverty have ranged from $1,000 to over $10,000 annual income for a family. John Kenneth Galbraith [John Kenneth Galbraith, *The Affluent Society* (Boston: Houghton Mifflin, 1958).] using the $1,000 definition in 1958 estimated that 20 million persons were below the poverty line; the Bureau of the Census in 1970 used $3,000 and reported over 33 million people as below the poverty line in America.

Obviously, whichever definition is preferred is dependent upon the purpose and motivation of the user, and it has not been exactly unknown for a politician to use one base for defining poverty before an election, then another after the election to show how the situation has improved (or worsened).

Several criticisms have been leveled at the fixed definition approach to poverty. (1) Since there are so many vested interests in the different definitions, there will never be any complete agreement as to which definition to use. (2) What may be considered an adequate income in one region might constitute deprivation in another—a family might survive on $3,000 in Idaho where they can glean the potato fields and shoot venison for food, but that amount may barely pay the rent for a decent housing unit in a New York ghetto. (3) Each region has its own particular household and family needs—winter clothing and fuel are more costly in Minnesota than in Mississippi. Thus, many prefer a relative definition of poverty that is based upon family needs for a particular region.

From the relative needs perspective a family would be provided with the basic necessities to live a comfortable but simple life. The children's allowance would be sufficient to provide them with adequate school clothes and medical care, the family would have enough income to rent a decent home and furnishings (a stove, refrigerator, bedroom furniture, and indoor plumbing), and enough extra to allow job training and advancement to self-sufficiency in life. Life would not be luxurious, but adequate to meet the basic needs and to allow the family to escape from the confines of deprivation.

Liberals often prefer the latter definition with the argument that this is the least that the richest nation on earth should provide for its population. However, to accomplish such would require a considerable reordering of national priorities to finance the program.

Indicate whether each of the following statements is true or false by writing "T" or "F" in the space provided.

1. _____ Governmental officials have developed reliable methods for determining the number of poor people in America.
2. _____ Most middle-class people in the United States are really not aware of the proportion of poor people, because the poor are largely invisible.
3. _____ Sociologically, a definition based upon "relative income" is more meaningful in estimating poverty, than a fixed income definition.
4. _____ Public interest in poverty as a social problem comes and goes, but some degree of poverty always remains.

Now turn to Answer frame 1[9] on page 56 to check your answers.

Frame 2[9]

SYSTEMIC AND INSTITUTIONAL FACTORS OF POVERTY

The sociological approach to social problems is concerned with examining the effects of the structure and organization of society upon the creation of the social problem. There are both systemic and institutional factors that influence the state of poverty.

Institutional factors. Foremost among institutional factors that cause poverty is the nature of the economic system. From this perspective, poverty exists because of basic social and economic inequalities that are built into the economic order. The American economy is based upon capitalism, and as such, each person is dependent upon himself to provide for his own needs. The pure capitalistic ethic contains no

Answer frame 1⁹

1. False. The number of poor in America is dependent upon the definition used, and may vary 20 percent or more in either direction.
2. True. The poor usually live away from the regularly traveled routes or in facilities that people often assume are abandoned. Thus, the poor remain invisible.
3. True. Fixed income definitions do not consider regional variations, thus relative income definitions are usually more meaningful.
4. True. Public interest in poverty follows almost a generational cycle, but there always remains the poorest one fifth of the population.

If you missed any of the above, reread Frame 1⁹ before starting Frame 2⁹ on page 55.

Frame 2⁹ continued

provision for the care of the needy or indigent, and each person's success (or failure) is viewed as his own responsibility. The government's only obligation is to protect the freedoms of the person, so as to allow him to succeed or fail on his own. This philosophy is also sometimes referred to as social Darwinism, whereby the age old rule of "the survival of the fittest" is applied to social behavior as well as nature. The capitalist philosophy never sought the approximate economic equality found among some primitive societies, or the economic equality proclaimed but not fully attained by socialist or communist societies.

Nor was the ruthless individualism implicit in theoretical capitalism ever practically true. Various kinds of assistance to the poor, while not very effective, were a part of the capitalist system throughout its history. The Christian ethic suggests that people should be humanitarian and provide for the needs of people who cannot care for themselves. The combination of these two somewhat contradictory social ethics, the capitalist ethic and the Christian ethic, has produced a social philosophy that holds that the government should provide for the basic survival needs of the disadvantaged, but beyond these minimum needs, each person is responsible for his own comfort. In America the government usually provides for the minimum needs of the disadvantaged (through welfare, aid to dependent children, and old-age assistance), but does not provide welfare for able-bodied persons who can work for themselves. However, institutional forces will continue to create poverty in America as long as the economic system allows a differential in the ability or opportunity for some persons to acquire wealth and power in the society.

Other institutional forces that enhance the problem of poverty in the American society involve the relatively low priority of values for social welfare. For the most part, the economic and governmental institutions support technological development (such as the space program and defense) and physical developments (highways, buildings, and airports) more than programs for the social welfare of the population (job retraining, educational programs, and old-age assistance). These priorities are justified with the argument that technological and physical developments stimulate commerce and provide an immediate return on investments, while investments in social welfare return few capital gains. Again, the problem of poverty will continue until there is a drastic reordering of national priorities to favor social rather than physical development in the society.

Systemic factors. In addition to the institutional factors that promote poverty, certain systemic factors contribute to the problem. Foremost among these factors are technological unemployment, inflation, and social inequality of opportunity.

Technological unemployment is created when technological change renders a category of workers obsolete and unusable. The most prominent group of technological poor in the American society are the rural poor, who continue to try to wrest a living from a marginal piece of land without the capital and machinery necessary to transform the operation into an economically profitable unit. Often these farmers are self-employed sharecroppers (either with a landholder or the bank), who remain poor as they attempt to apply 19th century technology to 20th century agriculture. Often these families survive only through the contributions that family members make from outside employment, but as a group their plight worsens each year through debt or age. Most marginal farmers are middle-aged or older, have no marketable skills, and have little formal education, making them poor prospects for job retraining. They "hang on" until retirement age, when their farms are combined with adjoining lands to make up farms of average size.

Technology constantly decreases the need for unskilled or manual labor, and steadily shrivels the opportunities for the uneducated or poorly trained workers. Occasionally a shift in institutional priorities may cause temporary technological unemployment (such as the reduction in the space program which created a glut of unemployed Ph.D.'s), but usually these persons can move into other occupations within a relatively short period.

Inflation. Although inflation affects all socioeconomic groups, the elderly who are living on fixed incomes are the most affected. Within the last few years the cost of living and medical expenses for the elderly have increased at roughly three times the rate of increase in social security and old-age assistance payments, which rapidly drains any reserves that older people have accumulated for retirement. Increases in inflation are increasing the proportion of elderly poor at rates which may soon make them the largest poverty-stricken group in the American society. It is noteworthy that in the price inflation of 1973–74, the price of the economy foods (potatoes, beans, cheaper meats) rose much more rapidly than the luxury foods. The poor are inflation's greatest victims.

Social inequality. Social inequality may flow from a variety of sources—race, sex, age, ethnic origin, and so on, but also these factors may interact to create compound effects. In proportion to their presence in the total population, non-whites and women are highly over-represented among the lower income groups, and the combination of these statuses along with a low income may present barriers that become insurmountable. Thus, some groups in the American society suffer the effects of double-discrimination for being the wrong race, the wrong sex, and the wrong family background. These factors often limit the possibilities for educational or occupational advancement to positions that would place the family above the poverty line. The occasional person with superior abilities and great determination may be able to surmount these handicaps; but average ability and average effort leave most of the children of the poor in lifelong poverty.

Indicate whether each of the following statements is true or false by writing "T" or "F" in the space provided.

_____ 1. Poverty in the American society is a direct product of the capitalistic economic system.
_____ 2. The institutional values of the American society support economic and technological development more than social development.
_____ 3. Poverty affects all age and status groups equally.
_____ 4. Technological unemployment tends to create a new category of poor people each generation.

Now turn to Answer frame 2⁹ on page 58 to check your answers.

Answer frame 2⁹

1. True. Capitalism produces inequality among people, causing some to be more successful than others. This creates "relative" poverty for some people in society.
2. True. Technological and economic programs are supported financially to a much greater extent than are social welfare programs.
3. False. While all groups are affected to some extent, the young and old and marginally educated are most affected.
4. True. Today's largest group of technological unemployed are the marginal farmers, but the next decade may see other highly trained specialists becoming technologically unemployed.

If you missed any of the questions, reread Frame 2⁹ before beginning Frame 3⁹ below.

Frame 3⁹

The nature of poverty. There are many popular fallacies about the nature of the poor; that unemployment is the basic cause of poverty, that able-bodied men are drawing welfare, that if the poor would only work they could escape poverty, and so on. However, a more critical analysis would suggest that unemployment is not the fundamental cause of poverty (over 87 percent of the poor who are able to do work regularly). Statistical data from the Office of Economic Opportunity show that 56 percent of the poor are underaged children, another 15 percent are elderly and over age 65, and another 12 percent are ill or disabled. Less than 12 percent of those who were able did not work on a regular basis, and of this group less than one percent were unemployed males.

Of those who work regularly, a quick mathematical analysis shows us that even working full time, many families cannot escape a state of poverty. A man employed at the minimum wage (which is common for most manual or migrant labor) and working full time (40 or more hours a week) would earn only $80.00 a week or just over $4,000 a year before deductions. This level is only $600 above the Welfare Administration's requirement to receive welfare. Thus the fundamental cause of poverty for those who do work is *underemployment,* or employment at a wage that does not even allow people to escape the confines of poverty.

A second group of myths about poverty pertains to those who are receiving welfare. Often it is stated that welfare families are just loaded with kids, and like rabbits they produce more just to increase their monthly allotment; that most welfare children are illegitimate; that if the poor were given any extra money they would just squander it; that most welfare families are black; and that the welfare rolls are full of able-bodied loafers who are cheating the government.

Statistical data indicate that each of these presuppositions is factually incorrect. [See "Welfare Myths vs. Facts," a pamphlet by the Department of Health, Education, and Welfare, U.S. Government printing office, Washington, D.C.] Over one half of welfare families have only one or two children and 56 percent spend less than two years on welfare. In most states the monthly allotment for additional children is less than $1 per day, and the author suspects that there are few mothers who voluntarily would wish to feed and babysit a child for only $7 a week! Further, almost 70 percent of all children receiving Aid to Families with Dependent Children were born to married parents who were subsequently divorced. Thus, relatively few mothers appear to abuse this welfare program.

The majority of people on welfare in the United States are white (48.3 percent), while blacks represent 43.3 percent, and other racial groupings represent 8.4 percent. Of those on welfare, less than one percent are men who are physically capable of working and less than one half of one percent of welfare recipients have been prosecuted for defrauding the government.

Finally, of those receiving welfare, 56 percent will graduate to self-dependency in less than two years. Only about 6 percent of those receiving welfare will spend ten years or more on public assistance.

Poverty lifestyles. Middle-class persons are often prone to criticize lower class people for their seeming lack of motivation and interest in conforming to middle-class traditions. And, in many cases, the middle class are often correct in what they observe, but usually they fail to understand the reasons for lower class behavior. Many of the actions of the poor are reasonable and logical reactions to their current state of relative deprivations, and in part, can be accounted for in terms of *situational* explanations, and in terms of the formation of a *culture of poverty*.

The situational explanation of poverty lifestyles suggests that lower class behavior is a direct adaptation to their immediate situation and environment. The poor are often unstable in their work patterns, largely because unskilled or manual employment is temporary and sporatic in nature. The poor often do not express attitudes of deferred gratification (to save for tomorrow), because all resources the family might acquire are needed for survival today. The poor typically have no confidence that they can do anything to change their fate; instead they tend to accept and endure whatever happens. The poor are rarely interested in politics or social reform, because they have neither the energy or ability to influence community action. Thus, often the poor do become short sighted, fatalistic, and concerned only with the present, largely because the future holds little promise for improvement.

Oscar Lewis, in observing the attitudes and behavior of the poor, proposed that these attitudes and patterns have become so ingrained into the poor lifestyles that they have created (in effect) a "culture of poverty." [Oscar Lewis, *La Vida: A Puerto Rican Family in the Culture of Poverty—San Juan and New York* (New York: Random House, 1966).] These cultural values incorporate attitudes which accept "welfare as a way of life," defeatist attitudes toward education and self-improvement, and condone an animalistic mode of existence. This culture of poverty should be recognized as an intelligent and rational adaptation to poverty; it enables one to survive and endure a wretched life. But, while the culture of poverty has survival value, it also incapacitates one from taking advantage of opportunities when they present themselves. Thus poverty in the presence of opportunity tends to be self-perpetuating.

Although this explanation may be applicable to a small section of the "hard-core" poor in the American society (who live on welfare through the generations), many sociologists are quick to point out that the vast majority of the poor aspire to middle class status and lifestyles and strive continuously to move out of their lower class status. As pointed out above, over half of the poor receive welfare or public assistance for less than two years then are moved upward to a higher status and self-sufficiency. This pattern of upward striving is particularly apparent for the young, but often it is reversed for the elderly or the infirm.

The future. It has been suggested by more than one academician that structural and systemic changes in the institutions which encourage the existence of poverty will not occur until the poor organize to create a reordering of national priorities. From this perspective, the poor will have to initiate a social movement in the American society in the same fashion that other minority groups have done.

Critics are quick to point out, however, that the poor constitute such a heterogeneous group (the young, the old, infirm, and racially mixed) that there is little basis for a common identity to inspire to group unity, thus any widespread social action is very unlikely. The precedence of the past suggests that no such movement will occur, but we also must recall that the future is always uncertain.

Indicate whether each of the following statements is true or false by writing "T" or "F" in the space provided.

_____ 1. The basic problem of poor people is that they fail to hold consistent employment.

_____ 2. Poor people often use child assistance payments as a means of supplementing their income.

_____ 3. Blacks and other minorities constitute the largest number of persons receiving public assistance in the American society.

_____ 4. The poor often establish living patterns that create in effect, a "culture of poverty."

Now turn to Answer frame 3[9] on page 62 to check your answers.

chapter 10

SOCIAL DEVIANCE

Frame 1[10]

All societies are "organized." By "social organization" we mean the pattern of roles and relationships between persons and groups according to which they interact with one another. Each day people go about their assigned tasks and expected roles with only occasional deviation—they show up for work at the prescribed time, they perform the expected tasks, they pay their bills, and otherwise follow the conventional patterns of daily living for the American people. These people maintain the social organization of the society by following expected, prescribed, and conventional roles.

However, other people fail or refuse to conform to conventional patterns of behavior, and these persons are called deviants. *Deviance is behavior that does not conform to the conven-* *tional norms,* whether it be jaywalking, using illegal drugs, or participating in exotic sexual behavior. Why do people become deviants when all the obvious and apparent rewards are for conformity in the society? For the answer to this question, we must turn to the sociology of deviance.

There are several theories that seek to account for deviant behavior in one fashion or another, but perhaps the most prominent body of theory at present involves a combination of *differential association* (as described in Chapter 12) and *learning theory,* along with social and psychological reinforcement of the behavior. From these perspectives, a person is attracted to a deviant act through the expectation of receiving some reward—be it emotional gratification, social prestige, power, or economic gain. Thus, the person commits the deviant act with the expectation of receiving something he or she desires, whatever it might be.

Deviance in society. When a pattern of deviant behavior becomes widespread, and people become uncertain as to how to respond to the new form of behavior, a condition of *social disorganization* has developed. When many people are uncertain about a behavior pattern, or are in sharp disagreement with others over it, a potential social problem is created. Thus, alcoholism, illegal drugs, and homosexuality have been social problems for a long time, while the youthful practice of living together instead of marrying, the no-work ethic of estranged youth, and the practice of exotic sexual behavior have become social problems more recently.

The social organization-disorganization-deviance process therefore involves the following stages: (1) a stable equilibrium in which the norms, values, and institutions of the society are well harmonized with one another, and most people conform unquestioningly to these norms; (2) a disruption of this equilibrium through social change, so that the traditional norms, rules, and values seem inapplicable in the new situation; (3) growing doubts and uncertainties about the old norms together with behavioral deviation from traditional expectations, and experimentation with new forms of behavior; (4) the eventual institutionalization of some of the new forms of behavior, which become the conventional norms of a new equilibrium. Thus, (1) the old norm of parental control over children until their maturity, (2) became inapplicable when most children began leaving the farm for jobs, college, and other places where parents could not easily supervise them, (3) with growing doubts about parental authority and increasing relaxation of strict parental controls, and finally (4) the current institutionalization of greater independence for older children (lowering the voting age, drinking age, the end of "in loco parentis" rules on campus, and so on). In this way, new norms arise through the social change—disorganization-reorganization cycle—which is in progress continuously on a dozen or a hundred different fronts.

To some extent, the social organization of modern societies tends to create or encourage the development of deviant patterns of behavior. As our nation moves toward a mass metropolitan society, the extent of personal *anonymity* is increased as people become invisible among the masses. Deviant behavior is less frequently noted when one cannot attach a name or a face to the behavior, thus deviance becomes less susceptible to notice and control. The pressure for achievement and success among the middle class majority pushes individuals to seek innovative (and often illegal) means to achieve societal goals of success in life and business. As the American society becomes more technological, more urbanized, and as human relations become more impersonal, feelings of *anomie* increase (feelings of alienation, estrangement, and indecision as to what norms to follow). All of these factors create a fertile ground for the growth of deviant behavior.

Learning deviance. If the reward or gain from committing a deviant act is perceived by the person to be greater than the cost (negative sanctions imposed by others; feelings of guilt), the stage is set for repeating the act at the next acceptable opportunity. As this process is repeated, persons are gradually enticed into a pattern of deviance. But the process is hardly this simple. Learning theory [See Howard S. Becker, *Outsiders; Studies in the Sociology of Deviance* (New York: The Free Press, 1963).] suggests that a person must *learn* the technique and acquire the skills necessary to commit the act. (For example, most persons would have no idea at all how to prepare heroin for injection.) They must also *learn* the attitudes that support the act (that drinking or drugs is fun, and so on), and the rationalizations that justify the act (it's really the "now" thing to do). Finally, the deviant must define the final result as desirable and worth the effort, or else the act is not worth repeating.

Often, once others come to know the person as following a deviant pattern, they tend to *label* the person as drinker, pothead, or addict, and treat him as if he always follows the pattern. This leads to the important concept of *primary and secondary deviation*. [See Edwin M. Lemert, *Social Pathology* (New York: McGraw-Hill Book Company, Inc., 1951), Chap. 4.] *Pri-*

Answer frame 3⁹

1. False. Over 87 percent of the poor who are able to work do work regularly. However the wages that they earn are insufficient to provide a standard of living that allows them to escape poverty levels.
2. False. Child assistance payments are so small that hardly anyone could view them as a means of additional income, other than in desperation.
3. False. The largest majority of persons receiving public assistance in America are white.
4. True. This is the thesis of Oscar Lewis, and in many ways, the poor do create a culture of poverty.

If you missed any of the above, reread Frame 3⁹ before working Examination 3 on page 137. Then begin Chapter 10 on page 60.

Frame 1¹⁰ continued

mary deviation is deviant behavior which is not recognized and labeled (the secret homosexual, embezzler, or peeping tom), and which is therefore relatively independent of the rest of an individual's behavior. But when deviation is discovered and labeled as deviant, the rest of the individual's life is affected. He may lose his job, be rejected by his family, and be excluded from conventional society. When he begins to reorganize his life in response to this labeling process, this is called *secondary deviation*. When his conventional ties and associations are cut off, and he is thrust into dependence upon deviant associations, deviance has now become a central feature of his life organization. Thus, the reactions of others may lock him into deviance and make any return to conformity very difficult. Through the process of secondary deviation one may progress from an occasional or incidental deviancy to a *deviant career*. When significant portions of the population begin following deviant careers, a social problem has developed.

Indicate whether each of the following statements is true or false by writing "T" or "F" in the space provided.

_____ 1. People commit deviant acts out of the expectation of receiving some reward from the act.

_____ 2. Social change tends to disrupt the social organization of society, creating opportunities for deviance to develop.

_____ 3. Social disorganization and reorganization are a constant process occurring in society.

_____ 4. People learn to commit deviant acts in the same fashion as they learn to commit any other behavior.

Now turn to Answer frame 1¹⁰ on page 64 to check your answers.

Frame 2¹⁰

ALCOHOLISM AND ADDICTION

Which is the number one drug problem in America? Most people are inclined to answer this question with heroin, marijuana, or one of the other illegal drugs. Actually, alcoholism is America's biggest drug problem, and in the opinion of many experts, it affects more people, is more costly, and does more damage to the fabric of the American society than all of the illegal drugs combined!

Most people are not inclined to think of alcohol as a drug, but clinically, a drug is any chemical substance that when ingested, alters the nature of physiological processes. There is an abundance of evidence (much by popular experience) to confirm that alcohol stupefies the mind, can cause physical deterioration of the brain, liver, and intestinal tract, and results in a wide variety of behavioral manifestations that are more problem-creating than the physiological effects. Over two thirds of the adult population are either casual or chronic drinkers; police report that drinking is involved in over half of all automobile accidents; and for perhaps one in ten people who drink, alcohol becomes a major problem in their life. Although estimates vary widely, it is likely that over 9 million people in America are excessive or problem drinkers.

Why then, if people are well aware of the undesirable or harmful effects of drinking, do people continue to consume ever-increasing quantities of alcoholic beverages? Drinking is a social pattern which, for some people, becomes a psychological or physiological phenomena. Thus it is appropriate to examine the social aspects of drinking in order to understand the psychological and medical aspects.

While many people today are of the opinion that the constant rise in the consumption of alcohol is a reflection of an increased level of permissiveness in modern society, or represents a decline of traditional values, a more objective analysis suggests that alcohol is used as a means of escape, used somewhat in the same fashion as other medicinal drugs. All persons use one means or another to escape from the daily frustrations of life, and drinking is easy, relatively safe, legal, easily accessible, and certain in its effects. Drinking easily becomes a reward for successes, a security blanket for failures, and a social lubricant for interacting with others. Once people have learned to drink and define the result as enjoyable, they then are embraced by the subcultural group to reinforce the pattern.

Causes of alcoholism. Current thinking suggests that there are almost as many types of alcoholism as there are alcoholics. The motivations to drink are many and varied, since each alcoholic has his own particular set of problems to overcome. Research does show that some persons, and maybe some races (particularly Orientals) are more sensitive to alcohol than others, but the effects of consumption still largely remain an individual factor. For a long time it was thought that the tendency toward alcoholism was inherited with a heavy bias toward the father's lineage, but this tendency is better explained through behavioral patterns. If the parents tend to resort to drinking as a means of escaping daily frustrations, the children easily learn the pattern from their parents.

Peer group and occupational associates have some influence, but no other variable shows as high an association with youthful drinking patterns as parental drinking patterns.

With a few exceptions, minority groups in any culture tend to have a higher rate of alcoholism than majority groups; the rate of alcoholism among blacks, Indians, and Chicanos in the American society far exceeds that of whites. However, this difference is better explained by the greater frustration that minority groups encounter than by any racial factor. The simple factor of being employed reduces the time available for drinking and perhaps also other tensions that encourage drinking (such as the accompanying frustrations of meeting creditors' demands).

The rate of alcoholism varies considerably by different nationalities and religions; although about the same proportion of Canadians drink as Americans, the rate of alcoholism in the United States is almost twice as high. Both the Italians and French consume about the same quantity of wine, but France (where drinking is a social pattern) has several times the alcoholics as Italy (where people drink only with meals). Wine is an integral part of the Jewish religious ritual, but alcoholism among Jews is almost unheard of. Protestants and Catholics are more prone to alcoholism than Jews or Mormons; the Irish are more prone than the English, men are more prone than women, and urban dwellers are more prone than farmers. Alcoholism is rare when the beverage is consumed only with meals or for religious purposes, but the incidence increases rapidly when it is consumed for social occasions or for escapist functions.

Although there is not yet any exact scientific criteria whereby one can judge if a person is an alcoholic (most alcoholism is a progressive

Answer frame 1¹⁰

1. True. Although other people may not agree that the reward is desirable or worth the effort, deviants commit the act because *they* see it as rewarding.
2. True. Social change often makes traditional norms inapplicable, creating a normless period which is conducive to the development of deviance.
3. True. Social change is constantly changing the nature of society, creating a constant process of disorganization and reorganization.
4. True. Learning theory suggests that people must learn the technique to commit the deviant act, the attitudes which support the act, and to define the reward as worth the effort.

If you missed any of the above, review Frame 1¹⁰ before starting Frame 2¹⁰ on page 62.

Frame 2¹⁰ continued

pattern that takes from 5 to 15 years to develop), the National Council on Alcoholism has compiled a checklist to represent the tendency toward alcoholism. The questions include: Do you black out occasionally after drinking? Do you ever sneak drinks when no one is watching? Are you sensitive about others talking about your drinking? Can you stop when you start drinking? They state that a "yes" answer to only a few of the questions may indicate a psychological tendency toward alcoholism.

Society offers powerful temptations to those who are susceptible to alcoholism, and usually a person is unaware of the compulsion until the pattern is well established. A wide variety of treatment techniques have been tried (aversion therapy with electrical shocks, implanting Antabus to create nausea at just the smell of alcohol, and a varied selection of group therapy efforts such as Alcoholics Anonymous). However, few programs have been successful in more than 30 to 50 percent of the cases.

Some researchers are of the opinion that motivations for drinking are not greatly different in substance than for the use of other illegal drugs, only different in their manifestations. The patterns of addiction appear to be somewhat similar, and both are conducted with a subcultural reference. However, one quite significant difference remains that drinking is becoming more popular, while the use of illegal drugs is declining!

Indicate whether each of the following statements is true or false by writing "T" or "F" in the space provided.

_____ 1. Illegal drugs are the number one drug problem in America.
_____ 2. There is only one reason for drinking, and one type of alcoholic.
_____ 3. Most youth learn to drink from their parents.
_____ 4. Cultures in which the consumption of alcohol is associated with dining have fewer alcoholics than cultures where drinking is a social pattern.

Now turn to Answer frame 2¹⁰ on page 66 to check your answers.

Frame 3¹⁰

SEXUAL DEVIATION

The early 1970s has been a period of sexual upheaval of sorts. Young couples are playing at marriage; gay liberationists are petitioning universities to be listed as an extracurricular organization; and college freshmen are almost embarrassed to report on research surveys that they are still virginal. Octogenarians have found that they can receive more social security from illegal unions than a legitimate marriage, and parents give a sigh of relief when their daughter finally announces a wedding date. What do these new trends mean?

Sociologically, there is little in the realm of sexual behavior that has not been tried before somewhere and at some time in history, but since they are new for Americans now, they become deviant patterns.

Societal factors. Although traditionalists are prone to lament that the emerging patterns reflect the rebirth of a new Sodom or Gomorrah, a more objective analysis would suggest that sexual deviance is a normal product of the changing structure and organization of society. A spirit of individualism flourishes in a period of industrialization, and with the anonymity that urban life provides, there is ample opportunity to engage in extreme behavior without the scrutiny of others. Anonymity in the city produces opportunity, as exemplified by conventioners who cast off moral restraints when they get away to the big city.

The push of modernization and technology encourages people to always seek ever new and wilder experiences. All of these forces push for ever-higher levels of permissiveness in society, and liberal sexual behavior is only a reflection of these trends. In spite of new emerging trends of sexual permissiveness, however, the majority of the population is quite conservative and traditional in their sexual behavior. Most people are socialized to moral and traditional norms; although youth may "sow their oats," over 90 percent of them marry by the mid-twenties and settle down to a staid and traditional family life. Thus, for the vast majority of the population, the dire consequences of the sexual revolution have not had the disorganizing impact that moralists predicted.

Homosexuality. For decades in America, homosexuality has been viewed as a degenerate disease or mental affliction. Nonhomosexuals simply could not accept the possibility that homosexuals could be normal people, and governmental and private agencies scorned to hire suspected persons. Recently, however, riding the crest of libertarian social movements, gay liberation groups have petitioned for recognition and acceptance. Thus a behavior that has long been closeted is now brought to the forefront of public awareness.

Research shows that about one third of males, and one tenth of females report at least one or more homosexual experiences during their lifetime, but only a few of these become frequent or exclusive homosexuals. The proportion of the population in each generation who become homosexual appears to have remained relatively constant, regardless of the social policy or moral climate of the society.

Although there are a variety of biological, psychological, and sociological theories that attempt to account for homosexuality, the most prominent body of theory suggests that it is mainly a problem of socialization to and identification with opposite sex norms. While most people internalize the norms of heterosexuality, homosexuals do not do so. It appears that a major portion of homosexuals had an extremely dominating cross-sex parent and a passive same-sex parent, but this is not true in all cases. Authorities report that men often participate in homosexual behavior while in prison, or at an isolated post in the military (where no heterosexual contact is possible), but revert back to heterosexuality when the opportunity to do so becomes available. Thus, while homosexuality may be a psychological compulsion or a basic psychological orientation for some, for others it is simply a means of achieving sexual gratification.

A violent controversy rages over homosexuality. The orthodox psychiatric view of homosexuality as a personality disorder, rooted in some *failure* of the socialization process, is vehemently rejected by the gay liberation movement. Activist homosexuals insist that homosexuality is not a disorder, but is simply a different, but equally viable and healthy, lifestyle. They resent all attempts to "treat" or "cure" homosexuals as insulting and oppressive. Such attempts have, in fact, rarely been successful.

Legal, economic, and social penalties for homosexuality have declined rapidly in recent years, but not yet disappeared. Earlier debates on whether homosexuals should be "punished" are largely replaced by arguments over whether homosexuals should be "treated" or should be ignored.

Answer frame 2¹⁰

1. False. Although most people are prone to think that illegal drugs are the number one drug problem in America, the use of alcohol and the resulting problems are more damaging than are illegal drugs.
2. False. There are many reasons for drinking (social acceptability, prestige, and escapism, and so on), and scientists are now of the opinion that there may be many types of alcoholics.
3. True. Although the peer groups and occupational associates may reinforce drinking, initially most youth learn to drink from their parents.
4. True. In cultures where drinking is only done with meals or for religious purposes, the rate of alcoholism is much lower than cultures where drinking is a social phenomenon.

If you missed any of the above, reread Frame 2¹⁰ before starting Frame 3¹⁰ on page 64.

Frame 3¹⁰ continued

Pornography. The debate over the virtue or vice of pornography has raged for over a century, but only recently has there been any significant research data on its effects. The President's Commission on Obscenity and Pornography could find no evidence that pornography stimulated sex crimes, sex deviations, or sex delinquencies. Its only significant effect was to stimulate greater sex behavior within the person's established pattern of sex conduct. While this research may not be definitive, it provides no support for the censors.

Research shows that almost everyone indulges in brief pornographic fantasy upon occasion, but most people are soon saturated or their curiosity is satisfied. For these persons, the availability of pornography has little importance.

Actually, pornography may be an acceptable alternative for people who are impotent in interpersonal relations, or who cannot establish a healthy heterosexual relationship, since it can provide an opportunity for achieving sexual outlets through fantasy. In Denmark, where pornography was recently legalized, authorities report an actual decrease in child molesting and voyeuristic activity. For opponents, on the other hand, pornography challenges deeply felt moral convictions, and is feared to have the potential for creating unhealthy attitudes. At present research has shown no significant social harm to arise from pornography, and the public debate appears to be a battle over aesthetics, not public morals.

Indicate whether each of the following statements is true or false by writing "T" or "F" in the space provided.

_____ 1. Standards for sexual permissiveness are becoming *more* stringent than in the past.
_____ 2. Permissiveness in society is an indirect product of industrialization and modernization.
_____ 3. There has been a rapid increase in the number of homosexuals in the American society.
_____ 4. Research clearly shows that pornography tends to encourage sexual deviation.

Now turn to Answer frame 3¹⁰ on page 68 to check your answers.

chapter 11

CRIME IN SOCIETY

Frame 1[11]

Crime is an enduring social problem. As long as there are laws, there will be people who violate the laws.

Whenever anyone examines the social problem of crime in society, several questions soon arise: Why is there so much lawlessness in our society? Why do persons violate the law? What possible solutions might there be to the crime problem in America? To understand the social problem of crime in society, it is important to examine (1) the nature of law and its enforcement; (2) theories of criminal behavior; and (3) the nature of criminal behavior itself.

Laws are necessary to maintain the organization of large complex societies. Sociologically, laws are formalized norms that are enforced by a duly appointed policing agency. In a democratic society, laws are passed by a legislative body, thus representing some shared consensus of approval of the larger population. In other words, *society makes the laws, the violation of which constitutes crime in society.*

Small groups or tribal societies have little need for formalized or written laws as the social codes of the group encourage conformity and proper behavior. If there is any deviation, the group punishes the offender itself, and no policing agency is required for law enforcement. For example, in several societies in the Pacific islands, an offender is rarely executed for major crimes, as he is expected to take his own life after being judged guilty by the community. Among the Australian aborigines, the injured person is allowed to exact his own punishment by throwing three spears at the accused, after which the guilty person (if he survives) is fully pardoned.

Sumner reports in his ethnographic study of societies around the world that almost any pattern of behavior may be considered proper or improper in some society somewhere. [Sumner, *Folkways.*] This variability in laws is perhaps most noticeable in the United States where each state is allowed to develop its own legal codes to supplement federal codes. This leads to several ironic interpretations of moral behavior; prostitution and gambling are legal in Nevada, but not in neighboring Utah. Not long ago, possession of marijuana was a felony in Texas with a penalty of ten years to life imprisonment, but was only a misdemeanor in some communities in Michigan, punishable with $5 fine. Whistling under water is a misdemeanor in Iowa, and wearing a Smokey the Bear emblem without authorization is a violation of a federal statute.

Legally, a crime is defined as any violation of a law, whether it be littering with a candy wrapper or armed robbery. Laws in most societies are broken down into categories according to the perceived threat of the behavior to the society. The most prominent categories are *crimes against property* (theft, robbery), *crimes against the person* (assault, injury, or defamation of character), and *crimes against the state* (treason, espionage, and so on). Societies differ widely in the emphasis they place upon the different types of crime, in that capitalistic nations tend to emphasize crimes against property, while communistic nations emphasize crimes against the

67

Answer frame 3[10]

1. False. The American society is becoming less stringent and more permissive in regards to sex standards than in the past.
2. True. Industrialization and modernization tend to encourage standards for individualism and permissiveness.
3. Research does not show any great increase in the number of homosexuals in society, only a greater public awareness of the condition.
4. False. Although it is often popularly assumed that pornography tends to encourage sexual deviation, research does not suggest that this is true.

If you missed any of the above, reread Frame 3[10] before starting Chapter 11 on page 67.

Frame 1[11] continued

state. Tribal societies which have limited property or state government tend to emphasize crimes against the person.

In the United States, crimes are further broken down into misdemeanors (jaywalking, speeding, loitering, and petty theft) which are punishable with a small fine and/or a short jail sentence. Felonies are more serious and receive heavier punishments. Felonies involve property crimes above some established figure (often $100) or are major threats to the person (armed robbery, assault, and so on).

In most westernized nations, laws are enacted and enforced in the name of the community, thus protecting the people collectively. Early Judeo-Christian law was individualistic in that the wronged person exacted his own punishment against the offender (an eye-for-an-eye). Although many laws in America reflect a standard of morality derived from the Judeo-Christian heritage, there is nothing absolute or finite about laws; they vary with the time and need in society.

Indicate whether each of the following statements is true or false by writing "T" or "F" in the space provided.

_____ 1. Sociologically, there will always be crime in society.
_____ 2. Any single pattern of behavior may be considered proper or improper in some society somewhere.
_____ 3. Capitalistic nations tend to be more concerned about crimes against the state than communistic nations.
_____ 4. Many laws in America flow from the Judeo-Christian tradition.

Now turn to Answer frame 1[11] on page 70 to check your answers.

Frame 2[11]

TYPES OF CRIMINAL BEHAVIOR

Apparently since the origin of civilization man has been searching for an explanation of why persons commit crimes or do not conform to the values and normative ideals of the society. Numerous theoretical explanations have been proposed, many of which accounted for some types of criminal behavior, but none has fully accounted for all types. The failure of most theories of criminal behavior is found within the different motivations for violating laws. Premeditated crime involves the intent of committing the crime as well as careful planning for the event. Our society is most concerned with premeditated crime and punishes it more severely than any other type (armed robbery and premeditated murder carry the heaviest penalties of all crimes).

Situational crimes occur as a result of an unfortunate combination of circumstances. Rarely does the person intend to commit the crime, and there is no premeditation. Situational crimes usually occur in instances of passion, rage, or negligence: the husband kills his wife in the heat of a marital dispute, an alcoholic hits a child while driving home, or a speeding driver loses control and hits another car and kills its occupants.

Civil suits may also be considered as situational crimes. Civil suits are generally considered as noncriminal in nature or intent, but appeal to an issue of morality whereby the aggrieved (injured) party charges the offender with inappropriate conduct. The court judges the issue, and then renders a judgment in favor of the most moral party, or perhaps awards damages to the aggrieved. Property disputes, violations of contract, and disturbances of the peace may be included in civil offenses.

White collar crime is conducted in the normal operating procedures of businessmen or employees carrying out their occupational roles. Criminologists estimate that the cost of white collar crime is several times the amount of all other types of crime combined. Common examples are price-fixing in business, failing to honor guarantees on merchandise, or misrepresenting the quality of products sold to the public. The doctor who gives false medical testimony in a damage suit, the business operator who uses fictitious warehouse receipts as collateral for bank loans, or the political campaign manager who solicits illegal campaign contributions from businessmen all illustrate white collar crime.

White collar crime is not only conducted by businessmen; taxpayers who fail to report all their income, and employees who pocket a few office supplies are also included within the classification of white collar crime. Such behavior is usually rationalized by the employee under the guise of "employment compensation" or "everyone else is doing it" to diminish feelings of guilt, but it is illegal just the same.

White collar crime is rarely punished to the extent of other premeditated crime because it is conducted by otherwise moral and responsible persons who are the basic working force of our society. Such people often express alarm at the "lawlessness" of our society today, while continuing their own white collar crimes.

Psychopathic crime is attributed to a biological or psychological condition in the person, which he cannot normally control. It rarely involves rational premeditation or intent, and the punishment for psychopathic criminals is usually commitment to a mental institution rather than imprisonment.

The psychopath is directed by a compulsion that he cannot deny, and he usually derives some distorted sense of power or revenge from his acts. The pyromaniac may set fires then help the fire department put them out; the kleptomaniac steals a whole trunkful of the same item; or the sex deviant may steal women's undergarments from the clothesline, creating considerable distress but little damage.

Psychopathic crime provides sensational news and usually receives considerable publicity, but the psychopathic criminal constitutes a very small minority of the criminal population. His acts are sometimes dangerous (sadistic killers, violent rapists) but are more often trivial (peeping toms).

Civil disobedience consists of premeditated violations of the law with the intent of challenging the validity or legitimacy of the law in order to bring about some change. Civil disobedience is most commonly supported by a protesting group and the actions are designed to bring public attention and recognition to perceived inequities in the law. Although the protest itself may be physically threatening, the legal penalties for civil disobedience are rarely severe. Here again the intent of the criminal act is an important consideration in understanding the nature of law enforcement itself.

Organized crime. The amorphous, invisible nature of organized crime easily instills fear and concern in the minds of the public, perhaps because it emerges where people least expect or they fail to prove its existence when they do expect its presence. Sociologically, organized crime consists of "power structures" or groups in a community that use illegitimate means to acquire wealth or position.

Answer frame 1[11]

1. True. Crime is any violation of a law, and societies must make laws in order to maintain their social organization. Thus there will always be some crime in societies.
2. True. There is considerable variation in what is considered proper behavior in the different societies, and what is legal, moral, and proper in one society may not be in another.
3. False. Capitalistic societies tend to be more concerned about crimes against the person, while communistic nations tend to be more concerned about crimes against the state.
4. True. Many of the moral standards of American law were taken from Judeo-Christian law.

If you missed any of the above, reread Frame 1[11] before starting Frame 2[11] on page 68.

Frame 2[11] continued

To much of the public, organized crime is associated with the Mafia or la Cosa Nostra, which were criminal "brotherhood" groups formed in Sicily during the late 1800s. As Sicilians emigrated to the United States, some of them imported the "brotherhood" concept. However, the popular conception of a secret nationwide organization ruled by a hierarchy of family patriarchs appears to be more myth than fact.

Most criminologists agree now that there are organized syndicates in major cities that control certain illegitimate operations, but the scope of these syndicates is limited and not centralized under a formal nationwide syndicate with tentacles reaching into every business and city office in the area. Each metropolitan area may have multiple syndicates, each dominating a specific enterprise; one syndicate may control the vending machines and juke boxes of the city, another may control the cement and construction market, another may dominate the prostitution or drug market.

Organized crime is hardly a Sicilian invention. Daniel Bell notes that the ethnic identification of organized crime is related to immigration patterns; Irish syndicates were followed by Polish syndicates, who in turn were followed by Italian syndicates, and these Italians likely are soon to be replaced by blacks and Puerto Ricans. [Daniel Bell, "Crime as an American Way of Life," *Antioch Review*, 13 (June 1953): 131–54.] The patriarchs of organized crime today may be Irish, Polish, Chinese, or any other red-blooded American who is also engaged in legitimate business, politics, or entrepreneurial activity. In either event, organized crime exists because of persons attempting to acquire money or power through illegitimate means.

Much of the success of organized crime in America is due to the services they provide to a hungry public. The largest growth of criminal organizations occurred during the prohibition era when bootleggers such as Al Capone created systems of procurement and distribution for illegal liquor. When prohibition was repealed, the organizations shifted their supply of services to other illegal activities—prostitution, gambling, and usury. Thus the organizations function to provide the services that the public cannot otherwise legally obtain, and they could not survive without the public's tolerance.

Organized crime is difficult to control because the victims are willing participants, creating *victimless crime*. The gambler must seek out the "action," prostitution requires a clientele, and the drug user requires a source of supply—but who among the victims is likely to complain to the authorities?

Bell concludes that organized crime, as it has existed in the past, is eroding away. It appears that the nature of organized crime is changing toward a mixture of quasi-legitimate business endeavors that defy prosecution in the courts. Value changes in the society are eliminating traditional sources of illicit profit (such as prostitution) and the various ethnic groups upon which much of the organization depended are being assimilated, destroying the traditional bases of power. As the structure of society changes, so does its organization and the groups therein.

Indicate whether each of the following statements is true or false by writing "T" or "F" in the space provided.

_____ 1. Situational crimes are usually intended and premeditated.
_____ 2. White collar crimes are crimes conducted by anyone who is a businessman.
_____ 3. It is clear now that there is a nationwide organized crime syndicate that controls all criminal activities.
_____ 4. Organized crime flourishes because most of the victims are people who desire the illegal service.

Now check your answers with those in Answer frame 2[11] on page 72.

Frame 3[11]

THE STATISTICS OF CRIME

An abundance of statistics is available on crime, but also perhaps no other social data are more confusing and misleading as to the true nature of the problem they purport to describe. First, there can be no accurate estimate of the extent of lawlessness in society because not all the laws of a community are enforced and not all the violators are apprehended. Numerous studies have shown that many persons violate a variety of laws each day, but most persons go for months or even years without receiving a traffic ticket or arrest for a simple misdemeanor. Further, surveys of community police departments suggest that less than one fourth of all crimes are reported in official reports. Arrest rates may vary with a variety of factors; as an example, a UPI story reports that police in Chicago "showered motorists with tickets to force salary negotiations with police organizations." [United Press International, September 28, 1972.] Arrest rates thus become more of an indication of the current concerns and activity of police and officials rather than reflecting the actual rate of violation of a law.

Second, there can be no fully accurate estimate of the cost of crime in society. Much of organized and white collar crime is quasi-legal and escapes public or official recognition. Thus there is no realization of its cost to the public.

Third, punishment for crime appears to vary almost inversely with the financial value of the crime; representative of common examples is a recent case in which an armed robbery in a small town netted less than $120 and brought a prison term of six years. During the same month, a bank official embezzled over $200,000 and received one and one half years, and during his arraignment he was reelected president of a prominent community business organization. Thus it makes a difference what crime is committed by whom!

Most crime that is reported is never solved or results in conviction. FBI statistics show that for each 100 crimes that are reported to police, less than 22 percent result in arrest, of those arrested only 16 percent are held for prosecution, of which 8 percent are referred to juvenile courts, 3 percent are acquitted, and only 5 percent are finally found guilty as charged. Thus the chances for committing a major violation and escaping free are quite good—at least favorable enough to encourage persons to commit over 8 million major crimes per year.

Demographic variables in crime. Although people commit almost all types of crimes in all regions of America, the types and rates of crimes most often committed vary significantly by different demographic variables.

AGE AND SEX. Although people of all ages and both sexes commit crimes, young men appear to be the most active. Criminal behavior appears to peak during late adolescence and early manhood, then declines steadily with advancing age. Young men are most prone to commit crimes against property (80 percent of all arrests). The more sophisticated crimes require maturity and experience; thus fraud and embezzlement peak at age 45–50.

Answer frame 2[11]

1. False. Situational crimes usually occur by accident, and are unintended and not premeditated.
2. False. White collar crimes are conducted as part of the normal procedures of business or by employees carrying out their occupational roles, illegally. Thus, murder conducted by a businessman is not white collar crime, but failing to honor guarantees is white collar crime.
3. False. On the contrary, organized crime does exist, but its organization is composed of a collection of small organizations scattered throughout the society.
4. True. This is known as victimless crime, because the victims themselves must seek out the criminal activity.

If you missed any of the above, reread Frame 2[11] before starting Frame 3[11] on page 71.

Frame 3[11] continued

However, along with the emergence of the equal rights movements, women are narrowing the crime gap. Female arrest rates since 1970 are increasing some 6 percent faster than male arrest rates. Whether this reflects increased female criminal activity, or growing sex equality in prosecution, is not known.

URBAN-RURAL. Urban areas generally show higher rates of crime than rural areas because of the greater degree of *anonymity* and *heterogeneity* of the population found in the cities. Town gossip spreads rapidly in small communities, and deviating acts are quickly noted and repressed by townfolk. The high degree of *observability* in small communities exercises strong restraints upon deviant or criminal behavior. Crime can be reduced in an area by increasing the observability of the deviant behavior, whereupon persons either refrain from the deviation or migrate to urban areas where such deviation is less conspicuous.

REGIONAL VARIATION. For reasons not quite clear, the southern states tend to have slightly more crimes against the person while the north has more crimes against property. However, regional factors appear to have less impact in accounting for variations in criminal activity than the existence of metropolitan areas within the regions. Cities tend to attract the criminally prone because of the anonymity that the city life provides.

CLASS VARIATION. Criminal statistics clearly show a major social class difference in crime rates; the lower class has a much higher arrest rate than the upper social classes. This difference is due to two causes. First, the lower class is more prone to committing the crimes that are most likely to result in arrest and conviction. Because of the threat to public security, armed robbery, and assault are more likely to be prosecuted than embezzlement, white collar crime, or other organized crime.

Second, people of the higher social classes can more easily avoid prosecution if they are arrested. They are more likely to have an educational advantage, prominent standing in the community, connections to important public figures, and the financial resources to hire a good legal defense. These factors also influence juvenile delinquency arrests because upper class youth are more likely to be returned to the parents' custody than remanded to the juvenile court.

In consideration of these factors, upper class persons do not appear to be any less criminal than the lower class, just less likely to be apprehended, arrested, convicted, or sentenced.

MINORITY STATUS. Minority groups tend to be highly overrepresented in arrest and conviction statistics. Several factors appear to cause this difference. First, most of the overrepresentation can be explained when one controls the variables of social class and lifestyle. The concentration of minority people into lower income and unemployed status exposes them to the types of crime which are most likely to attract police attention. Statisticians have found more variation within racial groups than between groups, thus adding additional credence to the class factor as an explanation of "racial crime."

Second, the greater degree of visibility of minority persons makes them more vulnerable to arrest. Third, discrimination does appear to be a factor in the likelihood of being arrested and convicted. [William J. Chambliss and Richard H. Nagasawa, "On the Validity of Official Statistics," *Social Forces* (Winter, 1969): 71–77.] Although there is no conclusive evidence that minority groups are more criminal than other groups, minority status does increase the likelihood of being arrested, convicted, and serving a longer sentence. This is, however, a diminishing factor in crime rates. Earlier studies, before 1960, showed unmistakable evidence of discriminatory law enforcement, while the more recent studies suggest that such discrimination is disappearing.

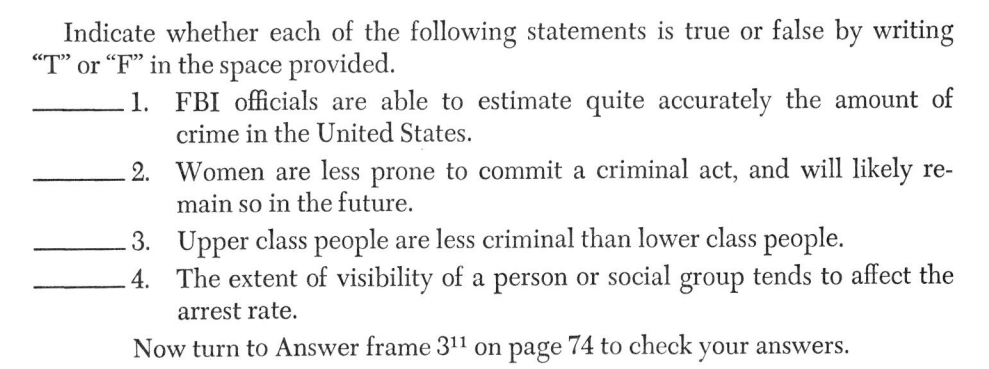

Indicate whether each of the following statements is true or false by writing "T" or "F" in the space provided.

_____ 1. FBI officials are able to estimate quite accurately the amount of crime in the United States.

_____ 2. Women are less prone to commit a criminal act, and will likely remain so in the future.

_____ 3. Upper class people are less criminal than lower class people.

_____ 4. The extent of visibility of a person or social group tends to affect the arrest rate.

Now turn to Answer frame 3[11] on page 74 to check your answers.

Answer frame 3[11]

1. False. The majority of crime that is committed is never reported or prosecuted, thus FBI statistics give only a relative indication of the amount of crime in the American society.
2. False. Women are less prone to commit a criminal act, but statistics show that the number of crimes committed by females is increasing some 6 percent faster than males each year.
3. False. Research suggests that the upper class people are just as criminal as lower class people, but they are less likely to be arrested and prosecuted for the crimes that they commit.
4. True. High observability tends to increase the likelihood of arrest, particularly if the person is of lower class or minority status.

If you missed any of the above, reread Frame 3[11] before beginning Chapter 12.

chapter 12

THEORIES AND TREATMENT OF CRIMINALITY

Frame 1[12]

Early theories of criminal behavior tended to emphasize biological or spiritual causes. Early Puritans thought that crime consisted of sinful behavior that was inspired by the devil; thus religious repentance was the solution to the crime problem.

BIOLOGICAL THEORIES

In the early 1900s various biological explanations of criminal behavior were developed. Cesare Lombroso, a phrenologist who is often credited with founding the field of criminology, proposed a theory of "constitutional inferiority," whereby some persons were born with criminal tendencies. Lombroso thought that these tendencies could be identified by physical anomalies of the person—the shape of the head, muscular build, or bone structure. William Sheldon later proposed a theory of body structure categorizing certain physical types—the endomorph (a short, fat, rotund person), the mesomorph (a strong muscular, heavy-boned person), and the ectomorph (a lean, fragile, and frail person). Although the "body type" theory of Sheldon provided good stereotypes for Damon Runyon characters, criminals come in all types and shapes and there is little proof that specific body types can account for criminal tendencies.

More recently (the late 1960s) another biological theory suggested that criminals may have an extra "Y" chromosome which predisposes some persons to commit criminal acts. Although the chromosomal theory received considerable attention, there as yet has been no proof that criminals are any more likely to have an extra chromosome than the noncriminal population.

Today, most criminologists agree that biological theories have questionable validity, except that such biological factors as strength and sex may predispose some person to commit certain types of criminal acts—the frail ectomorph is rather unlikely to commit assaultive acts (as he is likely to get the worst end of the effort), and it is unlikely for a woman to be imprisoned for rape.

PSYCHOLOGICAL THEORIES

The early biological assumption that the criminal was abnormal or deranged in some fashion carried over into the psychological theories of criminal tendency. Early psychological theories also sought to identify the one undesirable characteristic that inspired criminal behavior. Various theories were proposed; among the first was the IQ theory that prisoners were mentally retarded and could not learn proper behavior. Considerable testing of prison populations did indeed show that prisoners were generally of lower IQ than the normal population. Although the conclusion was correct, the method was not; later research indicated that the mentally retarded were simply more likely to be caught and imprisoned while the more intelligent escaped prosecution. Current evidence strongly indicates that intelligence is not associated with any criminal tendency.

Other attempts, generally called "the personality trait" theory of criminal behavior, have been made to identify personality traits that were associated with criminal behavior. Hundreds of traits were identified and researched—introversion-extroversion, masculinity-femininity, deference, and so on, but in general, criminals were found to hold approximately the same mixture of personality traits as the noncriminal population.

The 1930s also saw the growth of Freudian psychoanalytic explanations for criminal behavior. Freud theorized that the deep-seated and perhaps unconscious emotional problems of insecurity and inferiority, coupled with uncontrollable impulses of aggression created personality disorders in the criminal mind. From this perspective, criminal behavior simply represented symptoms of underlying emotional problems, requiring psychoanalytic analysis and treatment. Although many criminal acts are perhaps motivated by unconscious emotional conflicts, psychoanalytic theory fails to account for vast areas of criminal conduct—white collar crime, organized crime, and situational crime.

Indicate whether each of the following statements is true or false by writing "T" or "F" in the space provided.

_____ 1. Some persons are born with criminal tendencies.
_____ 2. There are no biological influences at all upon criminal behavior.
_____ 3. Research clearly shows that most criminals are psychologically abnormal.

Now turn to Answer frame 1[12] on page 76 to check your answers.

Answer frame 1[12]

1. False. Although some youths may learn criminal patterns from their parents, they are not born with criminal tendencies.
2. False. Although most of the biological explanations of criminal behavior are not now accepted as valid, such biological factors as strength and sex are predisposing factors to some types of criminal behavior.
3. False. Although many attempts have been made to establish that criminals are psychologically abnormal, no specific trait or characteristic has been found to cause criminality.

If you missed any of the above, reread Frame 1[12] before starting Frame 2[12].

Frame 2[12]

SOCIOLOGICAL THEORIES

Although biological and psychological theories adequately account for certain types of criminal behavior, no one theory accounts for all types of crime—premeditated, white collar, organized crime, and so on. Sociological theories attempt to provide social explanations of crime and criminal behavior, starting from the question of how social structure and society influence criminal behavior. The most prominent sociological explanations are (1) Merton's *goals-means* theory, (2) Sutherland's theory of *differential association*, (3) *delinquent subculture* theories, and (4) *control* theory.

Merton's goals-means theory. Robert Merton [Robert K. Merton, *Social Theory and Social Structure* (Glencoe, Ill.: The Free Press, 1964), pp. 131–60.], taking his cue from the early French sociologist Émile Durkheim, notes that society provides a set of socially approved goals for its people to achieve (for example, comfort, pleasure, material goods, and status), and a set of socially approved means to accomplish the goals (getting an education, working for a living). Most people in society accept the traditional goals and conform to socially acceptable methods for accomplishing the goals; they work diligently, pay their bills, and respect community norms. Some persons, however, accept the goals but fail to achieve them through the legitimate means. These people turn to illegitimate means to attain the goals, which produces criminal deviation. From this perspective, the solution to the crime problem is to encourage conformity to the cultural goals and to the legitimate ways of achieving these goals. Among groups who have limited access to socially approved means because of barriers of race or class, high crime rates can be expected.

Sutherland's theory of differential association. Sutherland's theory of differential association is a social-psychological explanation of how persons learn to develop patterns of criminal behavior. As described in earlier chapters, there may be considerable variability in what is considered to be crime (an act may be illegal in one state or time but legal in another), thus Sutherland argues that any theory of criminal behavior must focus upon the deviant patterns of behavior rather than considering the law as absolute and never changing.

Sutherland outlines his theory with nine propositions. [Edwin H. Sutherland and Donald R. Cressy, *Principles of Criminology*, 7th ed. (Chicago: J. B. Lippincott Co., 1966), pp. 81–82.] The first is that *criminal behavior is learned* the same as any other pattern of behavior. Most crimes require a certain amount of skill to commit successfully, and the skill must be learned—not inherited. For example, a corporate executive is unlikely to know how to crack a safe, but he may know how to commit stock frauds and embezzlement. Few women have the skill or interest to strip a car, but they can shoplift goods from a store. Thus, the tendency to commit a crime, or the types of crime committed, depends upon the knowledge and abilities of the person.

Second, *criminal behavior is learned in interaction or association with other persons,* in that the skills are learned through communication with others. Third, *the principal learning of criminal behavior occurs within intimate personal groups.* Criminals acquire the skills and abilities necessary to commit criminal acts from those around them. Fourth, *the learning includes the techniques of committing the crime, as well as the motives, drives, and supporting attitudes.* Fifth, *the direction of the motives and drives is learned from definitions of the legal codes as favorable or unfavorable.* If one accepts the law against theft, he generally will not steal.

Sixth, *a person becomes delinquent because of an* excess *of definitions favorable to violation of the law over definitions unfavorable to violation of the law.* This is the principle of differential association—that the differential between rewards and costs is sufficiently favorable to encourage the criminal act. Criminals must believe that the chances are favorable for receiving more reward than cost, or they would not commit the crime.

Seventh, *the differential association may vary in frequency, duration, and intensity.* The greater the contact with criminal deviants, the greater the likelihood of learning and performing criminal acts. Eighth, *the process of learning criminal behavior by association with criminals involves all of the mechanisms that are involved in learning any other activity.* Ninth, *criminal behavior is an expression of the same general needs and values as noncriminal behavior.*

Thus, to Sutherland, the difference between acceptable behavior and criminal behavior is mainly one of direction, in that one behavioral pattern is illegal, while the other is legal. From this perspective, persons may pursue criminal careers with the same diligence as legal and proper careers.

Sutherland's theory has wide application in that it explains the process of learning the motivation for committing crime, as well as accounting for the method of acquiring criminal skills, the type of crime committed, and the problem of whether a person is likely to follow a criminal career. As such, his theory is applicable to premeditated crime, white collar crime and organized crime. It cannot, however, account for situational crime that involves no premeditation.

Subculture theories. A variety of theories have been proposed to describe the emergence of criminal groups in society. Most theories start with the recognition that middle class norms and values tend to predominate in society and become the standards of morality. These norms embody the Protestant work ethic, and the standards for thrift, honesty, and virtue. The middle class is achievement-oriented and supports individual responsibility.

However, not all groups in society have equal opportunity or access to the societal means to obtain the middle class goals of achievement and success. Thus, as a result of the limited opportunity available to them, lower class or marginal groups may develop subcultures of contranorms or values with alternate structures of status and prestige. These groups often become known as delinquent groups, and when the norms pervade the whole immediate community, they may become delinquent subcultures. [The reader may refer to the novel, *Manchild in the Promised Land* by Claude Brown for a good description of life in a delinquent subculture.]

The members of these groups with these subcultures tend to be characterized by sporadic or low-status employment, and feelings of defeat or rejection from the middle class and its standards. Since these groups have little opportunity to succeed through conventional means, they often turn to illegitimate means to accomplish the goals of comfort, pleasure, and material possessions. In other words, deviance and crime become a way of life for the groups and a means for subsistence.

Indicate whether each of the following statements is true or false by writing "T" or "F" in the space provided.

_____ 1. Sociological explanations of criminality examine the effects of the social structure of society upon criminal behavior.

_____ 2. Robert Merton in his "goals-means" theory would suggest that criminals hold the same goals as other conforming persons in society, but use illegitimate means to achieve the goals.

_____ 3. Sutherland's theory of differential association suggests that criminals have to *learn* criminal behavior.

_____ 4. Subcultural theories of criminality focus upon the formation of deviant groups in society.

Now turn to Answer frame 2¹² on page 80 to check your answers.

Frame 3¹²

JUVENILE DELINQUENCY

In examining the emergence of delinquent subcultures, Albert Cohen suggests that lower class youth are ill-equipped to achieve in a middle class status system, thus they sometimes join together in delinquent gangs to at least share a common plight. [Albert K. Cohen, *Delinquent Boys: The Culture of the Gang* (New York: Macmillan, 1955).] Alternate status systems are constructed which emphasize toughness, masculinity, smartness (beating the straight man at his game), and delinquent role behavior. Thus, by rejecting middle class values and substituting an alternate status structure, the delinquent can at least achieve the goals of stature and prestige among the members of the subculture.

Cloward and Ohlin describe three types of delinquent subcultures that appear in metropolitan areas—the theft, conflict, and escape subcultures. [Richard S. Cloward and Lloyd E. Ohlin, *Delinquency and Opportunity: A Theory of Delinquent Gangs* (Glencoe, Ill.: Free Press, 1960).] The theft subculture emphasizes stealing as an acceptable mode of survival. The conflict subculture is oriented around the possession of and protection of a turf or territory from competing groups, and controlling the "action of the area." The escape subculture is composed of members who reject both societal and delinquent subcultural goals and means and withdraw into their own world. Hippies, drug addicts, and social misfits are the "double losers" who reject the whole society and are often classified into this group.

For the youth born and raised in the delinquent subculture, delinquency (as defined by middle class standards) is viewed as the normal and expected role behavior for delinquent subcultural youth. Delinquent subcultures are more likely to develop in metropolitan ghetto areas with large numbers of nonworking class families. Bandura and Walters note that the fathers in such families provided ineffective role models for their sons to emulate in achieving conventional societal goals. [Albert Bandura and Richard H. Walters, *Adolescent Aggression* (New York: Ronald Press, 1959).] The role models of success become the pimp, the pusher, and the con artist who "makes it off the straight [person]." Deviant patterns become the proper and expected (although socially disapproved) mode of behavior for the ghetto dweller and marginal members of society. Thus, the delinquent subculture perpetuates itself through the generations.

Control theory. A newly emerging body of theory, *control theory*, rejects the delinquent subculture and learning theory approaches to criminality, and suggests that the criminal or delinquent is poorly integrated into the social system and has very weak ties with the major social institutions (churches, schools, and community organizations) that control the behavior of the rest of the population. Delinquents fail to follow institutionalized norms for behavior and consciously devise sets of counter norms that condone criminality for themselves. Thus, from the control theory perspective, the delinquent is not to be viewed as an unfortunate, maligned child who was deprived of opportunity in life, but rather as one who was poorly integrated into the social system and consciously chose his course of action.

It is hard to know which of the above theories are most useful in accounting for delinquent and criminal behavior. The motivations to commit a crime are many and varied, and an explanation that would account for one event or time may be insufficient to account for others. We could only suggest that there is more than a grain of truth in each of the theories and that perhaps the theories should be used differentially according to the motivations and circumstances of the criminal event.

Punishment and imprisonment. The American conception of punishment by institutionalization follows a long tradition formed in early Europe and England. The principle was based upon the assumption that if a lawbreaker was institutionalized and allowed the opportunity to reflect upon his "sins" (as well as adding a little physical pain and discomfort for encouragement), he would surely see the virtue of following the straight and narrow path. Two thousand years of the practice, however, does not seem to have taught many criminals many lessons; petty theft, larceny, and even murder is still as common today as ever.

The fallacy in the above principle is that criminals really do not expect to be caught when they violate the law, or else they would not commit the crime. Punishment is effective when there is a strong likelihood of getting caught (notice how drivers slow down immediately when they spot a radar equipped police car), but professional criminals are well aware that they stand only a 5 percent chance of being imprisoned for a crime, even if they are caught. For them arrest is simply an occupational risk.

The effectiveness of punishment for criminal behavior is somewhat related to the degree of commitment to the crime; housewives who are caught shoplifting are often too embarrassed to try stealing again, but for career criminals the profitability of crime, and for juvenile delinquents, the excitement of delinquency outweighs the cost (the reader might refer back to Sutherland's differential association theory once again for the rationale and process for developing a criminal career).

A wide variety of techniques for reforming habitual law offenders has been tried (education, religion, guidance and counseling, psychoanalysis, prison reform, and even physical mutilation), but none have found much success. In three out of four cases, the convicted felon returns to the criminal pattern and is imprisoned again.

Currently the trend is going away from imprisonment as a solution to the crime problem (penologists now realize that incarceration often serves as a graduate level course in higher crime for young criminals), and many penal reforms are being oriented toward retraining the criminal in new occupational roles and trying to build alternate socially acceptable lifestyles that allow the person to be integrated into society when he is paroled. Although no program is fully successful in achieving criminal reform, this approach offers more promise than others tried in the past.

Indicate whether each of the following statements is true or false by writing "T" or "F" in the space provided.

_____ 1. Youth who are raised in delinquent subcultures are abnormal.
_____ 2. Youth in delinquent subcultures often create alternate status systems which justify their delinquency.
_____ 3. Control theory suggests that delinquents have no control over themselves.
_____ 4. If punishment were only severe enough, people would never commit any crimes.

Now turn to Answer frame 3[12] on page 80 to check your answers.

Answer frame 2[12]

1. True. The sociological perspective assumes that the social structure of society causes some forms of criminal behavior.
2. True. The use of illegitimate means is what produces criminality.
3. True. It takes skill to be a successful criminal, and persons must acquire the skill and learn the attitudes and values that support the criminal behavior.
4. True. Subcultural theories suggest that criminal subcultures form in society that support criminal behavior.

If you missed any of the above, restudy Frame 2[12] before starting Frame 3[12] on page 78.

Answer frame 3[12]

1. False. Although they may be abnormal by prevailing middle class standards, they may be normal for the environment in which they were raised.
2. True. The status system in a delinquent subculture may support delinquency, theft, and other malicious acts.
3. False. Control theory would suggest that delinquents are persons who are poorly integrated into the larger social system, and are fully aware of the effects of their actions.
4. False. Punishment is effective only when there is a certainty of punishment, or if the person is not fully committed to the criminal act.

If you missed any of the above, reread Frame 3[12] before working Examination 4 on page 139. Then begin Chapter 13 on page 81.

chapter 13

RELIGION

Frame 1[13]

It is an axiom of functional theory that for an institution to exist it must fulfill a function or purpose, or else it will cease to be maintained. Religion serves a variety of purposes in society —it is a haven for the weak or troubled, a force of community organization and stability, and helps to establish the moral standards for the society. Although some functions of the church are timeless and never change in substance, other functions are influenced by the forces of social change, which in turn influence the nature and role of organized religion itself. To understand the problems of churches in modern society, it is important to examine the purposes and functions they serve, both in the past and in modern society.

FUNCTIONS OF RELIGION

Although religion perhaps has a different meaning and purpose to each person, there are some general common functions it serves for all people. Malinowski (an English anthropologist) studied the Trobriand Islanders in the Pacific to ascertain the origin of their religious faith and magical practices. He observed that when the natives prepared for a dangerous fishing expedition upon the ocean, all preparations were accompanied with considerable religious ceremony and magic; however, when they fished in the relative safety of the island lagoon, no ceremonies were conducted. Ceremonies were conducted for the planting and harvesting of crops and other uncontrollable or hazardous events (births, deaths, marriages, sickness, and so on), but not for regular or nondangerous events in life.

Malinowski noted that the biggest concerns the natives expressed in life were that of *contingency*, or the problem of meeting uncertainty and the unknown dangers in life (sickness, death, starvation); *powerlessness* in coping with contingency; and *scarcity* (the problem of fulfilling the daily needs for food and shelter). He concluded that the practice of magic and religion provided a means for meeting the problems of life by invoking the assistance and guidance of supra-empirical or deistical powers. (*Religion* is sociologically defined as a body of beliefs and practices concerning supernatural powers and ultimate values. *Magic* is a body of techniques for manipulating or controlling supernatural powers, and is often, but not always, a part of religion.)

Religious institutions serve the function of providing a means for coping with the fears of contingency, powerlessness, and scarcity for people in society. Since these conditions are equally present in modern as well as primitive societies, religion will continue to serve these functions. Other functions served by religion, however, are rapidly changing, and are having a significant impact upon churches today.

Social functions. Although it was not anticipated, the invention of the automobile and the TV has perhaps had a greater impact upon reducing the role of the church as a center of social activity in American society than any other factor. Early in the development of rural America, the church served as the major center for social activity (and in most small communities the only center of activity). Historians report that the weekly or monthly church service often assumed almost a festive atmosphere; occasionally they were accompanied by boxing matches, horse auctions, and naturally, a social luncheon. Many churches in early America could not afford a full-time minister, thus they either shared a circuit preacher or had both the church and the minister also serve as school and schoolmaster. These functions naturally placed the church at the center for all social activity for many communities across the nation.

However, with the development of industrialization and urbanization, many of the social functions of the church were diminished. Urbanization provided an abundance of recreational and entertainment facilities which distracted people from church activities. People across America came to prefer personal pleasure and satisfaction rather than piety. The mass production of the automobile and a hard-surfaced highway system encouraged people to escape to the countryside on weekends rather than unite in communal worship. Movies and television programs rapidly preempted the weeknight prayer and Bible study sessions. In short, industrialization caused churches to lose much of their influence over the population and in turn, somewhat diminished their position as a center for social activity in American life. The role and function of the institution of religion in society changed accordingly.

Education. Throughout history, churches have served as the center for education in many societies as well as attending to the spiritual needs of the people. During the middle ages in Europe, the church was the sole repository for knowledge, and the priesthood supplied almost all the teachers for the few who became educated. Because of this, churches were able to exert considerable influence upon the state of knowledge and the selection of students, thereby influencing the nature of societies in general.

The involvement of churches in education in America has followed similar lines. The close and intimate involvement of the churches in school activities allowed them considerable influence upon the people and the community, particularly in such matters as legislation, the expenditures of public funds, and the establishment of standards of morality.

However, several forces were to change the relationship between the church and its educational function. The expanding industrial economy of the 1800s required an increasing supply of trained skilled laborers and waves of uneducated and illiterate immigrants came to America to seek employment. The massive migration of rural poor to urban areas provided additional millions of people who required resocialization and training into an urban-technical environment. Thus, changes in the composition of the American population produced a need for a large-scale system of public schools, and reduced the role of churches in public education.

Political and moral leadership. When churches were the center for educational and social activity they could easily influence the social life and atmosphere of small town communities. Commonly, church elders were also community leaders, and religious standards and community standards were usually inextricably mixed. Religious standards for morality were often transformed into legal standards for the community creating the current structure of laws which regulate personal behavior in sexual matters, moral conduct, and issues that pertain to the sanctity of life. However, social change in the values of the society toward individualism and personal satisfaction produced a proliferation of different value positions and standards for morality, and large proportions of the population became more eclectic in their choice of moral standards. The emergence of "situational ethics" (that the right or wrong of the event should be determined by the nature of the situation, not by absolute standards) prompted major portions of the population to disregard theologically oriented church standards of morality. Thus, support for religious institutions diminished as church members often found themselves at variance with the standards of their particular churches.

Several social problems were created over the resulting conflict of moral values—the controversy over abortion and birth control challenges long established standards over the sanctity of life, and the issue of prayer in the schools continues long after the U.S. Supreme Court ruled on the matter. Increasingly, people raise questions as to the extent that private behavior should be regulated by church doctrine. As values in the society change, conflicts between old and new values emerge producing the basis for social problems. As new issues emerge in the future, more social problems will be created.

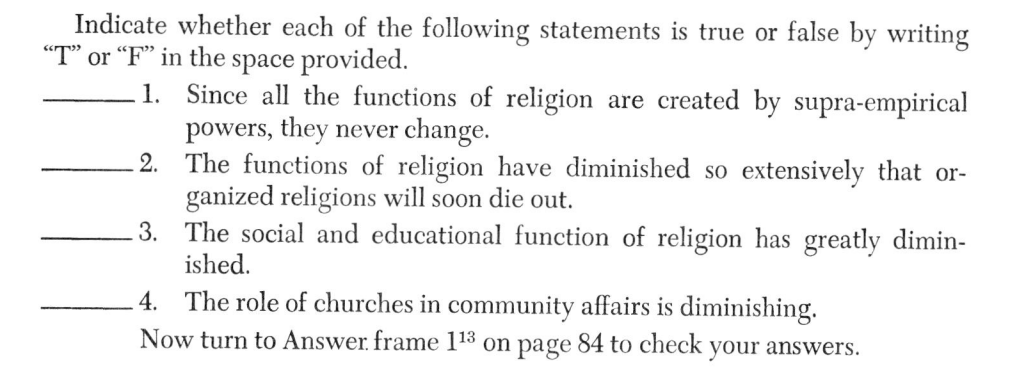

Indicate whether each of the following statements is true or false by writing "T" or "F" in the space provided.

_____ 1. Since all the functions of religion are created by supra-empirical powers, they never change.

_____ 2. The functions of religion have diminished so extensively that organized religions will soon die out.

_____ 3. The social and educational function of religion has greatly diminished.

_____ 4. The role of churches in community affairs is diminishing.

Now turn to Answer frame 1[13] on page 84 to check your answers.

Frame 2[13]

A major factor in the development of social problems of religion involves a change in fundamental religious values and the conditions to which the values pertain. The success of early Protestantism in America can be largely attributed to the extent that Lutheran and Calvinist doctrines coincided with the needs of a frontier-agrarian society.

The origin of most Protestant values can be traced to the period of the Reformation. During the Middle Ages, the Roman Catholic Church predominated in European societies and fostered a *church-centered* approach to religion. The church organization was the center of all religious worship and faith, and Papal officials determined church doctrine and practices. Ecclesiastical rule superseded individual interpretation, and church members were bound by church rules.

Although a combination of factors created the basis for the Reformation, the evolution of science was a primary factor. Scientific conclusions on the nature of man, the universe, and the story of creation frequently contradicted church doctrine, and the "church-centered" orientation required intellectuals to either accept church doctrine or abandon their religious affiliation. Since neither alternative was attractive or desired, intellectuals of the period led the search for a new doctrine that could accept the tenets and conclusions of science without conflicting with their religious commitment. To Martin Luther and his followers, one's religious commitment was a matter of individual conscience and decision; thus, a person could seek his own peace with God without adhering strictly to church doctrine. To the "protestors" against the established church, the church and the person were separate, and each individual had the obligation to seek his own communion with God. From the Protestant view, the church served as a means toward the communion, but it was not the total religious relationship in itself.

This does *not* mean that the new Lutheran and Calvinist movements were any more tolerant of dissent than the Catholics had been. Luther, who narrowly escaped the stake himself, agreed to the burning of his assistant, Michael Servetus. But the Protestant idea of individual conscience inevitably led to the eventual toleration of dissent, despite the intolerance of the early reformation leaders.

Meanwhile, the Calvinists added the values of thrift, hard work, clean living, personal responsibility, and achievement to Protestant doctrine, creating what has now become known as the "Protestant ethic."

Early Protestantism thus became *individual-centered* in that it emphasized the personal relationship with God rather than approaching God

Answer frame 1[13]

1. False. The functions of the church have been greatly changed by industrialization and modernization.
2. False. Although the functions of religion have greatly changed, the basic functions are no less important today than before industrialization.
3. True. Many of the social functions of religion have been assumed by the recreation industry, and public education has assumed much of the educational function once carried out by churches.
4. True. Although churches still play a major role in community affairs, their role is diminishing.

If you missed any of the above, reread Frame 1[13] before starting Frame 2[13] on page 83.

Frame 2[13] continued

only through the church. This philosophy coincided nicely with the needs of early American pioneers, who were largely dependent upon their own resourcefulness to survive in a primitive and unsettled land. Later, as the German philosopher Max Weber observed, the individualistic philosophy also complemented the emerging philosophy of capitalism that swept Europe and England during the period of developing industrialization. Under capitalism, each person was personally responsible for his own welfare and achievement. Protestantism was reinforced by the religious values, lifestyle, and economic philosophy of the frontier people in America, and thus it is no surprise that it became the dominant religion for frontier America.

However, the balance of church power was soon to shift on the American scene. In the late 1800s, a rapidly growing industrial economy encouraged the large-scale immigration of European workers. As the people emigrated, they also brought their cultural values and customs, and the Roman Catholic and Jewish religions (as well as a variety of others) were imported along with their adherents. The different cultural origins of America's religions created considerable variety in religious ideology and differences in value positions. The "individualistic orientation" of Protestants placed them at odds with "collectivist-oriented" Catholics, and "separatist-oriented" Jews. America became pluralistic in its religious ideologies as the different churches settled into more-or-less peaceful coexistence together.

Structural changes. The very values that facilitated the emergence of Protestantism in early America are now creating social problems in society. Prominent among the value conflicts is the battle that has emerged between the fundamentalists and modernists. The fundamentalists' doctrine grew out of early rural American society and represented rural values for a spartan life, hard work, thrift, and strict adherence to doctrinal beliefs. Fundamentalists believe in a literal interpretation of the Bible, that it represents the absolute true words of God, and that the only path to heaven is to become a "true believer." Fundamentalist denominations are still heavily rural based today, with the urban fundamentalist churches attracting mainly the first and second generation rural migrants.

Religious liberalism or "modernism" grew from two main roots. The findings of natural and social science conflicted with the literal interpretation of the scriptures, while the values of urban, industrial society conflicted with fundamentalist pietism. The modernists accepted a liberal interpretation of the Bible and believed that it represented more a philosophy of life than a set of literal directives, that proper living was more important than the faith one professed, and that religious doctrines and practices should be revised when they conflicted with the findings of science. The difference in fundamentalist and modernist ideological interpretations have become manifested in current social problems over abortion and divorce and the extent that the government should regulate the private life of its citizens (prayer in the schools, sexual behavior, and taxation of church property).

RELIGIOUS TRENDS TODAY

Churches today are facing a variety of crises. Old Protestant values are strongly challenged by emerging permissive patterns of urban lifestyles, splitting groups into those favoring older traditional lifestyles and those favoring modern patterns for living. Although the individualistic philosophy of Protestantism allows it to be open to considerable doctrinal change, many Protestants feel that modernist religions leave little of substance to adhere to. As a result, current fundamentalists reject liberal Protestantism.

Liberal churches have grieved little over the loss of fundamentalist members, as they were often viewed as "decadent discontents who were out of tune with social reality." The disagreements over the interpretations of Biblical law and modern needs split almost every modern church in recent history, and caused a fragmentation of denominations. This resulted in the formation of several hundred smaller churches and a corresponding decentralization of church organizations. The fragmentation inevitably created feelings of estrangement and uncertainty among church members and was eventually manifested in a general weakening of religious commitment among the population.

The church-centered denominations were also forced to make some overtures to change. The Roman Catholic Church modernized its rituals and relaxed age-old canons for priestly conduct; Judaism became more tolerant of nonorthodox practices of family worship and intermarriage; other orthodox churches slowly melted into oblivion as they lost their members through death and disinterest. However, in spite of vast reforms, church-centered religions have been only moderately successful in maintaining their youthful following as compared to the past.

However, the above is not to suggest that the institution of religion is dying or is rapidly decaying; trends in religiosity have shifted widely and frequently on the American scene. Between 1900 and 1930, the values for early Protestantism shifted and the social gospel became the new vogue in religion. The social gospel sought to reform society, cure its ills, and reorganize society to serve humanistic needs. During the 1940s and the 1950s, the social gospel gave way to the "age of revivalism" as churches made massive efforts to return to the people through tent meetings and city-wide religious crusades (as exemplified by Billy Graham and Oral Roberts among others). The 1960s and 1970s might be called the age of the "Jesus Cults" or "Charismatics," as many college students across the nation flocked to "high voltage" spiritual sessions and formed campus communes across the nation.

Modern cults may assume many forms, but the majority of those presently emerging tend to be neopentacostal in belief. These are attempting to return to the "true meaning of the Bible." Other cults have reverted back to semiprimitive magical-cultist faiths that may include the speaking in tongues (glossolalia) and even perhaps some vestiges of serpent worship. Still others are preoccupied with mysticism, yoga, or occultism, in a number of varieties. Today's cults, however, are somewhat unique as they appear to be attracting middle-class and educated members, making inroads into "mainline" churches, while earlier cults mainly appealed to the lower class uneducated or marginal members of society. The exact reason for this difference is somewhat unclear, but as Malinowski points out, it may be that while primitive cultists practiced magic in hopes of acquiring the material needs of life, modern cultists appear to be seeking new, greater levels of spiritual experience. Whatever may be the future for religion in America, we might presume that the "fragmentalization, decentralization into cults, and recentralization into new religions" process will continue to produce new religions and faiths on the American scene.

Indicate whether each of the following statements is true or false by writing "T" or "F" in the space provided.

_____ 1. Protestantism was created in early America.

_____ 2. Protestant religions are usually "church-centered" in organization and structure.

_____ 3. The success of Protestantism in America is largely because its values support a frontier-agrarian society.

_____ 4. Religious modernists believe in a literal interpretation of the scriptures.

Now turn to Answer frame 2[13] on page 88 to check your answers.

Frame 3[13]

RELIGION IN THE SCHOOLS

The concept of the separation of church and state in America is that the two entities should be operated independently and without interference from the other. In principle, this separation of churches from the state was meant to protect the pluralism of religious faiths, and operated on the premise that the only way the government could protect the religious freedoms for all was to favor none.

Early American schools were generally expected to intermix religious and secular education. Laws forbidding religious instruction in public schools began to be passed late in the 19th century, in response to pressure from Catholics who wished to protect their children from Protestant indoctrination. But in many areas where Catholics were not influential, religious instruction continued. Many disputes arose over the proper place of religion in the schools.

The issue was dramatized in the famous *Scopes Trial* in 1925, in which John Scopes, a science teacher, was arrested and convicted under state law for teaching Darwin's theory of evolution in a Tennessee high school. The state law derived from the fundamentalist religious view that the Bible's account of creation should not be contradicted. Although secularists lost the case, the trial did arouse public interest in the question of the extent that the church might be involved in school affairs. Strong counter movements arose to challenge the church's position.

During the 1950s, concern over the growing secularism of society led to a concerted attempt to require morning prayers and Bible study in the public schools. Several means were proposed to facilitate the practices—released time for religious instruction, the incorporation of religious instruction into school curriculums, and increased financial support for parochial schools. This demand cut across denominational lines and aroused considerable controversy and heated debate as competing groups both within and outside the church argued over the selection of "acceptable" prayer, literature, and curricular content. Further legal complications arose over the use of public funds for parochial schools, as the practice provided financial advantages to some groups at the expense of other religious groups.

Finally, the U.S. Supreme Court decided to clarify the issue and in 1962 ruled to remove all religious instruction and participation in the public schools. Formal prayer or religious instruction was not permitted; however, there were no restrictions placed upon private prayer or study. In 1973, the Court addressed the question of financial support to parochial schools and ruled that no public funds might be expended for the operation of nonpublic or parochial schools.

Considerable dissent still exists over these opposing value positions and, in view of the deep emotional and value commitment to the respective sides, it is unlikely that the interest over this issue will decrease soon. At least the problem will not be fully resolved until one group abandons its value position.

Establishing the public morality. In at least one respect, churches and society are opponents: church leaders are faced with the impossible task of "saving" members one by one while society can "corrupt" persons by the thousands. Thus, it is to the churches' advantage to help establish the moral climate of the society.

One means of accomplishing this is for churches to formalize moral standards into law, thus at least requiring moral conduct by the population. This process works well for small, simple communities with a single faith and in which the mechanisms of social control work effectively; however, industrialization and urbanization has brought forth a high degree of complexity in society with diverse lifestyles and a larger variety of behavioral patterns. Widespread value change in the society has accompanied the change in the organization of society, favoring individualism, personal choice, and freedom to do your own thing. These values are often incompatible with church doctrine, producing value conflicts between churches and society.

Church and government. Churches and government have several points of conflict, but foremost among the issues is the taxation of church property. Although churches are not required to report assets for tax purposes, it has been variously estimated that religious institutions in America may own between $80 and $100 billion in assets which could yield tax revenues of some $5 billion or more per year. Few people object to the tax-exempt status of church buildings used for religious worship, but many object to the exemption being extended to television stations, real estate developments, and panty-hose factories.

It is often a fine line that is drawn between the appropriate and judicious use of tax exemptions for religious purposes and the blatant exploitation of a tax loophole. In many cases, the exemptions are well justified—the welfare programs of the Catholic and Mormon churches are well known and their contributions to welfare clients often exceed that of governmental agencies in the area. Thus, in these instances, the exemptions are well used and result in a saving to the government. However, the use of the exemption to purchase real estate on picturesque islands for speculation may be an abuse of the privilege.

Critics of the churches often charge that the exemptions provide an unfair competitive advantage when churches enter commerce, as the tax savings provide inordinate profits and allow the accumulation of additional assets at governmental expense. In either event, the majority of the population still feels that the benefits of current tax exemptions of church property outweigh the cost, thus the practice will continue until the attitudes change.

Indicate whether each of the following statements is true or false by writing "T" or "F" in the space provided.

_____ 1. The principle of separation of church and state was originally devised to protect religious pluralism in the American society.

_____ 2. Churches often attempt to change the nature of society by formalizing moral standards into law.

_____ 3. Widespread value changes in the society favoring individualism creates church-society conflicts.

_____ 4. Only church buildings used for worship are tax exempt.

Now turn to Answer frame 3[13] on page 88 to check your answers.

Answer frame 2¹³

1. False. Protestantism was a product of the reformation, which occurred in Europe. It was later imported to America.
2. False. Protestant religions tend to be "individual-centered" in that they believe that each person must establish his own relationship with God.
3. True. The Protestant values supported an agricultural society and were particularly appropriate for settling a new land.
4. False. Modernists usually view the scriptures as a philosophy for life, rather than accepting them literally.

If you missed any of the above, restudy Frame 2¹³ before starting Frame 3¹³ on page 86.

Answer frame 3¹³

1. True. Since America had several religions, only by protecting the freedom of all religions could any single religion be protected.
2. True. Creating a law is one means by which churches can attempt to change the public morality of society, although such actions often meet considerable public resistance.
3. True. Values of individualism often conflict with the churches' desire for commitment, creating conflicts throughout the society.
4. False. Currently all church property (including publishing houses and factories) operated for the benefit of the church receives some tax advantage, creating, in the opinion of some persons, a conflict with private enterprise.

If you missed any of the above, reread Frame 3¹³ before beginning Chapter 14.

chapter 14

EDUCATION

Frame 1[14]

Virtually everyone thinks he knows what is wrong with our schools. While most people are pleased with some aspects of the educational system in America, few are completely satisfied. Some people want to return to the "quality" education of yesteryear; others seek to implement "more relevance" for a modern age; practically everyone wants something changed.

Many of the problems associated with the educational system in America can be conceptualized as value conflicts over (1) the philosophy of education (what goals the educational system should accomplish); (2) the quality and content of education (curriculum and teaching methods); and (3) the method of school administration and operation.

PHILOSOPHIES OF EDUCATION

After at least a century of arguing over the philosophy of education, we seem to be no closer to resolving the issue than we were a century ago. The difficulty in resolving the problem lies within the changing needs of American society. One philosophy may be preferred for an agrarian-frontier society, while another may be more appropriate for an industrialized-urbanized society. Thus in order to understand the nature of the value conflict, it is necessary to examine the historical development of philosophies of education in America.

Elitism. The predominant philosophy of education between 1600 and the early 1800s in America was elitist. Only a few elite members of the upper class in society were educated. Since most people were either farmers or laborers in an agrarian society, children learned most of what they needed to know by simply watching and taking part in whatever was going on.

A small number of highly educated statesmen and clergy in the United States were needed to manage the government and provide the moral direction for the society. Under the elitist philosophy, students were trained in the esoteric subjects (foreign and classical languages and literature) which was suitable for the upper class but had little relevance for the common man. Under the elitist philosophy of education, only about 5 percent of America's youth acquired any higher education, and much of this was acquired in European or English colleges. Thus, early education in America was heavily influenced by the classical nature of European universities.

Pragmatism. The growth of industrialization in the late 1800s in America drastically changed the educational needs of the population. Industry and commerce needed people who were trained in basic academic skills (reading, writing, and arithmetic) as well as a large variety of manual skills (woodworking, metalcrafting, and many others). These needs were more pragmatic in nature in that they could be used directly to earn a good living and to enjoy a good life. Thus, the pragmatists rejected the elitist philosophy of classicalism in education and promoted courses in science, mathematics, and engineering which eventually replaced the classical courses in Latin and Greek.

The need for a highly trained labor force in the new industrial society encouraged the democratic ideal that every person was to be given an opportunity for education, and this became translated into a new form of schools—that of the *common* school. In the common school, each child was to be given an equal opportunity to be educated, rich and poor alike (but not necessarily white and black alike). During the early 1900s, the government passed legislation which required schools to operate for the benefit of the common person and to build thousands of new schools across the landscape of America. In the common school, boys were trained in skills to enable them to earn a good living, and girls were trained in homemaking skills to teach them to provide a happy home for their husband and family. With the influence of John Dewey, the focus of education shifted toward educating the "whole person," which included both the mental and physical development of children. Thus, public schools added courses in driver's training, sports, and band (instead of orchestra) to produce the well-rounded person.

Eclecticism. Although the pragmatist philosophy still largely prevails in modern education, it too has been transformed to meet the needs of a sophisticated industrialized society. Modern education still emphasizes the academic basics, but has added the dimension of educating the social person to fit into and survive in a modern sophisticated and highly specialized society. The high degree of specialization required in an industrialized society requires each student to be highly trained in a few specific subjects, producing a wide variety of different needs and interests for students. Thus some educationists feel we may be changing our educational philosophy toward *eclecticism*, or allowing each student to select the educational program that best fits their own unique personal and social needs. Thus, today schools have added highly specialized courses in the sciences, as well as courses in creative dance, golf, music appreciation, foreign travel, and Dale Carnegie-type courses designed to help students find the identity that they presumably have lost in modern society.

We can see how the American educational system has evolved through a series of educational philosophies, and each philosophy grew out of a different combination of needs in society. No doubt, new educational philosophies will evolve in the future as new societal needs emerge. Value conflicts emerge as people of different social positions assume different philosophical viewpoints; upper class parents may tend to prefer an elitist approach to education in society to produce another Maria Callas or an American Nureyev; backwoods conservatives wish to stick to the basics and quit teaching communism, radicalism, and atheism; and the middle class establishment calls for a system that turns junior into a nuclear physicist and teaches little Mary to perform on her flute for the local PTA. Here again, social problems are created when people hold conflicting viewpoints as to the preferred nature of the social order.

Indicate whether each of the following statements is true or false by writing "T" or "F" in the space provided.

_____ 1. Elitism is a particularly appropriate philosophy for educating the masses.

_____ 2. The pragmatist philosophy states that schools should teach the necessary skills for a person to achieve a successful career and a satisfying life.

_____ 3. It appears that education in America is gradually shifting its philosophy toward eclecticism.

_____ 4. There is usually a high degree of agreement as to the educational philosophy preferred in the American society.

Now turn to Answer frame 1[14] on page 92 to check your answers.

Frame 2[14]

EDUCATIONAL OPPORTUNITY

One of the most controversial issues to emerge within the last two decades in the American society involves inequality of educational opportunity. We revere the ideal of equal opportunity while the reality is that children do not have an equal opportunity to succeed in life, for some groups are born to an advantageous position (in family, social class, race, wealth, or position), while other children are less fortunate.

The importance of this difference is shown in research conducted through the U.S. Office of Education, which indicated that the family background of children was highly significant in influencing the levels of academic performance, which in turn influenced the life opportunity of children. This research also suggested that the social composition of the student body had an impact upon performance levels, in that segregated schools typically were less successful than racially and economically integrated schools in influencing the level of academic performance for disadvantaged students.

In substance, the tendency for many cities across the nation to segregate minority and inner-city poor students into separate schools had the effect of permanently limiting these students in the quality of education and life opportunities they might receive. This practice violated the conscience of equalitarian-minded people in that the schools were encouraging and perpetuating the development of inequality in society, in specific violation of the Civil Rights Act of 1964.

Arguments over the preferred policy for reform were soon reduced to two conflicting value positions—the advantaged groups wished to maintain separation of students in the schools to preserve the quality and social homogeneity of local or neighborhood schools, while disadvantaged and equalitarian oriented persons sought to gain the educational and social equality that they had been denied.

Recent Supreme Court rulings have ordered all public schools to eliminate discriminatory practices and to discontinue any practices that tend to promote educational or social inequality (such as tracking, reordering school districts to segregate students, or providing unequal special services). Public school systems must also take positive steps to increase the level of opportunity for disadvantaged students (busing, providing special services, and reorganizing school districts).

Several means have been proposed to increase the level of opportunity for disadvantaged students. The most widespread but controversial practice is busing children to various schools so as to achieve a balanced mixture of children from all racial and social class groups. Advocates of busing contend that this allows each child an equal chance to maximize his or her abilities, while opponents argue that busing destroys the autonomy of neighborhood schools and forces an unnecessary inconvenience upon parents and children.

A second possible means of resolving educational inequality is to issue educational vouchers which children (and parents) can "cash-in" at the school of their choice. Students could then select a school according to its location, by the special courses it offers, or simply the school that interests them most.

A third alternative is the "deschooling" of society. Ivan Illich [Ivan Illich, *Deschooling Society* (New York: Harper & Row, Inc., 1970).], its most prominent advocate, suggests that the conventional schools are too highly structured and formal to meet the actual needs of students in today's society. He suggests that most students find school to be tedious, boring, irrelevant, and meaningless; so in light of this personal factor, education should be made more pertinent to student needs today. To accomplish this, formal schooling would be removed in society and replaced by personalized and individualized instruction in a free school setting. Students would simply drop into the school when they wanted to learn about a particular topic, and education would become a lifelong process of learning. Illich proposes that administrative bureaucracies could be dissolved through encouraging adults to volunteer their services as teachers and youth could teach each other on a personal basis.

Answer frame 1¹⁴

1. False. With elitism, only a small portion of the population are educated (the socially elite), thus the philosophy is not appropriate to educate the masses.
2. True. The pragmatist believes that schools should emphasize practical skills in education.
3. True. Eclecticism allows each student to choose his own course of specialization, which complements the trend toward individualism associated with industrialization.
4. False. The different groups in the American society have different goals and purposes, and there is usually considerable disagreement as to the preferred educational philosophy.

If you missed any of the above, restudy Frame 1¹⁴ before starting Frame 2¹⁴ on page 91.

Frame 2¹⁴ continued

Classicists disagree with Illich and argue that the free school would only promote marginal mediocrity in education and produce no certification of ability. Further, critics question if the free school could be organized on a national basis to educate the masses of the population. As yet, the free school has inspired much interest, but little action, on the national scene.

Indicate whether each of the following statements is true or false by writing "T" or "F" in the space provided.

_____ 1. Family background has little effect upon the educational performance of children.

_____ 2. Many of the current operating practices of public schools have the unintended effect of creating social inequality among students.

_____ 3. Experts agree that "deschooling society" is an economical and efficient means to educate all of America's youth.

Now turn to Answer frame 2¹⁴ on page 94 to check your answers.

Frame 3¹⁴

ADMINISTRATION AND OPERATION OF THE SCHOOLS

Financing. Financing the public schools has always been a bone of contention in American society. The first schools were almost entirely dependent upon local financing by parents who had children enrolled in the schools. This practice worked fairly well in small, one-room schoolhouses, where itinerant teachers (the same as doctors and ministers) could be paid partially with farm produce and services. However, with the advent of urbanization and the need for massive large-scale school systems, it became necessary to establish schools by the thousands and hire droves of teachers and administrators. The primitive barter system of financing was highly inappropriate for industrialized-urbanized society.

As communities across America grew and the one-room schoolhouse became transformed into large multigraded systems, it soon became necessary to develop improved means of financing the schools. Since parents and landholders were expected to benefit most from the growth of the schools, a property tax system was developed. Local support of the schools was viewed as appropriate and desirable, in that the parents who received the benefits helped finance the system, and it also gave the local community a means of control over school policy and administration. Thus, each community preserved its autonomy and could operate the schools as the people deemed appropriate.

However, of late, the property tax as a means of school financing has come under increasing criticism; school expenditures across the nation have increased at more than three times the rate of growth in revenue or the taxable property base of communities. Thus, the vast majority of communities are finding themselves in a financial bind and are forced to increase levies at inordinate rates to remain solvent in light of the increasing cost of maintaining both school and governmental services. Since school appropriations are the only tax levies that are voted upon by the public, the citizenry have recently begun to vote down school appropriations as a means of protest against increasing federal and state taxes. Through little fault of their own, schools suffer as they become the instruments of protest against the tax policies of federal and state governments.

The impending financial crisis creates several dilemmas for both the schools and the communities they serve. The increasing cost of providing school services must be met in some fashion and more specialized services are required each year, but the increased property taxes inhibit economic development and expansion in the communities which could provide the additional revenue needed for a healthy rate of economic growth. Financing local schools through local property taxation also creates great inequalities between "rich" and "poor" school districts. The only alternative available to many schools is to turn to state and federal financing, but this practice also limits the autonomy of the local schools and removes administrative power and authority to "outside" agencies. Simply put, the dilemma is that many local communities cannot continue to bear the tax burden for local support of the schools, but they also do not wish to relinquish their autonomy and local control to state and federal agencies. Social problems are created as people attempt to maintain the traditional values for local autonomy and control in the schools in the face of mounting organizational and economic pressures for the removal of local control.

Administration. One emerging problem of education in modern society is the extent of centralization or decentralization of school administration. It has been a Jeffersonian ideal that the people should retain local control and administration over their school, and they have largely done so through the incorporation of local school boards who establish policy for the operation of the school. This process worked fairly well for the little one-room country school where the teacher variously served as janitor, cook, nurse, and principal, as well as attending to the educational and aesthetic needs of her charges.

With the development of urbanization, however, school administrations grew as it became necessary to establish a plethora of school districts across the nation. The problem of school administration became particularly acute in metropolitan areas, as major cities might have anywhere from several hundred to a few thousand schools to administrate (metropolitan New York City has some 3,000 elementary and secondary schools).

The essence of the problem is that centralization is necessary to provide the coordination of school activities and the economies that can be gained through purchasing and providing specialized services. However, with centralization, there is an inevitable loss of local community control.

Thus, the stage is set for continuing conflict. School administrators are often forced to increase the degree of centralization in order to improve efficiency and economy of operation, while parents desire decentralization in order to retain local control over school policy and operation. Since the purposes of each group are mutually incompatible, it is unlikely that either group will ever be fully pleased, and inevitably some compromise must be made. The value conflicts, however, will likely continue and probably increase as we move toward a more urbanized and organized society.

Answer frame 2¹⁴

1. False. Family background often determines the quality of education a child will receive, the motivation for learning, and attitudes toward the value of education for the future.
2. True. Such practices as "tracking," although intended to improve the quality of education, often function to limit the opportunity that minority students might receive.
3. False. There is considerable disagreement among experts whether free schools would be effective on a large scale, or that it would be an effective substitute for the public school system.

If you missed any of the above, reread Frame 2¹⁴ before starting Frame 3¹⁴ on page 92.

Frame 3¹⁴ continued

Indicate whether each of the following statements is true or false by writing "T" or "F" in the space provided.

_____ 1. The growth of the taxable property base of most communities has kept pace with the increase in school expenditures.

_____ 2. School bond issues are one of the tax measures on which the public are allowed to vote.

_____ 3. The property tax basis for financing public schools often creates inequities in financing different school districts.

_____ 4. The extent of community control over separate school districts will likely increase in the future.

Now turn to Answer frame 3¹⁴ on page 96 to check your answers.

chapter 15

POPULATION

Frame 1[15]

Population as a social problem is both one of the oldest and also one of the newest social problems on the American scene. Ever since 1798, when Malthus brought forth his dire predictions about the future course of events for mankind, the subject has been widely discussed, but few people have taken the problem seriously. As recently as 1971, a Gallup poll showed that only 41 percent of Americans considered population as a major problem requiring immediate action.

DEMOGRAPHIC FACTORS

Three major factors of the world's population problem are (1) size and rate of growth, (2) age and sex composition, and (3) distribution.

It took approximately two and a half million years for the world population to reach the first billion. This was achieved about 1850. Within the next 100 years (by 1950) the total world population was estimated at two and a half billion, an increase of one half billion people in just 20 years. Estimates for world population for the year 2000 (only some 25 years away) range between 5 billion and 7 billion people, or about double the present population.

The world crisis is accentuated by the relatively preindustrialized state of the world's most populated nations. Recent world average birth and death rates have been high, particularly in undeveloped nations. With the innovation of improved sanitation and health care (brought by emerging industrialization and improved technology) the death rate per 1,000 people has been falling rapidly while the birth rate remains high. This differential produces a rapid increase in world population growth, and stability can be achieved only by reducing the birth rate to correspond with the lowered death rate.

Demographers use a variety of statistical classifications to describe the population problem. The crude birthrate is the number of births each year per 1,000 people, and the death rate is interpreted in the same fashion; the ratio of the two rates gives an indication of the rate of growth of the total population.

The fertility rate consists of the number of births per 1,000 *women*. This gives an indication of the number of fertile women who could procreate in the future. *Fertility* refers to the actual number of children born to mothers while *fecundity* refers to the number of children women are biologically capable of producing (which is about one per year between the ages of 14 to 45, if the woman does not die). Obviously very few women achieve their maximum procreative potential, and those who do earn notice in Ripley's "Believe It or Not," or *Guiness Book of World Records*.

Currently, the world population is increasing some two percent per year, while in the United States, the total population is increasing at about 1.2 percent, with the rate of growth declining somewhat in recent years.

Composition. The sex ratio consists of the ratio of men to women; a ratio of 95 would mean 95 men to 100 women. In spite of the social desirability of a balanced ratio (100), several factors tend to disturb the balance; more male babies are born than female, but their mortality

Answer frame 3[14]

1. False. Recently, school expenditures have increased two to three times the rate of increase in the taxable property base, creating a financial bind in many school districts.
2. True. Since school bond issues are one of the very few tax measures the public is allowed to vote on, they often become the only means by which the public can protest increases in taxes.
3. True. Districts with a large industrial base often have much more school revenues than do marginal farming areas.
4. False. As school districts grow larger, the extent of community control tends to decrease. There is a definite trend toward a greater degree of centralization in most school districts.

If you missed any of the above, restudy Frame 3[14] before beginning Chapter 15 on page 95.

Frame 1[15] continued

is higher at birth and later in life. The societal implications of the sex composition of a population is portrayed in the population pyramids of countries involved in major wars. Germany, ravaged by two world wars, lost more than half of her young male population. This naturally resulted in a shortage of manpower to rebuild the economy, limited the future birthrate as widows were left without husbands, and produced a predominantly female population. This can result in rather extreme changes in public policy and standards of morality (Stalin suggested in the Soviet Union after World War II that illegitimate conception was a woman's duty in order to replenish the armies for the state).

The age composition of the population affects such factors as the future birthrate, the availability of manpower for economic growth, and the composition of the consumer products that the public will need. A relatively young population will desire more and better housing for expanding families, better schools, and more durable children's clothing. An aging population will need retirement centers, more nursing homes, and more sedate forms of recreation.

Undeveloped countries typically have a smooth pyramidal age structure, as can be seen in Figure 1. In 1870, the United States' population pyramid was evenly pointed, with nearly 75 percent of the population under 60 years of age. The pyramid for 1970 shows a definite increase in the older population and a smaller pro-

FIGURE 1
Distribution of the population, United States, by age and sex: 1870 to 1969

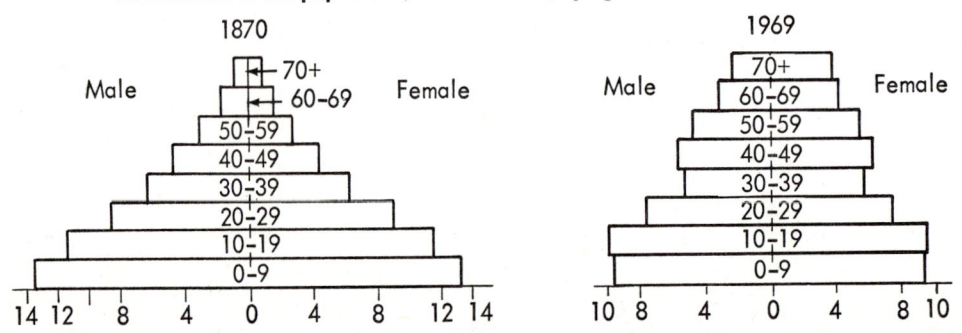

Percent of total population

Source: *Current Population Reports,* U.S. Department of Commerce Bureau of the Census, Series P-25, No. 441, March 19, 1970.

portion of children in the population. Thus it is readily apparent from these diagrams that the general population of the United States is becoming more mature, and that the rate of growth of the population may decline, because fewer people are in the childbearing years. As a result, more of the national income will be claimed for retirement pensions and services, while proportionately fewer working adults are paying the freight. This portends an interesting shift in social tensions. The future "conflict of generations" may be not between the youth and the adult generations, but between the working adults and the retired adults. The "accent on youth" may fade as an aging population shifts to adult-oriented tastes and services.

Distribution. People tend to migrate toward urban areas because of the employment opportunities, the excitement of city life, and the other attractions that cities provide. Several factors have influenced the migration trends in the United States. World Wars I and II encouraged a heavy migration of blacks from the tenant farms of the South to the industrial centers of the North. The mechanization of the coal mines in Appalachia caused a heavy migration of poverty stricken and unemployed coal miners to the steel plants of Chicago, Detroit, and Gary, Indiana. For the past few decades there has been a steady migration of skilled labor and professionals to the western regions of the nation to seek the employment opportunities of a new economic frontier.

Shifts in population may affect the health and stability of communities. The westward movement has weakened the economic base of once prosperous and thriving metropolitan areas—shifts in manufacturing centers have crippled the shipping industry of New York City, Chicago has lost its stockyards, and automobile production is being decentralized out of Michigan. New financial centers are attracting both money and talent westward, leaving decaying urban centers with declining tax bases to support poor and unemployed populations.

Many boom towns that grew around a new industry may find that they cannot build community services fast enough to meet the needs of a rapidly growing population, and often incur large excesses of long-term debts to finance the expansion of schools, churches, hospitals, and water and sewage systems. More than a few towns have found that their boom has dissipated, leaving a bankrupt city hall.

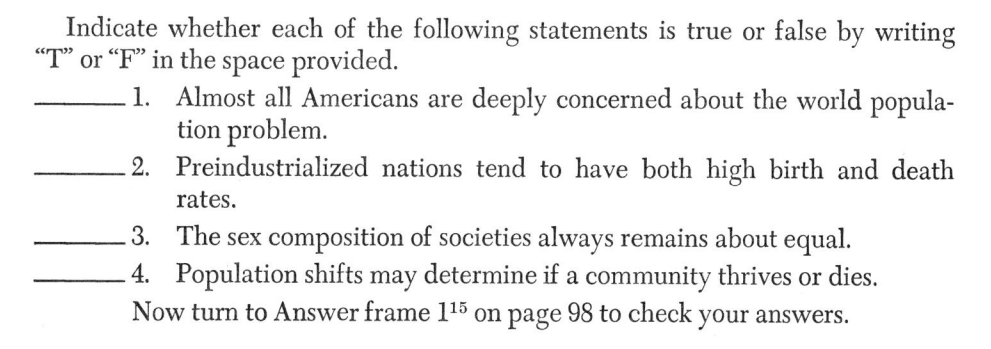

Indicate whether each of the following statements is true or false by writing "T" or "F" in the space provided.

_____ 1. Almost all Americans are deeply concerned about the world population problem.

_____ 2. Preindustrialized nations tend to have both high birth and death rates.

_____ 3. The sex composition of societies always remains about equal.

_____ 4. Population shifts may determine if a community thrives or dies.

Now turn to Answer frame 1[15] on page 98 to check your answers.

Frame 2[15]

POPULATION CONTROL THEORIES

The earliest and most famous theorist on population control was Sir Thomas Malthus, a 17th century English clergyman. Malthus observed that the human species reproduced at a geometric rate (1, 2, 4, 8, 16, 32, and so on), while the production of food and means for subsistence increased at an arithmetic rate (1, 2, 3, 4, and so on). In preindustrial societies, food production can be increased only by increasing the acreage planted, of which there was a limited amount in early England and Europe.

Malthus noted that there were natural *positive checks* upon population growth—deaths due to occupational dangers, disease, war, pestilence,

Answer frame 1[15]

1. False. In a recent Gallup poll, only about 41 percent of the population expressed any great concern about the world population problem.
2. True. Most preindustrialized nations have both high birth and death rates, creating a relative balanced population growth. This differential does not usually create a population problem unless one rate changes in comparison to the other.
3. False. The sex composition of societies may be influenced by wars, disease, and age composition of the population as women live longer than men.
4. True. Growing communities often attract young professional and working men, while declining communities are often left with aging and less prosperous families.

If you missed any of the above, reread Frame 1[15] before starting Frame 2[15] on page 97.

Frame 2[15] continued

and famine—and these forces keep populations from exceeding their means of subsistence, though often in a painful and brutal manner. Thus, he proposed the implementation of additional *preventive checks* for population control; that persons practice restraint in their sexual relations by delaying marriage until the mid-thirties, thereby reducing family size and keeping a population within its means of subsistence.

Although Malthus' intentions were humane, people had no enthusiasm for the self-restraint he proposed, and Malthus' theory had little impact upon the world population at the time. As a result, Malthus has often been accused of being wrong in his fateful predictions and for well over a century he was largely ignored. However, a view of present world conditions suggests that he may only have been premature in his judgments. The population problem of the 18th and 19th centuries was eased by spectacular advances in agricultural technology, transportation, food preservation, and by cultivation of vast new land areas in North and South America.

However, one may ask today whether technology and industrialization have solved the inevitable crisis, or merely delayed it. Technological advances have brought new means for reducing famine and disease, but this has resulted in a longer life expectancy for more people, increasing the total world population. At present, the world population is increasing at a rate of some 70 million people each year, or in effect, producing a new population the size of the United States each three years.

The impact of industrialization and technology.
Whether increases in population are beneficial or harmful is dependent upon the level of industrialization and the state of technology in a society. Technology provides innovations to preserve life and to allow a greater number of people to live in comfort and health. Industrialization provides the facilities to mass produce and preserve the means for subsistence, and as compared to the one-man-horse farm of Malthus' period, with an ever increasing efficiency. The agricultural revolution that began in the early 1800s allowed the world to increase its population size severalfold, and the improved processing of resources has provided a world standard of living that was never even envisioned in the 1700s.

However, not all nations have benefited equally from the technological revolution, producing acute crises in some nations. A growing industrial economy requires a balance of resources which can be developed—energy, land, water, forests, minerals, and a strong skilled labor force. These resources, combined with the technology, produce wealth which can be used to further expand the means of production. Nations lacking in some of these resources may be irreparably hindered in their development. The hungry masses of the Middle East, Asia, and South America consume resources faster than the resources can be produced. This prevents any stabilization of growth or accumulation of wealth. Thus the conditions of poverty and hunger perpetuate themselves in these nations.

Demographic transition. The theory of demographic transition suggests an evolutionary development of population control, that the forces of industrialization will eventually function to maintain stability in population size. As described above, the development of industrialization and technology is a major determinant of the number of people the land will support and the quality of life in a nation. However, these forces have other effects upon the *values* of the people, which in turn affect the birth rate and population stability.

The process of demographic transition consists of a series of three stages of development: (1) the first, the preindustrial (primitive or agricultural) stage, is characterized by high birth and death rates, and with little total population growth in the society; (2) the second stage consists of a period of developing industrialization, which starts with a high death rate, but as health and sanitary conditions improve, the death rate is reduced while the birthrate still remains high; (3) finally, modern industrialization produces a change in values favoring smaller families, and reducing the birthrate. Eventually both birth and death rates become stabilized at a lower level, reinstating a relative stability in the rate of population growth (see Figure 2).

There appears to be considerable empirical support for the demographic transition theory, but as yet there has not been sufficient time for many nations to enter stage III and to prove the validity of the theory. At present, most of the world is in stage II of population growth, resulting in a rapid rate of growth for developing nations. The recent reductions in the birthrate of some European nations and the United States suggest that these nations may be entering stage III. In either event, the total world population will for some time continue to grow at a much higher rate than before the development of industrialization in the world.

The eugenics movement. In recent years, a very controversial movement began to advocate population control through "selective breeding" and limiting family size. The origin of the movement grew out of the belief that, historically, the poor were producing a disproportionate number of children, producing an inferior, socially undesirable population. In view of the inevitable overpopulation crisis, eugenicists advocated the selection of persons with "superior genetic qualities" to procreate (with a heavy bias toward the upper classes). Thus they thought to improve the quality of life for those who might survive the population crisis. Poor genetic or phenotypic specimens (people with low IQs, retarded, or deformed persons) would be sterilized in order to make room for the healthy. The age-old law of nature of "the survival of the fittest" would be manifested.

Eugenicists noted that the current structure of

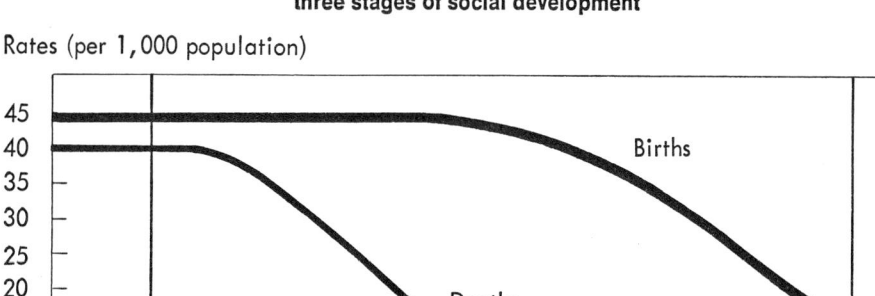

FIGURE 2
Demographic transition: Changes in birth and death rates in three stages of social development

society still supports large families through tax deductions for children and the public financing of schools, and they proposed to eliminate these "incentives" and limit procreation only to those who could financially "afford" children.

Much of the early impetus of the eugenic movement was weakened by a failure to gain widespread value support for the cause. The difficulty of agreeing upon the identification of the "genetically preferred" persons is all but insurmountable, and few persons who are marginal physical specimens are willing to forfeit their rights to the pleasures of parenthood. Sterilization is a sensitive question that involves complex religious, social, and moral questions so diverse that any widespread agreement is very unlikely. For example, recent instances of "voluntary" sterilization of mentally retarded welfare clients have aroused widespread concern.

The movement was also weakened by the spreading awareness that much of the post–World War II "baby boom" was initiated by middle or upper class families. Concern over the problem was also moderated by the realization that the public educational system and an expanding industrial economy allows for upward mobility of the poorer segment of the population. At present, the eugenics movement does not appear to be gaining in public or professional support.

Indicate whether each of the following statements is true or false by writing "T" or "F" in the space provided.

_____ 1. Malthus believed that the "positive checks" upon population would control population growth.

_____ 2. Malthus failed to anticipate the effects of industrialization and technology in his theory.

_____ 3. The theory of demographic transition suggests that industrialization will eventually cause a change in values toward favoring smaller families.

_____ 4. The eugenics movement has found strong support among scientists and professional people.

Now turn to Answer frame 2[15] on page 102 to check your answers.

Frame 3[15]

THE AMERICAN PROBLEM

Scientists have recognized the objective conditions and consequences of overpopulation for decades, but people on the American scene did not accept the subjective reality of the problem so readily. This failure was mainly due to the strength of early values for procreation in our nation, which supported large families and a high birthrate; during the 1700s, only about two out of three children would be expected to survive to adulthood. Thus it was necessary in that time to produce many children so that a few might survive.

Societal needs also reinforced the family values for procreation. There was a tremendous shortage of manpower to feed a new growing industrial economy, to stoke its blast furnaces, and to weave its cloth. The social and economic advantages of procreation were also reinforced by a Biblical mandate to populate and replenish the earth. Immigration was encouraged; America was thought to be the "land of plenty" for all. All of these factors supported the values approving large families and viewing rapid population growth as evidence of national vigor and progress.

However, old values die slowly and usually some event must force their change. The increasing awareness of today's energy crisis is causing many to realize that more people simply means an even greater amount of energy and resources will be consumed—and perhaps with questionable improvement in the health of our nation and its quality of life. The shortage of natural fuels is forcing people to realize that the supply of energy is not unlimited, and unless there is a phenomenal technological breakthrough, the supply of accessible, clean, natural fuels may be depleted within our generation. Food supplies, of which we have had a surplus for several decades, are now shortened, as well as the supply of minerals and other valuable resources.

However, in some ways, America's population problem is not exactly the worst of situations. The greatest severity of the crisis is yet to come and we are conveniently removed from the abject poverty of the teeming, starving masses found in other nations. America's biggest question at present is whether we can maintain the high standard of living and the level of industrial production to which we have become accustomed without destroying the environment in the process. In a broader reference, the question is whether we can survive as a strong, wealthy nation in an overpopulated world. Current disputes involve a lack of resources—the focus of future wars may be over living space.

America's population problems stem from three particular social conditions; first, sanitary engineering and preventative medicine have lowered the death rate without immediately reducing the birthrate. A falling death rate, without a commensurate decline in the birthrate, gives an explosive increase in the rate of population growth.

Second, more Americans are marrying at a younger age today and more young couples are producing families earlier in their lives than their European counterparts. Although it is clear that American values are changing toward favoring quality rather than quantity in family size, a greater total number of married women are producing children than a century ago resulting in a net increase in population growth.

Third, American belief in individual rights and the satisfaction of parenthood encourage procreation to maintain the family lineage. Although family planning has become an institutionalized and widespread practice in America, families are not abandoning the desire to have children—only to have them when they are desired or are more convenient. Family planning and the use of contraceptives may moderate the population problem somewhat, but in practice this will not eliminate the problem.

Medical innovations and social change. It is popularly presumed that medical innovations and social change will alleviate the population problem. But theoretical and empirical analysis suggest that though the use of contraceptives and abortion will have an impact, it will not necessarily be the one expected. The recent technological development and widespread acceptance of "the pill" and the IUD is frequently credited with *causing* the recent decline in the birthrate and average family size. Although contraceptive use has had an impact upon population growth, there is little evidence to suggest that the availability of contraceptives is the sole cause of the change. Ira Reiss, using census data, shows that the birthrate and average family size started to decline almost a decade before the current popular contraceptives were available for use, suggesting that a change in social values toward smaller families is more important in reducing birthrates than the availability of medical means. [Reiss, *Family System*, p. 291.] Reiss cites the restraining factors of industrialization, urbanization, and a general increase in the educational level and affluence of the population as being more important factors in determining the birthrate than the availability of medical means of contraception.

Abortion. Many people expect that the legalization of abortion will eliminate the unwanted births and solve the population problem. Although there is no question that the rate of abortion *could* influence the birthrate, most couples still desire to have children, and continue to procreate. It is not clear yet whether the legalization of abortion has increased the total number of abortions performed, or has merely replaced illegal abortions with legal abortions.

Women's liberation. Whatever the actual prospects for today's woman, many people predict that she will abrogate her motherhood role and create a sterile childless population. A more critical evaluation would suggest that these predictions are more melodramatic than realistic. Numerous research analyses of college females (the most liberal segment of the female popu-

Answer frame 2[15]

1. False. Although the positive checks would function to somewhat limit population growth, Malthus believed that they would be insufficient to control population growth.
2. True. The enormous productivity achieved by industrialization and technology in the 19th century allowed world agriculture to feed a much increased population.
3. True. The theory of demographic transition suggests that first the death rate will fall, producing a rapid increase in population growth, but then a value change favoring smaller families will occur to reduce the birthrate.
4. False. Although some scientists and professional people may find the eugenics movement ideologically attractive, few find the movement practical.

If you missed any of the above, reread Frame 2[15] before starting Frame 3[15] on page 100.

Frame 3[15] continued

lation) repeatedly indicate that although today's woman desires social, political, and economic equality of opportunity, she has not abandoned the ageless maternal desire for procreation. In fact, research shows that a greater proportion of women today expect to marry and have a family than in the past. Thus, it is not that the modern-minded woman does not desire to have children, but rather that *she* will decide when and how many. Although the women's liberation movement may have had an impact in encouraging childspacing and reducing the average family size, it is not expected to solve the problem of population pressure.

Indicate whether each of the following statements is true or false by writing "T" or "F" in the space provided.

_____ 1. In the past, a high rate of population growth has been viewed as an indication of national vigor and strength.

_____ 2. America's population problem largely stems from a high reduction of the death rate, without a corresponding reduction in the birthrate.

_____ 3. The innovation of the birth control pill has *caused* the reduction in the birthrate in America.

_____ 4. The legalization of abortion in America is expected to cause a sharp reduction in the birthrate.

Now turn to Answer frame 3[15] on page 104 to check your answers.

chapter 16

URBAN AND RURAL COMMUNITIES

Frame 1[16]

One consistent theme that flows through all study of social problems is the impact of urbanism upon modern social problems. Urbanization consists of the massing of large heterogeneous populations into a compact spatial area. It also includes the development of diverse lifestyles and "progressive" values; it is technologically oriented; and it is the spearhead of social change. In a variety of ways urbanism is the antithesis of rural life, and many urban problems are created as a rural heritage is metamorphized into urban lifestyles and patterns of social relations. In order to understand the origin of modern urban conditions, it is necessary to examine the conditions of early rural America, and the rural-to-urban transition.

EARLY COMMUNITIES IN AMERICA

Many of the current problems of modern cities can be traced to the structure and organization of early communities in America. In a variety of ways, each community was a society in miniature, complete with all the elements of social organization, social structure, and social processes that might be found in the larger society. Early settlements in America were usually formed to accommodate the transportation systems of the period and might be located at the confluence of two rivers where freight would be reloaded for shipping, at natural harbors which provided a safe haven for ships, or at stage stops where passengers might rest or transfer routes.

In the midwestern agricultural states, towns were established according to the distance a horse and wagon could travel, transact business and return comfortably in the time between morning and evening chores (about 10 to 15 miles), or the distance a steam locomotive could travel before it needed more coal or water (30 to 40 miles). Typically the towns were small (rarely more than a few hundred people), and self-sufficient in that they provided all the services that the residents might need in a simple rural society. The size of counties within a state was generally determined by the maximum distance that one could ride a horse without undue hardship (about 20 to 30 miles square), with the county seat usually situated approximately in the middle of the county.

Thus, the geographical location of many of today's modern cities was determined in large part by factors convenient to an agrarian age rather than an industrial age. This is why few modern cities are designed to accommodate modern mass transportation systems or to serve the convenience of people in an industrialized society. As a result, many modern cities have to expand in a haphazard fashion that often makes little use of natural resources or terrain (stores and businesses are often sprawled along several miles of highway rather than being closely grouped for easy shopping).

As America became more industrialized, many small communities were drastically changed. Isolated small rural communities slowly began

Answer frame 3[15]

1. True. A high rate of population growth was desirable in the past in America, because we needed the manpower to work in the factories and farm the land.
2. True. Innovations in medicine caused a sharp reduction in the death rate, but extensive value change (a much slower process) had to occur before there was any significant reduction in the birthrate.
3. False. Although the pill is used to control pregnancy, the birthrate in America started to decline several years before the pill was available for use.
4. False. Although abortion could be used to reduce the birthrate, there is no evidence as yet that the rate of legal abortions has exceeded the earlier rate of illegal abortions.

If you missed any of the above, reread Frame 3[15] before working Examination 5 on page 141. Then begin Chapter 16 on page 103.

Frame 1[16] continued

to age and decline, as larger cities sapped the financial wealth of small communities close to the cities. Large, glamorous supermarkets and shopping centers were built to lure the purchasing power of the rural folk away from the neighborhood "mom and pop" grocery stores. Cities began to centralize the wealth, power, and laborers of the rural regions, while many small town businesses aged and painfully died, burned in "accidental" fires, or simply abandoned. Thus, the American landscape is dotted with small communities that have passed their prime as centers of commerce, and now have assumed the function of providing a haven for retired persons or suburbanites who seek to escape the pressures of urban life.

The urban migration. Although urban migration may have been encouraged by the attractions of city life, its basic cause was changing technology. Without a revolution in industrial technology, there would have been no great expansion of the nonfarm labor market to employ the youth who left the farm. Without a revolution in agricultural technology, which rapidly decreased the number of farm workers required to produce food, there would have been no surplus of farm youth to fill the demand for industrial workers. The market surplus of food (beyond the farm family's own food needs) produced per farm family has grown by over 100 times (more than 10 thousand percent) since 1790. Consequently, the farm population has shriveled as the number of farms declined and the average size of farms increased.

Changing lifestyles. The process of industrialization sounded the death knell for thousands of small communities across America as the youth fled the farm for the city. Eighteenth century America was a rural society. Nine out of ten workers were farmers, while most of the rest—ministers, blacksmiths, storekeepers—were a part of a rural lifestyle. Today, 1 out of 33 workers is a farm worker, and three fourths of the population is classed as "urban," and many of those classified as "rural" are suburban commuters. Early Oriental societies had cities, but for the first time in the world's history, we now have *urban societies*.

In an urban society, the urban lifestyle becomes *the* lifestyle of the society. The rural lifestyles were based upon what sociologists call a *gemeinschaft* community (small communities dominated by intimate personal associations based upon primary relationships of trust and simplicity of life). The personal nature of the rural relationships created strong bonds of social control over the population, as everyone knew just about everything about everyone else in the community. Any deviations from the norm were quickly passed through the gossip mills for the gratification (and embarrassment) of all.

Urban life, however, is impersonal and formal in nature. The heterogeneous masses of people lead to a greater diversity of behavior, creating what is known as the *gesellschaft* community. As gemeinschaft communities are based upon primary group relationships, gesellschaft communities are dominated by secondary group relationships. Urban life is characterized by highly formal and specialized relations, impersonal and contractual in nature, with a high degree of anonymity for individuals. Business relations are highly standardized—everyone is treated equally, like a product being serviced on a production line. People come and go without meeting or knowing each other, because tomorrow might bring a new job, a new home, or a new family next door. The high degree of anonymity and lack of permanence tends to repress the mechanisms of social control over the population and allows a greater degree of deviation in behavior. This tendency, amplified throughout the population of metropolitan areas, tends to enhance the degree of social disorganization that is found in urban society today.

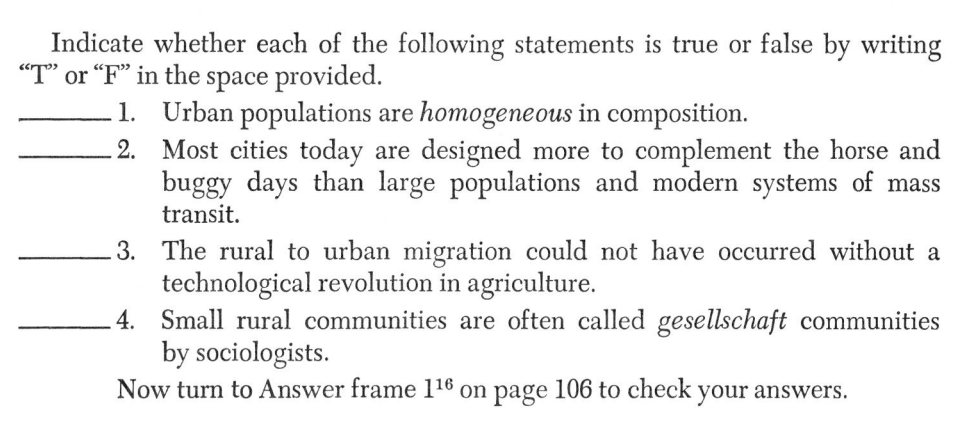

Indicate whether each of the following statements is true or false by writing "T" or "F" in the space provided.

_____ 1. Urban populations are *homogeneous* in composition.
_____ 2. Most cities today are designed more to complement the horse and buggy days than large populations and modern systems of mass transit.
_____ 3. The rural to urban migration could not have occurred without a technological revolution in agriculture.
_____ 4. Small rural communities are often called *gesellschaft* communities by sociologists.

Now turn to Answer frame 1[16] on page 106 to check your answers.

Frame 2[16]

COMMUNITY ORGANIZATION AND JURISDICTION

In early rural America, cities were usually separated by miles of farmland, prairies, and forests. Townships and even many counties were so sparsely settled and so well separated that conflicts or disputes were infrequent. With the advent of urbanization and improved systems of transportation, however, metropolitan areas began to extend their boundaries to engulf entire townships, and in a few cases, whole counties (metropolitan Chicago and New York extend far beyond the boundaries of their counties). The development of "strip cities" (small incorporated municipalities that spring up along transportation arteries between metropolitan areas) and bedroom communities (suburban areas where people live who travel to the city to work) created a maze of jurisdictional boundaries that complicates the administration of city governments and utilities (water and sewer systems, police and fire protection, and so on).

In these situations, city planning is often hopelessly stalled in jurisdictional disputes which may cause children living on different sides of the street to be bused to schools on opposite sides of town, or which prevent city firemen from crossing the city boundary to save a burning home. Overlapping jurisdictional boundaries can and often do lead to the duplication of administrative and public services, creating inefficiencies of operation and the unnecessary expense of maintaining duplicate facilities. Many cities today find themselves surrounded by a ring of incorporated communities that feed off the resources of the larger city. Suburbanites earn their money in the central city and use its facilities, but return little in tax revenue. Suburban communities were often formed by residents seeking to escape the congestion and high taxes of the larger city, but who also wish to be close to the facilities that the large city offers. Any attempts by the central city to increase the tax base by expanding their boundaries are usually met with vigorous opposition by suburban residents who wish to retain the administrative autonomy, low taxes, and good (but often segre-

Answer frame 1[16]

1. False. Urban populations tend to be heterogeneous (composed of many diverse personality types), while rural populations are homogeneous (composed of people who are quite similar in personality type and lifestyle).
2. True. The majority of American cities were designed several decades ago, with little forethought for systems of mass transit or for the expansion of population.
3. True. Farming in early America required considerable labor, and the technological revolution in agriculture freed the laborers to work in industry.
4. False. Sociologists usually classify small rural communities as *gemeinschaft* communities because people tend to be informal and personal in their relationships.

If you missed any of the above, reread Frame 1[16] before starting Frame 2[16] on page 105.

Frame 2[16] continued

gated) schools that the small community provides. The more prosperous residents move to the suburbs, while the central city tends to fill up with the poor who produce less tax income but consume more services. As a result, central cities often languish under the burden of high and increasing expenses, while their taxable base of property erodes away; aging and once proud townhouses are ruthlessly chopped into multi-family slum dwellings, factories move to the suburbs to escape urban congestion and taxes, and major department stores build suburban shopping centers to be closer to the customers, while abandoning "downtown" stores to discount houses and pawn shops.

Several attempts have and are being made to meet these organizational and jurisdictional problems. Federal and state revenue sharing is an attempt to delay the economic crises many major cities are experiencing. At best, however, revenue sharing cannot be expected to resolve the problem, but only to forestall the problem until cities can develop metropolitan or regional planning and zoning programs. This process, too, is hindered by the large variety of vested interests each community serves, and any advancement in planning and zoning will not be accomplished without considerable effort and cooperation from all.

Increasingly, modern cities are being forced to develop city-wide, county, or even regional planning and zoning for the future. Such planning must take into account the interrelationships among cities within a region to maximize the use of natural resources (energy, power, and water), the development of systems of transportation and shipping (highways, railroads, and airports), and the placement of industry so as to maximize the productivity and the convenience of the population. Some regional planners have proposed a grid system of organization whereby small, self-sufficient communities of 10,000 to 30,000 people will be located every five to ten miles apart. With this design, each community would be self-contained with its own industry, schools, and utilities. Another design consists of a doughnut-type ring of residential communities encircling a centralized industrial area. In both cases the purpose is to design a convenient and ecologically attractive community that provides the most appropriate use of natural resources and terrain for the economic and social benefit of all.

Indicate whether each of the following statements is true or false by writing "T" or "F" in the space provided.

_____ 1. Overlapping jurisdictional boundaries often complicate the problems of city administration.

_____ 2. Suburban communities usually have a greater degree of autonomy in city administration than do metropolitan cities.

_____ 3. Most major problems of metropolitan communities today can be resolved through state and federal revenue sharing.

Now turn to Answer frame 2[16] on page 108 to check your answers.

Frame 3[16]

CONTROL AND DEVIATION

One can hardly pick up a newspaper today without noting the increasing problems of maintaining social control in urban areas. Stores and businesses are fighting an overwhelming tide of shoplifting; apartment dwellers are alarmed by the increasing rash of break-ins and petty thievery; city streets are unsafe; and simple arrests in ghetto areas often explode into street riots. As a result of the increased amount of crime, police budgets must be increased to add more patrolmen to fight crime; teachers fear for their safety as they try to teach in urban ghettos; and firemen find their hoses slashed when they try to fight fires in slum areas. It is no wonder that city fathers often feel helpless as they try to cope with the multitude of problems that confront the modern metropolitan areas.

Two theories about maintaining social control in urban areas are (1) the theories of *anonymity and observability;* and (2) the formation of *primary relationships* in urban life.

The theory of observability and anonymity. In rural areas, there is considerably less deviation in behavior, as (due to the small size of the community) any deviation in behavior is easily observed by the neighbors. Observability (the extent to which one is likely to be observed in his behavior) is high in rural areas and any anonymous intruder (outsider) is quickly noted. With observability comes social control, because if a person is assured that his deviant behavior will be observed and reported to others, he is less likely to behave in a deviant fashion. This principle is exemplified by the research findings that crime in high rise apartments is far more prevalent than in smaller complexes (four to six units), because families in smaller developments know each other personally and any intruder is quickly noticed, as a threat to all. Thus, the problem for urban areas is to increase the extent of observability and reduce the degree of anonymity in urban areas to achieve more social control over the population. This naturally is difficult to achieve in densely populated areas where neighbors move in and out on a weekly basis, but some cities are beginning to build smaller apartment developments and separate them into clusters so that each almost constitutes a small community within itself.

Other means that cities have used to increase the degree of social control are increasing the number and frequency of foot-patrols through high crime neighborhoods, increasing the amount of lighting facilities in alleys, parks, and vacant areas to allow a more complete surveillance by police and citizens, and removal of abandoned buildings and structures which might provide concealment to delinquents.

The primary relationship theory. Charles Horton Cooley (one of the first American sociologists) observed that social control is effective where interpersonal relationships are more primary in nature (persons relating on an intimate personal basis). As noted above, rural relationships are primary in nature, which supports a high degree of social control that is found in most rural areas.

On the urban scene, several changes might be made to increase the degree of primary relations in city life. Efforts might be made to reduce the extent of bureaucracy in city organization and decentralize the power and responsibilities for decision making in city management. This plan has met considerable success in England, where responsibility for city management is regularly rotated among the citizenry (even the positions of magistrate judges are rotated). As a result, a large proportion of the citizenry has experience in and shares the responsibility for city management, creating a high degree of intimacy and involvement in community problems.

A second means of enhancing primary rela-

Answer frame 2[16]

1. True. Overlapping jurisdictional boundaries often prevent city planning and reorganization, and complicate the process of administration of city utilities and services.
2. True. Suburban communities are usually more homogeneous in population and usually need fewer municipal services than metropolitan cities, thus allowing a greater degree of autonomy in their administration.
3. False. State and federal revenue sharing is only a temporary solution. Long range solutions usually require extensive city and regional planning and reorganization.

If you missed any of the above, reread Frame 2[16] before starting Frame 3[16] on page 107.

Frame 3[16] continued

tionships is to encourage the development of small subcommunities within a larger metropolitan area where families can come to know each other on a personal basis. Small communities tend to nurture a spirit of "neighborhood" that facilitates the maintenance of social control. This spirit often grows in many suburban developments but it might be enhanced if community leaders would encourage this factor in city planning and zoning.

Indicate whether each of the following statements is true or false by writing "T" or "F" in the space provided.

_____ 1. Typically, observability of behavior is *low* in rural communities.
_____ 2. As the degree of anonymity increases in a community, the likelihood of deviance and lawlessness also increases.
_____ 3. There is less deviance and lawlessness when people interact on a primary basis.

Now check your answers with those in Answer frame 3[16] on page 110.

chapter 17

ECOLOGY AND THE ENVIRONMENT

Frame 1[17]

The science of human ecology is the study of how people interact with and adapt to their environment. Ecology is a relatively new science and has achieved its greatest growth within the last two decades. [For a more extensive examination of ecology and the environment, see Phillips W. Foster, *Programmed Learning Aid for Introduction to Environmental Science* (Homewood, Ill.: Learning Systems Company, 1972).]

Ancient man did very little damage to the environment. Early tribal groups were quite small in size and the people consumed the products of nature that were replenishable. After burning the firewood and hunting the game of one region, they simply moved on, leaving the area to regenerate naturally. The ravages of nature and disease and a limited food supply kept the world population small and very nearly stationary.

As man learned to domesticate animals and to start agriculture, he was able to increase his food supply. This allowed people to settle permanently in an area and to live in larger groups. Some anthropologists believe that this created the basis for the emergence of civilization. However, this also caused one of the first alterations of nature—although agriculture produced more food and allowed more people to live in a limited area, it also depleted the soil of its fertile elements. As populations grew, increasing amounts of natural land cover were removed. Eventually this became so extensive that entire plant, animal, and insect populations and even weather patterns of continents were changed.

The gradual growth of larger populations paved the way for the growth of large civilizations which in turn encouraged the development of technology. The development of the wheel, the lever, and eventually steam power created the basis for the emergence of modern industrialization as it exists today. Although it took some 6,000 years for man to evolve from the period of the early Greek civilizations of 3500 B.C. to the expanding megalopolises of today, this period, when compared to the evolution of the human race, represents only the blossoming of the rosebud for man, but in the mind of some ecologists, a growing cancer for nature.

An inevitable product of large civilizations is the despoiling of nature and the alteration of the environment itself. Cities are creations of man and not of nature, and as such they do not fit well within the natural organization of nature itself. Cities require a constant water supply and a source of fuel or energy. Natural resources must be used to provide housing, streets, and buildings, and this requires that forests be harvested for building materials. Forests have many uses, and one use often unrealized is their function in moderating temperature extremes and producing rainfall in a region. They provide huge reservoirs for water which cools the summer air and produces temperature differentials that encourage rainfall. In many areas, land de-

109

Answer frame 3[16]

1. False. Observability is usually quite high in rural areas, and low in urban areas.
2. True. As the degree of anonymity increases, people are less accountable for their behavior, thus deviance and lawlessness tend to increase.
3. True. When people interact on a face-to-face basis (primary relationship) there is more social control than when people interact on a secondary basis.

If you missed any of the above, reread Frame 3[16] before beginning Chapter 17 on page 109.

Frame 1[17] continued

nuded of its natural covering soon reverts to desert, and man is actually increasing the amount of desert in the world when he cuts the trees, plows or overgrazes the grasslands, and overpumps the ground water (the growth of the Sahara desert is one such example).

Civilizations require that rivers (which once supported wildlife and produced an abundant supply of food for a small population) be dammed and diverted to irrigate the land for large populations. Often these rivers are polluted as they carry away the wastes of large cities. The mining and quarrying of natural resources for energy and minerals alters the natural terrain and pollutes the underground water supply. The inevitable product of these actions is to alter the cycles in nature and encumber the equilibrium that nature established for itself. This is not always undesirable, but the increased incidence of flooding, droughts, and air inversions that are occurring today are more a product of man's creation than of nature's.

The essence of the problem is not that man cannot live in harmony with nature, but rather the question is how people can live within a geographic area without disrupting ecological cycles. At the turn of the century in America the population was rural and widely dispersed, and the ecological systems could easily absorb the small amounts of pollution created by the small population (although even then the major cities were experiencing problems in disposing of their horse manure). The products that people consumed were mostly natural products that were biodegradable and replenishable.

However since then, modernization and technology have produced a plethora of new plastics, metals, and pesticides that are not biodegradable or easily disposed of. Their manufacture also produces highly toxic wastes that can disrupt ecological cycles, and that are gradually absorbed up into the food chain to contaminate man also.

In order to feed a growing population, ever-increasing amounts of land must be converted to monoculture (growing only a single species of crop such as wheat or corn) to increase the production of food, which also increases the chances of insect infestation and crop diseases. The 19th century potato famine in Ireland is a good example of the possible effects of overspecialization in a single crop.

Perhaps the most spectacular modern ecological idiocy is our practice of depleting soil fertility by growing crops, and then, instead of returning the crop wastes, and human and animal manures to the land, we dump them into the streams. Thus we deprive the land of needed fertility while we pollute the streams and oceans, thereby destroying yet another natural resource. Chemical fertilizers to replace fertility depletion are a temporary expedient, for they also use a nonrenewable resource. This practice of using our wastes to pollute instead of renew, if continued indefinitely, will absolutely doom the human race to a massive die-off (which may, in fact, be almost upon us).

There are a few signs that people in America are slowly realizing the relationships between population, modernization, and environment, and there has been a subtle but significant shift of attitude from one of superconsumption a decade ago to attitudes favoring superconservation today. But the unanswered question that still remains is whether or not there has been a sufficient shift of attitude soon enough to moderate the environmental problem.

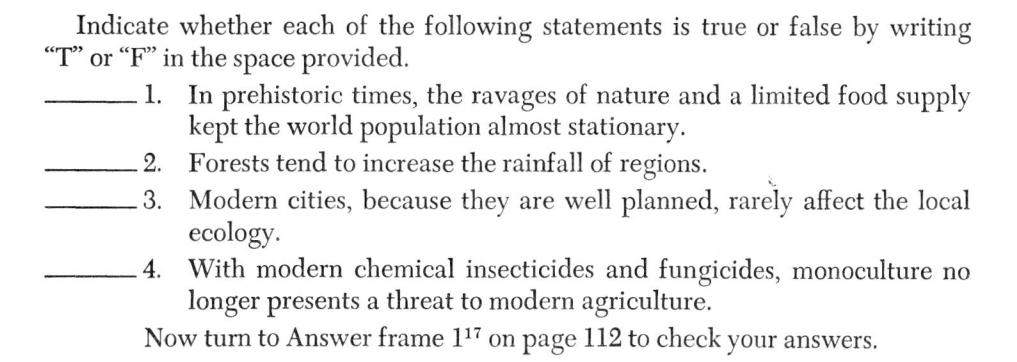

Indicate whether each of the following statements is true or false by writing "T" or "F" in the space provided.

_____ 1. In prehistoric times, the ravages of nature and a limited food supply kept the world population almost stationary.

_____ 2. Forests tend to increase the rainfall of regions.

_____ 3. Modern cities, because they are well planned, rarely affect the local ecology.

_____ 4. With modern chemical insecticides and fungicides, monoculture no longer presents a threat to modern agriculture.

Now turn to Answer frame 1¹⁷ on page 112 to check your answers.

Frame 2¹⁷

The recent emergence of the phrase "Spaceship Earth" reflects the increasing awareness that the earth is actually a closed biosphere traveling through space. Before the last few decades, man held the general perception of the earth as a vast and endless domain, created for man, and to be used by man for his convenience. Little thought was given to the need to conserve resources as it was generally believed that there was an abundance for all. There were always new frontiers to open, new forests to harvest, and new mines to strip for their wealth. If anything, the abundance of natural resources was sometimes an inconvenience, because man had to slash and burn the forests to increase farmland, dig ditches for drainage, kill off herds of buffalo and other wildlife to gain grazing land (without any regard for the hearty, viable, and natural food source that the wildlife itself presented), and destroy natural vegetation in order to plant a single species of plant.

What was not considered or realized was the intricate interrelation of all elements of nature. Barry Commoner [Barry Commoner, *The Closing Circle* (New York: Alfred A. Knopf, 1971).] postulates four basic ecological laws of nature that cannot be disregarded.

(1) *Everything in nature is connected to everything else.* This is the law of interdependence, that a change in one plant or animal population inevitably produces a change in another population. For example, the hunting of alligators in the Florida Everglades caused a reduction in the number of alligators which kept drainage ditches open to allow a flow of fresh water; thus alligator reduction caused a reduction in the fish population. In another bizarre case, a domino effect was created as the World Health Organization pursued its humanistic purposes by spraying remote areas in Borneo with DDT to eradicate malarial mosquitos. However, cockroaches and other insects developed an immunity and concentrated the DDT; in turn, the cockroaches became a deadly poison to the lizard population. Local cats discovered the lizards easier to catch than the local rats, and both lizard and cat populations died in due course. As a result of the decimation of the cat population, the rat population grew profusely and spread a greater variety of human disease than had existed before the spraying.

(2) *All chemical or natural elements in nature enter into the system somewhere* (and not always in a beneficial manner). Here is the principle of interdependence affecting food chains, when one animal or his waste becomes the food supply for another. Chemicals and inorganic salts in the water become the nutrients which nourish bacteria which are consumed by protozoa and higher life forms, which are eventually consumed by fish, which are consumed by birds, animals, and man, which in turn provide a new supply of inorganic wastes to regenerate the cycle.

Toxic industrial wastes, however, may kill off a species and destroy a link in the chain, and toxic chemicals often accumulate in a lower species to eventually become toxic to higher species. For example, the radioactive wastes of a nuclear power plant in the Columbia River Basin

Answer frame 1[17]

1. True. The world population did not show any large increases until man developed agriculture.
2. True. Forests provide huge reservoirs for water, which evaporates and produces temperature differentials, which in turn encourage rainfall.
3. False. Cities are not natural products of nature; the concrete buildings and highways collect heat and change the temperature of regions, the waste produced by large populations pollutes watersheds, and often construction alters the natural terrain. All of these factors and others change the natural ecology of regions.
4. False. Although monoculture increases the food supply, it also increases the possibility of a widespread crop failure (particularly from bacteriological sources which are often more difficult to control than are insect infestations).

If you missed any of the above, restudy Frame 1[17] before starting Frame 2[17] on page 111.

Frame 2[17] continued

were diluted in water to eliminate any possible danger to man or wildlife. However, biologists report that river plankton had soon concentrated the strontium some 2,000 times, and the fish who fed on the plankton concentrated it some 40,000 times, and finally, the egg yolks of water birds had concentrations of more than a million times greater than water concentrations. Thus, with time, man can easily accumulate dangerous concentrations of toxic materials. Some species of birds have already accumulated so much DDT that they lay soft-shelled eggs which cannot hatch.

(3) *The forces of nature act to maintain a dynamic equilibrium.* Here is the rule of the survival of the fittest, that if one species tends to come upon favorable (or unfavorable) environmental conditions, it increases (decreases) its population to maintain a relative balance. For example, in Northern Canada it was noted that the rabbit and lynx populations tended to vary with similar cycles—when the supply of rabbits increased, the supply of predators increased until, over the long run, a relative balance was maintained. Nature also moderates wildlife populations through other natural forces such as droughts and heavy winters to maintain a relative balance. In the state of nature, a population explosion of one insect is soon followed by a population explosion of predator insects, who eat up the first insect population; then the predator insects die off as their food supply becomes scarce and the equilibrium is restored.

(4) *Nature is an intricate web* in that a strain or imbalance in one area produces extraordinary changes in other areas. Thus, a pollutant that affects the growth of algae in a lake not only kills the fish, but waterfowl and other wildlife, and destroys the lake as a source of potable water. Excessive nutrients increase plant growth and eventually turn the lake into a marsh and finally into a plain.

Care must be taken to protect the natural cycles of nature—the water cycle, carbon cycle, nitrogen cycle, and, most importantly, the carbon dioxide and oxygen cycles upon which man is as dependent as are wildlife. However, wildlife do not threaten the cycles; man does! As the forests are harvested (forests covered 40 percent of America a century ago, but only 20 percent now) and as the oceans are polluted (algae in the ocean produce almost three fourths of the earth's oxygen), the available supply of oxygen is reduced. Meanwhile, automobiles and furnaces consume an increasing supply of oxygen and pollute the rest, causing a measurable increase in the proportion of carbon dioxide in the atmosphere. Although it is unlikely that man will run out of oxygen, the increase in carbon dioxide can act as a shield to cause the earth to hold more heat from the sun, creating a "greenhouse effect" that has already raised the average temperature of the world by two to three degrees. Some ecologists fear that an increase of only five degrees could cause the arctic ice caps to melt, and raise sea levels by several feet. If this occurred, up to one fourth of the current land masses would be inundated and every port city could be under water.

The balance of nature is complex and there is no question but that the human race will have to be more considerate of its actions if it desires to live for another century on earth.

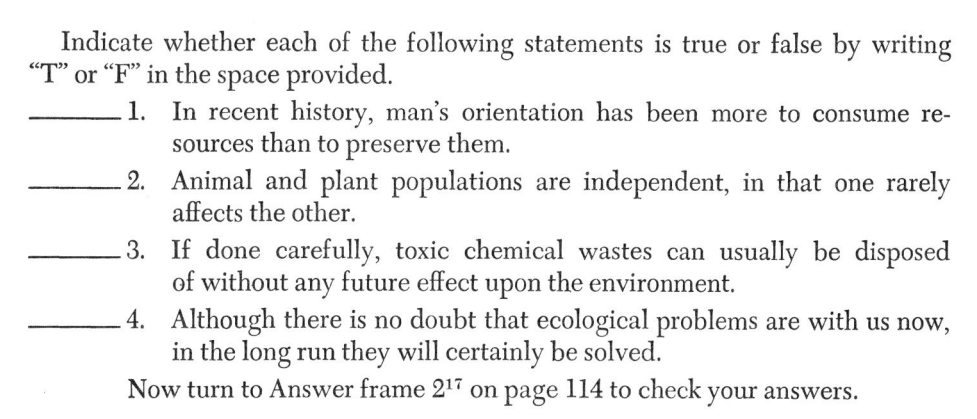

Indicate whether each of the following statements is true or false by writing "T" or "F" in the space provided.

_____ 1. In recent history, man's orientation has been more to consume resources than to preserve them.

_____ 2. Animal and plant populations are independent, in that one rarely affects the other.

_____ 3. If done carefully, toxic chemical wastes can usually be disposed of without any future effect upon the environment.

_____ 4. Although there is no doubt that ecological problems are with us now, in the long run they will certainly be solved.

Now turn to Answer frame 2[17] on page 114 to check your answers.

Frame 3[17]

Industrialization and modernization have produced an endless variety of products for man to aspire to possess and consume, and the minimal level of expectations for comfort and satisfaction in life have multiplied severalfold. The *changing level of expectations* in the American society has encouraged people to become highly consumption oriented, which in turn has had an adverse effect upon the environment. Aside from the walls, roof, and bed, the majority of products in today's household did not exist a century ago. Today's housewife, instead of using the old reliable (and noncontaminating) lye soap, now must have a minimum of 10 to 15 different detergents and cleaning compounds, each of which are major contaminants to the water supply. Instead of the old air-breathing horse of yesteryear for transportation, whose refuse nourished the local garden, most people have a gasoline-operated, air-polluting machine that can consume more oxygen in a day than a horse did in a year. Automobiles also produce up to two tons of carbon monoxide per year and other toxic compounds such as nitrous oxide, vaporized lead, and sulfur oxides, all of which are dangerous to man.

America has become, in the words of Thorstein Veblen, a society based upon conspicuous consumption—instead of having one good suit or dress, most people have 10 to 20. Instead of driving a car until it literally falls apart, people trade for newer models each two to five years. The *planned obsolescence* of nonreturnable and nonrepairable items has become so institutionalized that it is now taken for granted. Many appliances and subassemblies are not even designed so that they *can* be repaired, but must be discarded and replaced when they break down.

More important even than the *amount* of goods produced today is the *shift in product technology*. A century ago, one's sweater or jacket was knitted or woven from wool or cotton (both renewable resources) without the expenditure of very much energy. When finally discarded, cotton and wool easily and harmlessly degraded back into natural elements and reentered the ecological system. Today's garment is likely to be made from a synthetic fiber which, processed at the expense of large energy inputs, originated at a petroleum wellhead. Today's products typically use vast quantities of nonrenewable resources, require vast amounts of energy for their processing and manufacture, and end in a stubborn trash heap that resists reentry into the ecological system.

Industry has encouraged such indulgences, because they stimulate production, but they also consume natural resources at an ever-increasing

Answer frame 2[17]

1. True. Until very recently, there was always new land to open for agriculture and new natural resources to consume. Thus the consumption orientation prevailed over efforts toward preservation.
2. False. As Barry Commoner points out, animal and plant populations are *inter*dependent, in that a change in one eventually produces a change in the other.
3. False. Although in rare instances this may be true, for the most part, all chemical elements enter into ecological cycles somewhere and at some future time.
4. False. Ecological problems are slow to develop, and often when the process has started (such as the warming of the earth, the development of deserts, and the pollution of oceans), their effects are irreversible.

If you missed any of the above, restudy Frame 2[17] before beginning Frame 3[17] on page 113.

Frame 3[17] continued

rate. The traditional values of conservation and economic stability have been replaced with values of growth for its own sake in today's society—bigness is equated with quality, growth is equated with success, and happiness is equated with consumption.

"All of this costs somewhere" states Barry Commoner. The richest veins of iron ore have been mined and now lower quality ores must be concentrated into taconite pellets, a process that requires a much greater consumption of energy. The most productive and accessible oil wells have been pumped dry, and now must be drilled deeper or in the ocean to find new supplies. The consumption of natural resources has increased to the point where geologists estimate that current supplies of lead, tungsten, silver, and mercury will be exhausted within the next 40 years. Nature takes from one million to a billion years to produce petroleum and heavy metals, yet Americans, with only 6 pecent of the world's population, are consuming 25 percent of the world's raw resources each year. Meanwhile the rest of the world is catching up with the United States. Clearly nature does not possess unlimited wealth and inevitably the world's people will soon have to rethink the modern westernized concept of growth and consumption if industrialized societies are to survive for more than a few more decades.

Technology is often blamed as the major culprit in environmental problems, but a more objective view might suggest that it is man's use of technology that is the primary problem. The same as technology can develop pesticides, it can develop biological controls (for example, using sterile male insects who ignominiously breed to no avail) to control insect infestations. New research programs are focusing upon the use of solar energy and harvesting the winds and tides to produce electricity and hydrogen which would replace gasoline in automobiles and furnaces. In short, the same technology that produced the uses for natural resources can also assist their conservation; that is, if people are willing to pay the cost!

And this is the crux of the problem—people like the pleasure of consumption, but not the expense. Everyone is in favor of protecting the environment, at least until they figure the cost of such action. Commercial interests and the government tend to prefer short-term profits over long-range concerns, while environmentalists are sometimes ridiculed as anticapitalistic radical dissidents who have the weird conception that squirrels and song birds are more important than factories and highways.

The environmental problem may be an unwanted problem, but it cannot be avoided. Progress in achieving environmental reform is complicated and hindered because *environmental victories tend to be temporary in nature, while environmental damage is permanent.* Once the big shovels scoop off a mountain, a dam floods a valley, or a lake is polluted, the damage cannot be reversed. Contractors need win the battle only once to build their dam or apartment complex, while environmentalists must fight the battle every time a project is proposed. The "developers" can afford to lose every battle except the last one.

Considerable progress has been made within the last decade in implementing environmental standards and reforms, but most people are still unaware of the magnitude of the problem. Programs which are based upon *voluntary compliance* with environmental standards have been all but insignificant in their effect, and most ecologists are convinced that a system of *forced compliance* is the only solution.

The social problem of ecology is more than just a value conflict between people who wish to protect the forests, rivers, and wildlife of America, and those who wish to exploit the earth's resources now. This social problem threatens the whole of man's future existence on this earth. Environmental concerns will increase for at least as long as world population grows and the "revolution of rising expectations" continues.

Indicate whether each of the following statements is true or false by writing "T" or "F" in the space provided.

_____ 1. Conspicuous consumption is practiced only by the upper class in the American society.

_____ 2. In modern America, corporate growth often has become equated with financial success.

_____ 3. It is clear that technology has simply run rampant and cannot be controlled.

_____ 4. With the current concern over ecology, environmentalists have finally acquired the upper hand in controlling environmental issues.

Now turn to Answer frame 3[17] on page 116 to check your answers.

Answer frame 3[17]

1. False. Although it perhaps originated in the upper class, the increased affluence of the middle and lower social classes has institutionalized conspicuous consumption at all levels.
2. True. Economic growth has become the primary goal of many corporations, and has reduced emphasis on quality, craftsmanship, and the public interest.
3. False. The problem is not with technology per se, but rather man's use of technology. Technology can pollute, but it can also eliminate pollution if man so chooses.
4. False. Although concern about ecology has increased, environmentalists have had little impact upon most ecological issues; for the most part, private interests have prevailed over the public's interest.

If you missed any of the above, reread Frame 3[17] before beginning Chapter 18.

chapter 18

VESTED INTERESTS AND PRESSURE GROUPS

Frame 1[18]

Alexis de Tocqueville is reported to have commented that whenever three Americans get together, they form an organization. Americans tend to be known throughout the world for their proclivity to organize into special groups to advance their own particular interests. Although vested interests and pressure groups do not constitute a social problem in themselves, a conflict of interest groups is found at the core of most social problems.

Each person has a variety of special or vested interests in life—occupation and home life, religious and political beliefs, conceptions of what is right and wrong with the government, ideas of what is good and evil in society, ideals that are desirable and undesirable in life, and so on. Churches have a special interest in influencing the morality of the people and protecting the institution of religion in society. Businesses have a vested interest in protecting their markets and profits, and labor unions have an interest in protecting the working man from being exploited by businessmen. Even the poor and disenfranchised have vested interests; to protect their meager position in the welfare establishment, to protect their homes and family, and to protect their right to be recognized as individuals.

The importance of recognizing special interests and vested interests in the study of social problems is that people's interests tend to determine their position relative to different social problems, and to determine the extent of personal involvement in the problem. If we are only indirectly affected by the condition, it rarely arouses much interest or action, but if one of our special interests is directly affected, we naturally are much more concerned. This is why not all people are equally affected by different social problems—the degree of involvement depends in part upon the special or vested interests held by that person.

Although people often use the terms "special interests," "vested interests," and "pressure groups" in an interchangeable fashion, each term has a precise and exclusive meaning. *Special interest groups* consist of people who share a common interest, be it birdwatching, photography, stamp-collecting, or worshiping God. Any person who shares the same interest is a member of the "interest group" and although members may sometimes join an organization which promotes the special interest (perhaps to receive the publications), the members themselves are not organized as lobbying or legislative bodies. There are literally thousands of special interest groups in the American society and each person may identify with a variety of such groups.

Vested interest groups, on the other hand, consist of members who have a particular investment or position to protect (money, power, or prestige). Vested interest groups usually work to maintain the status quo and will oppose any change which they perceive as a threat to their interests. Physicians gained greatly in income and prestige during the 20th century, due partly to changes in medical technology and partly to effective organizational strategies; today medical societies adamantly oppose changes which threaten this position. Every profession has a set of "ethics" which are supposedly intended to protect the interests of the clients, but which are even more directly intended to protect the economic status of the profession. Thus the legal profession has been largely successful in blocking the sale of "do-it-yourself" divorce kits, the use of which would reduce the market for legal services. Every vested interest, while acting in defense of its own interests, seeks to maintain a façade of selflessly serving the public interest.

Vested interest groups often *do* benefit the public while feathering their own nest. When medical societies promote laws that prevent untrained "quacks" from practicing medicine, this benefits both the public *and* the medical profession. Often a vested interest group's actions benefit one segment of the people while damaging another. For example, it is to the public's interest to have a highway trust that builds thousands of miles of new turnpike each year; yet, the highway trust, working against the public's interest, has lobbied against the development of alternate modes of economical and efficient mass transit. As a result, in the face of an energy crisis, America is left with a decayed system of passenger rail service and will have to spend millions of dollars to fulfill the emerging need for mass transit. Larger and busier airports are profitable, but their noise reduces the value of the homes surrounding them. Strip-mining provides cheap coal to consumers and profits to mine operators, but destroys the land. Vested interest groups provide desired goods and services to some segments of the population, but it usually must be at the expense of another segment. It is not that vested interests are good or bad in society; they are simply necessary and inevitable features of a complex industrialized society.

While vested interest groups most often appear as defenders of the status quo, it is not always the case that they are reactionary. Vested interests support change whenever they perceive that a proposed change is beneficial to them. Thus the most massive public works project of all time—the interstate highway system—was adopted speedily with little debate when several powerful vested interest groups, including automobile manufacturers, oil companies, and highway construction firms, decided to support it. Significant social change seldom comes from an aroused public overpowering the vested interest. Instead, what usually happens is that some powerful interest groups decide that a proposed change will benefit them and swing over to its support. For example, the St. Lawrence Seaway was opposed by both the east coast shipping interests, who saw the seaway as potential competition, and by the great lakes business interests, who saw it as a needless waste of governmental funds. But when the iron ore beds near Lake Superior approached exhaustion, these same great lakes area industrialists switched to support of the seaway. Seldom is any issue a simple contest between "the interests" and "the people." Instead, some vested interests are generally found on each side of any major issue.

Pressure groups are organized special interest or vested interest groups that are designed to apply pressure to achieve or protect a position of advantage with legislative bodies. Few persons by themselves can exert much power or political influence upon the government (unless they are a J. P. Morgan or a Nelson Rockefeller), but often through joining together in a concerted effort they can achieve power. Pressure groups usually operate a lobby in legislative bodies to convince legislators of the great benefits to society of measures which happen also to be in the pressure group's interests.

Pressure groups represent a wide variety of interests in the American society. They range from powerful groups such as the American Medical Association, the National Association of Manufacturers, and the AFL–CIO, each with an elaborately-staffed Washington office, to many small and relatively unknown groups, each of which helps pay for a small part of the total lobbying effort of a single "legislative representative." Pressure groups support a wide range of proposals; for example, Common Cause supports a variety of "liberal" causes, and the John Birch Society supports many conservative causes. Most pressure groups, however, have a limited specific purpose; for example, the American Mining Congress, which lobbies against restrictions upon strip or open pit mining. While some segments of the public often benefit to some extent from the victories of pressure groups, more often the sponsoring interest group is enriched at the expense of the general public good.

Contrary to widespread public conception, most legislators feel that pressure groups perform a valuable and necessary service to the government. Abraham Holtzman reports that most legislators view lobbying groups as a valuable source of technical information and statistics, and lobbyists can often help draft legislation and find compromises in areas where the legislators have little expertise. [Abraham Holtzman, *Interest Groups and Lobbying* (New York: The Macmillan Co., 1967), p. 75.] Thus, pressure groups in society become another means for reconciling the conflicting interests of the various segments of the population and providing a source of stability in society.

Indicate whether each of the following statements is true or false by writing "T" or "F" in the space provided.

_____ 1. Most social problems involve a conflict between interest groups in society.
_____ 2. Everyone holds a variety of special interests in life.
_____ 3. Vested interest groups always work against the public's best interest.
_____ 4. Although all pressure groups are special interest groups, not all special interest groups are pressure groups.

Now turn to Answer frame 1[18] on page 120 to check your answers.

Frame 2[18]

Vested interest and pressure groups exist in society because they serve a purpose or function. Some functions are desirable, in that they tend to create order and organization in the society. Other aspects, however, may be dysfunctional or disruptive as they increase the degree of social disorganization in society.

Functional aspects. Vested interest groups

tend to provide a focus for group interest and involvement, and as such they can serve as a mechanism for initiating social action. The National Association for the Advancement of Colored People (NAACP) has served to focus the energy and efforts of minorities across the nation into concerted action and to organize support for civil rights legislation. Although different people may disagree with the purposes and actions of the different interest groups, each still represents the views of a segment of the population and serves as a means through which different causes can be advanced.

Interest groups can unify people and create a sense of belongingness for the disenfranchised or marginal people in society. Associations for retired persons, veteran groups, and youth groups such as the Boy Scouts give meaning and purpose in life to large groups of people in the American society. When people join an organization they tend to incorporate the goals and purposes of the groups into their own minds, giving them a new sense of identity and purpose in their own life. Thus, a crippled and forgotten GI becomes a Veteran of Foreign Wars, an itinerant Mexican migrant proudly proclaims *la Raza Unida,* and women across the nation unite in the movement for women's liberation in their quest to escape from their subordinate station in life. Membership in a special interest group provides a source of dignity for persons who might otherwise be forgotten.

Vested interest groups serve to focus public attention upon social issues in the society and clarify different attitudes and value positions. One prominent example might be the "poor people's march on Washington" which was designed to attract the attention of legislators and stir the conscience of the people toward the plight of the poor and minorities in American society.

Vested interest groups may assist in promoting reform in society. Environmentalist groups have brought considerable public attention to ecological and pollution problems and have been instrumental in initiating actions to protect scenic mountains, rivers, and wilderness areas from exploitation and ruination by commercial interests. As a result, the American society is clearly more pollution-conscious than it was a decade ago.

Dysfunctional aspects. Vested interest groups are also formed to promote a particular interest or position, and upon occasion "what's best for General Motors" may not be best for the larger population. Vested interest groups generally seek to protect their own interests above all others, and upon occasion they may ignore the rights and privileges of the larger majority. Currently, big timber corporations in the western states are lobbying to increase the allotment of trees they may harvest from the national forests. But if their allotment is increased, the annual cut would exceed annual replacement growth. Dune buggy enthusiasts, trail bikers, and snowmobilers seek to open the national parks to motorized vehicles, while conservationists seek to prohibit their use altogether. Many beverages can be bought only in "no return" cans or bottles, yet a great deal of energy is wasted because bottlers find that the "no returns" are more convenient for organizing large-scale distribution and squeezing out small local competitors. In this instance, the energy shortage is aggravated and small businesses suffer so that big businesses can be enriched. The public must always be on guard to note whose interest is being promoted and at whose expense!

Pressure groups are organized to exploit a position of power and to impose their own preferences upon the majority of the population. Although most pressure groups are reasonably ethical (within the bounds of protecting their own interests), some groups may employ unethical or misleading advertising to lull the public into a false sense of security that may eventually be against the public's own best interests (for example, refineries which pollute local water supplies and drug companies which fail to test their drugs for side effects).

Vested interest and pressure groups may oppose change in the status quo in society where reform might be drastically needed. For years Detroit automakers enticed consumers into buying ever bigger and more powerful automobiles in the face of an impending gasoline shortage and pollution crisis with little regard for future consequences. Electrical utilities are still pro-

Answer frame 1[18]

1. True. It is the disagreement between interest groups that brings public awareness to the social problem.
2. True. Each person holds a variety of special interests in life: job, home, religion, personal safety, pleasure, and so on.
3. False. Although the majority of vested interest groups rarely seek the public's interest, the public also has vested interest groups (although usually less powerful than corporate vested interest groups) which promote and protect their special interests.
4. True. Special interest groups do not always join together to become pressure groups.

If you missed any of the above, reread Frame 1[18] before starting Frame 2[18] on page 118.

Frame 2[18] continued

moting the installation of electric heating in regions already experiencing "brownouts," and loan agencies often encourage borrowers to "consolidate your debts into one easy payment" and lock consumers into an even longer loan payment period. Meanwhile, credit agencies lobby against proposed legislation which would require the complete disclosure of credit contracts and costs that borrowers will have to pay. Such practices are clearly designed to favor corporate interests over the public's interests.

Indicate whether each of the following statements is true or false by writing "T" or "F" in the space provided.

_____ 1. Interest groups can serve an integrative function in society, but they also can create social disorganization.
_____ 2. One function of interest groups is to unify groups of people.
_____ 3. Pressure groups are organized to exploit their position of power.

Now turn to Answer frame 2[18] on page 122 to check your answers.

Frame 3[18]

Power groups. Social power is constantly changing in source and operation. In medieval society, power was rooted in land ownership and noble birth; today the "landed gentry" has virtually disappeared while the "tradesmen" have come up in the world. Power may flow from a variety of sources—money can bring power if it is used for that purpose, power may be vested in a political or bureaucratic office such as elected or corporate offices, or power may flow from the consensus and support of the people as they unite in following a charismatic leader (such as Jesus Christ or Martin Luther King).

Whatever the source, power and authority exist by *fiat*—it is granted only by the tacit approval of the majority. For example, a president can rule only as long as the people accept his legitimacy to rule, and this legitimacy is granted through obedience to his directives and the laws of the nation and through reaffirmation of approval in public elections. When troops refuse to obey their commander (which occurred to some extent in Vietnam), when the public refuses to obey an objectionable law (such as occurred during prohibition), or when the people lose faith in a charismatic leader, the power and legitimacy of leaders to rule is destroyed.

There are a variety of different power groups in the American society (corporate, political, military-industrial, religious, intellectual, public service); yet there is still considerable disagreement among scholars as to the true nature of the structure of power in the American society. Two conceptions or models of power tend to prevail in most discussions—the *pluralist* conception of power, and the *elitist* conception.

Pluralists generally hold the view that there is a wide and diverse organization of power groups in the American society, and that the power is widely dispersed among a variety of organizations, interest groups, and elected bodies. From this perspective, no single group can ever consolidate enough power to dominate or control the majority of people in society for long, because disenfranchised groups would soon act in coalition to divest the controlling group of its source of power (as has occurred when Congress enacted antitrust legislation, and the right-to-work laws). This effect is known as control by *countervailing power,* wherein the exercise of great power tends to stimulate the appearance and organization of opposing power structures. (Big factories eventually produced big labor unions; union power stimulated laws to limit union power, and so on. This principle was relied on by the early founders of the American Constitution when they created three separate bodies to rule the government—the legislative, the judicial, and the executive branches of the government. Each branch functions as a watchdog over the other branches, preventing the consolidation of excessive power within any one branch. Organizations of countervailing power facilitate a balancing of power groups within both the government and the society. [Arthur Schlesinger, the author of *The Imperial Presidency,* has suggested that the actions of congress in instigating the investigations into Watergate and the ITT scandal was inspired by the view that President Nixon was consolidating too much power in the executive branch of the government, thus legislators used the Watergate investigations to erode Nixon's position of influence over the legislative and judicial branches of the government.]

Pluralists often believe in and support the concept of representative democracy in which the public actively participates through the ballot in the decisions of government and the formation of policy. Critics of the pluralists philosophy note that only two thirds of the eligible voters vote regularly in national elections, that less than one half of the voters can name the congressman that was elected, and that very few voters are well enough informed on most issues to have any well thought-out opinion. Thus, elitists argue, the general public can hardly be expected to assume the massive responsibilities for running the national government.

The *elitist* conception of power (as described by C. Wright Mills) [C. Wright Mills, *The Power Elite* (New York: Oxford University Press, 1956).] envisions a pyramidal structure of power in society, divided into three levels of influence: the apex of power is dominated by the corporate rich (the major stockholders of large corporations and corporate executives), the executive branch of the government (the president and his advisors), and the military leaders (the generals and Pentagon leaders) who can virtually control the rest of the population and the economy. Here the elitist notes that only 200 corporations in America control virtually all of the markets and prices for smaller corporations; that the president can initiate and negate wars at his will (such as Vietnam and the 1974 Middle East conflict), establish foreign policy at his choice (for example, open the diplomatic doors to the Soviet Union and China), and dominate domestic programs (for instance, create or cancel the "Great Society" programs). Any of these actions can have a tremendous impact throughout the whole American society. The Pentagon can initiate military contracts that run into the billions and chart the future success of thousands of major corporations in the American economy (examples are the C5A and F-111 project) without any consultation with or foreknowledge by the general public. Without question, a considerable amount of power and influence is held within the hands of a very few people in the American society.

The second level of power under the elitist model is held by a collection of vested interest and pressure groups, such as the AFL–CIO, American Farm Bureau, and the American Medical Association, which control vast segments of the domestic sector of the American society.

The third layer is a wide base composed of the unorganized masses of society who rarely receive any information about what is happening at the higher levels until after it has already oc-

Answer frame 2[18]

1. True. Interest groups are often viewed as serving an integrative function by supporters, but others who are opposed to the group may view the groups as disruptive.
2. True. Interest groups can unify people by providing a sense of belongingness and assisting in giving people a purpose in life.
3. True. Pressure groups are organized to protect and promote their own particular interests and position of advantage.

If you missed any of the questions, reread Frame 2[18] before starting Frame 3[18] on page 120.

Frame 3[18] continued

curred. Under the elitist model, the people's lack of participation and knowledge allows higher level groups to rule by default in that they rarely if ever allow the general public to voice its preference on any vital issues, offering election choices between candidates and parties who show no real differences.

The importance of studying power groups in society is that such groups are in an advantageous position to influence or rectify a wide variety of social problems. However, since often the genuine resolution of some problems would necessarily restrict or limit different vested interests, power groups may act to stabilize the social problem as it now exists rather than take positive and costly action to seek its solution. Many social problems in America will persist until it becomes expedient for different power groups to resolve them.

Indicate whether each of the following statements is true or false by writing "T" or "F" in the space provided.

_____ 1. Sociologists are clearly in agreement about the nature of the power structure of the American society.

_____ 2. Elitists often employ the concept of countervailing power to account for the power structure of the American society.

_____ 3. Elitists believe that with the American system of representative democracy, the voters are the true source of power.

_____ 4. The resolution of any social problem requires the support of the power groups affected by the problem.

Now turn to Answer frame 3[18] on page 124 to check your answers.

chapter 19

CIVIL RIGHTS AND CIVIL LIBERTIES

Frame 1[19]

In the last decade in America there has been extensive and wide-ranging change in the specification of civil rights. Racial groups challenged long-standing practices of racial discrimination in employment, housing, and education; conscientious objectors challenged the compulsory draft system and widened the specification of rights of selective service registrants; and consumers united as never before against the purveyors of shady credit and shoddy merchandise. The news media took bold steps to reassert their right to a free press and to publish the news without subjugation to governmental censorship; and finally legislators used the Watergate caper to clarify the power of congress relative to the president and to define the limits of executive privilege, to restrict the use and abuse of political power and influence, and to require the disclosure of campaign contributions.

Almost from the signing of the Declaration of Independence, civil libertarians have had to fight the battle of protecting the civil rights of the citizenry. America is a nation of laws, more so perhaps than almost any other society in the world. The legal foundations of our government are based upon the principle that individual rights and privileges supersede the rights of the state; or in other words, that the state was created to serve the people, not vice versa. However, since governments are the force that unifies people and represents them, they often become the major organized body in a society and tend to assume greater power than the people individually. The underlying purpose of civil libertarians is to protect the rights of individuals from the organized oppressive elements of government and from those who wish to subjugate the rights of others. [For a more complete examination of the relationship between the individual and the state, see Charles Asbury, *Programmed Learning Aid for Basic Facts on the Relationship of the Individual to the State* (Homewood, Ill.: Learning Systems Co., 1975).]

The Bill of Rights for all citizens is found in the first ten amendments of the Constitution of the United States. Specifically, they include the right of freedom of speech and religion, the right of personal privacy, the right to a speedy and impartial trial, the rights of due process of law, and the rights of bail and fair and reasonable punishment for crimes.

These constitutional provisions were written to protect the rights of citizens, in terms of what were felt to be threats to the citizen's rights in the late 1700s. Since that time the courts have extended the definition and specification of rights to include the right to equal educational and occupational opportunity; the right to have legal services provided for indigents; the right to vote and to be treated as a person even though an individual may be receiving public assistance, be imprisoned or institutionalized (in mental hospitals), or conscripted in the military; and the right to personal privacy in the home and freedom from unreasonable governmental investigation.

Answer frame 3[18]

1. False. There is still considerable debate over whether the elitist or pluralist model of power is most appropriate for the American society.
2. False. The concept of countervailing power is a pluralist concept, whereby opposing power groups always arise to challenge any excessive consolidation of power.
3. False. Elitists would believe that the voters are rarely allowed the opportunity to participate in governmental decisions.
4. True. Power groups often determine whether the social problem will be resolved or simply ignored.

If you missed any of the above, reread Frame 3[18] before beginning Chapter 19 on page 123.

Frame 1[19] continued

The doctrine favoring individual rights over governmental rights arises from the Jeffersonian philosophy that the people are the ultimate repository of truth and virtue in society, and if only given a chance, the wisdom of the people will defeat error, and truth and justice will eventually triumph. Thus the protection of the rights of the individual is paramount to the protection of the government.

Another fundamental basis of American democracy is granting the minority the right of protest against the majority, as long as the minority does not practice revolution or overthrow of the government. Under this doctrine the majority group in society must allow the political or social minority groups the right to protest and persuade and to set forth their views, while the minority groups must forfeit any acts of violence or revolution that threaten or overthrow the government. It is the obligation of the government to protect the rights of the individual against larger organizations (even the government itself); however, from the point of view of most civil libertarians, this is a duty and obligation that is constantly eroded by the machinery of bureaucracy. Large corporations and vested interest groups tend to accumulate power in the American society and tend to enforce their will over the rights of the citizens. Thus the protection of civil rights and liberties is a constant battle through time.

The forces of social change are constantly creating new challenges for civil libertarians to defend. The growth of bureaucracy in an industrialized society imposes new rules and regulations that impinge upon individual freedoms and privileges. Bureaucracy is necessary in a complex society as it is the only means through which large-scale organizations can operate in a mass society. However, each new regulation calls into question some particular personal right—should the Internal Revenue Service have the right to search personal records? Should credit bureaus provide for a fee personal and intimate information to creditors who request it, but deny the same information to the person involved? And should the military (which is supposed to protect the people from foreign invasion) photograph and compile dossiers on domestic student demonstrators who are not even in the ROTC?

With each period of growth in size, complexity, or organization in our modern society, the problem of the protection of basic civil liberties becomes more acute.

Indicate whether each of the following statements is true or false by writing "T" or "F" in the space provided.

_____ 1. The American political process is based upon the principle that people exist to serve the government.

_____ 2. The Jeffersonian philosophy suggests that the people are the ultimate repository of truth and justice in society.

_____ 3. A basic principle of American democracy is that the rights of the minority to protest must always be protected.
_____ 4. The growth of bureaucracy tends to limit individual freedoms.

Now turn to Answer frame 1¹⁹ on page 126 to check your answers.

Frame 2¹⁹

There are easily hundreds, if not thousands, of issues which involve or threaten the civil liberties of the people in America. Some of the more cogent issues are discussed below.

The legal system. The enforcement of the law is a never-ending problem. America has so many laws and regulations that only a very few of the rules can be enforced with regularity. The question becomes "What purpose should the law serve?"

One purpose of the law and police is to detain those who habitually or negligibly violate the normative principles of the American society. Another purpose to protect the rights of the larger majority from subjugation or exploitation by lawless minorities. It is difficult at times to identify the greater good for the majority.

Law enforcement agencies, like firemen with fire prevention programs, would like to practice *preventive detention,* or arresting and "detaining" the presumed criminal before he commits the crime. However, such practices run the risk of equating the simple thought of the crime with the commission of the crime itself. Although this may be correct for some criminally-oriented persons, this judgment cannot be reasonably extended to the general population—many people upon one occasion or another have embodied fleeting fantasies of murdering a particularly obnoxious person or committing the perfect robbery. But for most persons rational judgment prevails over impulsive emotion. History shows that wherever police have had the power of preventative detention, presumably to protect people from criminals, they have always used this power to punish dissent and protect the rulers from the people. Nor can a person who conscientiously objects to a governmental policy be assumed to be a potential traitor, nor can a citizen's home legally be searched on the basis of *possible* cause. By these criteria, almost every person in America would qualify for some degree of preventive detention for contemplating some crime or another. Again, the guiding principles behind the protection of civil liberties is the enforcement of the law for the greatest good of the majority without transgressing the "inalienable rights" of the individual.

The freedom of information and the press. If one accepts the Jeffersonian ideal that the government exists to serve the people, then any actions it takes or policies it develops should be for the actual benefit of the people, and not simply to facilitate the administration of government or to benefit special interests. It is necessary at times for administrators or officials to withhold information to facilitate planning or administration. On the other hand, it is something else to deny information to prevent public accountability for administrative decisions.

In America, the press has assumed the role of watchdog over governmental action and public interests. The press is granted the same basic freedoms and liberties as the citizenry, and it is given the responsibility of representing the minority view without censorship or restraint.

Every president from Washington to Nixon has publicly defended the right of a free press (it is their constitutional duty to do so), yet many presidents have toyed with repressive constraints upon the press when they felt the sting of criticism. Many presidents have had their own embarrassments to conceal, and have sought to "bend" the principle that political interests must not supersede the public's interest. The Nixon-Agnew attack upon the mass media differed from those of other administrations in that it was vastly more extensive, concerted, and successful, in blunting media criticism. [See Benjamin H. Bagdikian, "The Fruits of Agnewism," *Columbia Journalism Review,* January/February 1973, pp. 9–23.] From the civil liber-

Answer frame 1[19]

1. False. The principle of American democracy is that the *government exists to serve the people,* not vice versa.
2. True. Jefferson opposed the development of big government, as it tends to usurp power from the people.
3. True. A principle of American democracy is that the minority's right to protest must be protected, as long as they refrain from attempts to overthrow the government.
4. True. Bureaucracy tends to create new rules and laws which often restrict personal freedoms.

If you missed any of the above, reread Frame 1[19] before starting Frame 2[19] on page 125.

Frame 2[19] continued

tarian point of view, the maintenance and protection of a free and unrestrained press is necessary for the protection of a free society.

A second dimension of the above problem is the individual's right to the content of information that various agencies hold on him. Credit bureaus compile mountains of intimate data about nearly every person in America, yet citizens are only allowed a limited privilege of directly inspecting or correcting the information themselves. The Internal Revenue Service is not required to divulge all their methods of decision making in auditing tax returns, nor can a citizen acquire a complete copy of FBI data sheets of himself. All of these issues have been the subject of civil liberties investigation and remain as potential social problems for the future.

Indicate whether each of the following statements is true or false by writing "T" or "F" in the space provided.

_____ 1. Preventive detention is a practical means to eliminate criminality in society.
_____ 2. Civil libertarians believe that the protection of a free press must be maintained to protect the rights of citizens.
_____ 3. In practice, all citizens have the right to any information that governmental agencies compile.

Now turn to Answer frame 2[19] on page 128 to check your answers.

Frame 3[19]

Political extremism poses one of the greatest threats to the protection of civil liberties. By definition, extremists do not rely upon persuasion, but attempt to impose their own views upon the society, and usually at some sacrifice of the rights of the rest of the population. Thus, the study of political extremist groups is central to the study of the problem of civil liberties.

Political groups are perhaps best explained by placing them along a continuum from right to left. *Rightist groups* tend to be reactionary in their political philosophy, to resist social change in society, to be nationalistic, authoritarian, less permissive, and hold a high faith in individualism. *Leftist groups* generally seek the overthrow of capitalist society, and replacement with a socialist equalitarian society in which all inequalities of race, class, or sex are eliminated. Intermediate between these polar extremes are the *conservatives,* who admit to the need for modest reforms only, and the *liberals*, who promote more sweeping reforms within the pattern of the existing capitalist society.

Political extremists on both sides tend to fancy themselves as embattled defenders of freedom and justice, assailed from all directions by the minions of evil. Extremists tend to reject reason, intellectuality, and objectivity in favor of faith and loyalty, and reject conventional means of achieving political action or reform. Their extremism leads them to distrust the current political establishment and the established social institutions, and often they see violence as the only feasible means to implement the transformation to their ideal of society.

The numerous groups along both political dimensions may total 2,000 or more in number. The vast majority are small one-horse operations (only a few members and a printing machine) and are limited in their impact to local communities or regions. Rightist groups tend to be anticommunist, antisocialist, and highly nationalistic. They are prone to such statements as "America first . . . ," "America, love it or leave it," stress rigid obedience to programs of law in society, and profess a stringent personal morality. Their philosophy emphasizes the work ethic (usually along with the spirit of capitalism), and condemns progressive programs for welfare, public assistance, or any governmental involvement in private enterprise.

The "responsible right" seeks reactionary goals, but uses legitimate political processes in seeking them, while the "radical right" is less squeamish in its choice of means. Clearly among the radical right are the Minutemen, whose extremism has pushed them to arm themselves with M–16s, antitank guns, mines, grenades, and other explosives (which are illegal in a democratic society) to be prepared for the *expected* invasion of America. Such groups see the government as continually being weakened by antidemocratic forces and anticipate the need to initiate an armed overthrow of the government for its own protection. Needless to say, these groups are regularly monitored by the FBI and other governmental agencies as they are seen to present a threat to the maintenance of the government in its established form.

The largest and most influential rightist group is the John Birch Society, although whether it belongs to the "responsible" or the "radical" right can be debated. The members of the John Birch Society share the rightist conviction that the communists are overrunning the world and that the United States is infested with traitors, but they generally adhere to normal political processes in pursuing the society's goals.

Among the leftists, the "Old Left" represents late 19th and early 20th century radicalism which variously may include elements of Marxism, democratic socialism, and in some instances, anarchism. Marxists and socialists seek to "return the government to the people" by nationalizing all the major industries and instituting a cradle-to-grave program of services. They see the competition and inequality inspired by capitalism as the cancer that will destroy humanity, and they seek to implement widespread reforms to create a new "equalitarian" society. Since the Russian Revolution, the Old Left in the United States has been dominated by the Communist Party of the United States.

The more recent "New Left" found much of its ideological basis within the Old Left movement, but added utopian social and esthetic values to the movement. The New Left seeks political revolution (either violent or nonviolent) to achieve a quasi-utopian society that would be devoid of the oppressive elements of big business, bureaucracy, and the military-industrial complex. It seeks the highest ideals of permissiveness and individualism, as exemplified by popular slogans and placards featuring "love," daisies, and "doing your own thing."

The most prominent New Left group, the Students for a Democratic Society (SDS), was born from the radicalism of the late 1960s. College campuses exploded as a 60 percent increase of the student population, the product of World War II's "baby boom," entered colleges and universities. The movement fed upon the growing abhorrence of the Vietnam War, the oppression of the military-industrial complex, and the questionable ethics of big government, and sought to recreate society along the equalitarian-permissive lines of a gigantic "Summerhill."

The ending of the Vietnam War, the gradual passing of the war babies past the tragic age of 30, and a general emergence of political and

Answer frame 2[19]

1. False. Preventive detention implies the equating of the thought of the crime to the commission of the crime itself, and if all persons who ever *thought* of committing crimes were detained, most people would be imprisoned.
2. True. The press serves as a watchdog over government, and it often is the people's only source of information about governmental actions.
3. False. Although in principle all citizens have the right to any information governmental agencies compile about them, in practice much personal information is withheld and not available to citizens.

If you missed any of the above, reread Frame 2[19] before starting Frame 3[19] on page 126.

Frame 3[19] continued

economic conservatism inspired by the reelection of President Nixon weakened the New Left movement so that now only its former shell remains.

Political extremism of all types tends to threaten the protection of civil liberties of the population, as the different groups attempt to impose their ideology upon the larger population. In practice, both leftist and rightist movements tend to be equally oppressive, although in different directions. They both seek to subjugate the rights of persons to the goals of the movement. Thus the protection of the civil rights and liberties of all people is a never-ending battle that will even become more important in the future as people seek an even greater level of individualism in modern society.

An emergent issue: "freedom from" and "freedom for." The historic civil liberties issues were mainly concerned with establishing the individual's right to noninterference. Freedom of speech, of press, of religion, of assembly, and so on were basically the right to be let alone—to proceed with one's activities without interference from others. Protecting these freedoms, and determining just when and how they must be limited in the interest of the freedom of others—this is an enduring question.

In recent years, a strong demand has arisen, mainly from liberal and leftist groups, for a recognition of the right to make demands upon others. It is asserted that society should recognize each person's right to demand a minimum income, a decent house, medical care, and so on, all to be provided at public expense. Some leftists assert a "right to economic and status equality" as the primary civil right, without which all others are empty and hypocritical.

This right to make demands upon others is not entirely new. The question arose more than a century ago, when tax monies began to be used for free public education. Just how many goods and services a free society must provide its less affluent citizens, at the expense of the rest of its citizens, is likely to remain one of our most bitter public controversies.

There are many other civil rights and liberties issues which this brief chapter cannot treat —including the right of privacy, to control the use of one's own body, to use drugs; the rights of women, children, aliens, convicts, the mentally ill; and many others. A full discussion of the liberties and rights of Americans requires an entire volume. [See Norman Dorsen (ed.), *The Rights of Americans: What They Are—What They Should Be* (New York: Random House, 1971).]

Indicate whether each of the following statements is true or false by writing "T" or "F" in the space provided.

_____ 1. Political extremist groups generally rely upon persuasion to institute their philosophy in society.

_____ 2. Political extremists usually reject reason and objectivity in achieving political action or reform.

_____ 3. Both rightist and leftist groups seek a complete change in the nature of the social order.

_____ 4. Rightest groups tend to favor the trend toward greater permissiveness in society.

Now turn to Answer frame 3[19] on page 130 to check your answers.

Answer frame 3[19]

1. False. Extremist groups usually rely upon force or subversion to institute their views in society, largely because their attempts at persuasion have failed.
2. True. Political extremists usually are blindly convinced of their cause, and are rarely responsive to arguments of reason or objectivity about their movement.
3. True. Both groups seek to reorganize the social order; they differ only in the nature of the reordering.
4. False. It is the moderate left groups that favor a greater degree of permissiveness in society; rightists groups generally oppose permissiveness.

If you missed any of the above, reread Frame 3[19] before working Examination 6 on page 143.

Examination 1—Chapters 1–3

CHAPTER 1

1. A social problem exists:
   a. When a particular group is concerned about the problem.
   b. Only when experts state that a social problem exists.
   c. When there is widespread consensus among the people that the problem exists.
   d. All of the above.
2. All undesirable conditions in society will be recognized as social problems.
   a. True.
   b. False.
3. According to the text, which of the following statements are correct?
   a. Social problems exist in primitive societies as well as modern societies.
   b. People readily agree about the selection of current social problems.
   c. Once a social problem is defined, it is permanent.
   d. All of the above.
   e. None of the above.
4. Modern social scientists tend to view social problems as pathogenic or diseased elements of society.
   a. True.
   b. False.
5. Once a majority of the population agree that a social problem exists, it will not change until there is a major reorganization of society.
   a. True.
   b. False.
6. To be "ethically neutral" and "value-free" means:
   a. That social scientists cannot hold values.
   b. That social scientists reject all the values of other people.
   c. That scientists try not to let their personal values influence or contaminate their research or analysis.
   d. None of the above.
7. Fuller and Myers define three stages of growth of social problems, which are:
   a. _____
   b. _____
   c. _____
8. The three major forms of change in society are:
   a. _____
   b. _____
   c. _____
9. Social problems usually involve (objective; subjective) _____ interpretations of (objective, subjective) _____ conditions.
10. The scientific method for the analysis of social problems is:
    a. _____
    b. _____
    c. _____
    d. _____
    e. _____

131

CHAPTER 2

1. Cultural integration refers to:
   a. The integration of organizations in society.
   b. The integration of racial groups in society.
   c. The integration of norms and values of a culture.
   d. None of the above.
2. Social disorganization refers to:
   a. Socially inept people.
   b. The disorganization of government and organizations.
   c. The lack of integration of norms and values in society.
   d. All of the above.
3. Cultural lag refers to the inability of technology to keep pace with social change.
   a. True.
   b. False.
4. A culture consists of _____.
5. A society consists of _____.
6. An institution is _____.
7. The three types of norms are known as:
   a. _____
   b. _____
   c. _____
8. Status acquired through one's own effort is known as _____ status, while a status that is unalterable by the person is known as _____ status.
9. Social, cultural, and technological change (increases; decreases) _____ the extent of cultural integration of society.
10. Social change tends to (increase; decrease) _____ the extent of social disorganization of society.

CHAPTER 3

1. Social disorganization and reorganization are continuous processes in all modern societies.
   a. True.
   b. False.
2. Social disorganization in society tends to produce personal disorganization among people.
   a. True.
   b. False.
3. The greater the complexity of a society:
   a. The greater the number of value conflicts.
   b. The smaller the number of value conflicts.
   c. The complexity of society is not related to the number of value conflicts.
4. Everyone is equally bothered or disturbed about the different value conflicts in society.
   a. True.
   b. False.
5. In comparing the value conflict and social conflict perspectives:
   a. The value conflict theorist seeks harmony in society while the social conflict theorist does not.
   b. The value conflict theorist focuses upon cultural values, while the social conflict theorist focuses upon conflicting interest groups in society.
   c. The social conflict theorist views conflict as abnormal and undesirable, while the value conflict theorist does not.
   d. None of the above.
6. Conflict is always undesirable in society and serves no useful purpose.
   a. True.
   b. False.
7. From the personal deviation perspective, people become deviant when they:
   a. Fail to follow accepted norms.
   b. Fail to accept the preferred norms.
   c. Join deviant groups.
   d. All of the above.
   e. a. and b. above.
8. Deviance can result when:
   a. A person attempts to achieve a position that is inconsistent with his ascribed status.
   b. An expected status is not fulfilled.
   c. When a person attempts to fulfill status expectations that are inconsistent.
   d. All of the above.

9. The labeling theorist:
   a. States that the deviant is anyone the group labels as deviant.
   b. Focuses upon the group applying the label, rather than the deviant person.
   c. Labels all deviants as moral degenerates.
   d. a. and b. above.
   e. All of the above.
10. List the five key questions in using the social disorganization approach to social problems.
    a. _____
    b. _____
    c. _____
    d. _____
    e. _____
11. List the four key questions in using the value conflict approach to social problems.
    a. _____
    b. _____
    c. _____
    d. _____
12. List the four key questions in using the value social conflict to social problems.
    a. _____
    b. _____
    c. _____
    d. _____
13. List the four key questions in using the value personal deviation to social problems.
    a. _____
    b. _____
    c. _____
    d. _____

Now check your answers with those on page 146.

Examination 2—Chapters 4–6

CHAPTER 4

1. Match the traits that characterize the *traditional* family in America.
   a. _____
   b. _____
   c. _____
   d. _____
   e. _____

   1. Small and independent.
   2. Large and extended.
   3. Patriarchal authority.
   4. Equalitarian authority.
   5. Family centered.
   6. Person-child centered.
   7. Marriage from necessity.
   8. Marriage from desire.
   9. Children are a luxury.
   10. Children are an economic asset.

2. Match the above traits that characterize the *modern* family in America.
   a. _____
   b. _____
   c. _____
   d. _____
   e. _____

3. In the traditional family, patriarchal rule predominated because:
   a. Men were natural born leaders.
   b. Men were usually better educated.
   c. The role and position of men reinforced their being head of the family.
   d. a. and b. above.
   e. b. and c. above.

4. Industrialization and urbanization in America caused:
   a. A redefinition of male-female roles.
   b. A redefinition of the role of children.
   c. A decline in patriarchal authority.
   d. The demise of the extended family.
   e. All of the above.

5. The change in female roles in the modern family is encouraged by:
   a. Women holding jobs and earning more money.
   b. Women assuming a greater role in home decisions.
   c. Men working in industry and away from the home.
   d. All of the above.
   e. None of the above.

6. The increased experimentation with alternate lifestyles among youth indicates that the marriage institution is dying.
   a. True.
   b. False.

7. The increasing divorce rate in modern society indicates that:
   a. People no longer respect marriage.
   b. Modern values favor individualism and personal satisfaction.
   c. Modern society is becoming more immoral.
   d. Religious institutions are no longer effective.

8. The major reason for marriage has always been "love."
   a. True.
   b. False.

9. Average family size has decreased in the modern family because:
   a. Greater emphasis is being placed upon personal development.
   b. Children are more expensive to rear and care for today.
   c. The function that children perform in traditional families has changed.
   d. There is less need for children in industrialized societies.
   e. All of the above.

10. Elders and grandparents perform a diminishing role in the modern family because:
    a. They are no longer capable of assisting young families.
    b. They chose to be separate.
    c. Modern cultural values no longer support the extended family.
    d. All of the above.

CHAPTER 5

1. Male roles tend to be (instrumental; expressive) _____, while female roles are more _____ _____ in the American society.

2. In most societies, the female's status is a direct product of the status of the work she does.
   a. True.
   b. False.

3. Sociologically, a child can learn both female and male sex roles, depending upon which role set the child is taught.
   a. True.
   b. False.

4. Sociologically, expressive sex roles are undesirable and unnecessary in society.
   a. True.
   b. False.

5. The concept of androgynous sex roles means:
   a. Abandoning *all* sex roles.
   b. Abandoning all sex roles except those required by biological differences.
   c. Teaching men to be more tolerant of women's needs.
   d. All of the above.

6. List the factors that are responsible for the changing role and status of women in the American society:
   a. _____
   b. _____
   c. _____

7. The core of support for the women's liberation movement comes from:
   a. Females of a racial minority.
   b. Semi-professional females.
   c. Highly successful females in high prestige positions.
   d. Females who are dissatisfied with their current role and status, regardless of the level of prestige.

8. Although the women's liberation movement is amusing and sometimes distressing to men in the American society, it really is not affecting male roles much.
   a. True.
   b. False.

CHAPTER 6

1. Two major differences between youth and adults in America mentioned in the text are:
   a. _____
   b. _____

2. The educational system has functioned to accentuate differences between youth and adults in America.
   a. True.
   b. False.

3. A college education tends to create common ground for communication between most youth and adults.
   a. True.
   b. False.

4. Youth roles in the American society:
   a. Are often unclear and poorly specified.
   b. Are often contradictory and inconsistent.
   c. Often are neither adult roles or child roles.
   d. All of the above.

5. Since most youth feel that their parents are outdated, they learn little from their parents.

Examination 2—chapters 4–6

    a. True.
    b. False.

6. Whereas the periods of Consciousness I and II were adult oriented, Charles Reich suggests that Consciousness III is more youth oriented.
    a. True.
    b. False.

7. A sociological analysis of youth in America would suggest that:
    a. The irresponsibility of youth is finally being institutionalized.
    b. Consciousness III is a direct effect of industrialization and modernization.
    c. Youth are taking over today's society.
    d. Youth reject anything that is adult oriented today.

8. The American society is becoming more youth oriented.
    a. True.
    b. False.

9. According to Moynihan, the social factors that created the period of revolt in the 1960s were:
    a. _____
    b. _____

10. The age of revolt of the 1960s has passed and left no significant effect upon the American culture.
    a. True.
    b. False.

Now check your answers with those on page 147.

Examination 3—Chapters 7-9

CHAPTER 7

1. Smaller groups always possess less power than larger groups.
   a. True.
   b. False.
2. Which of the following produce physical and intelligence differences among the races?
   a. Genetic inheritance.
   b. Anatomical specialization.
   c. Diet and climate.
   d. b. and c. above.
   e. All of the above.
3. Most people are able to ignore the factor of social distance and accept all nationalities equally.
   a. True.
   b. False.
4. List five characteristics of prejudice in people:
   a. _____
   b. _____
   c. _____
   d. _____
   e. _____
5. Although people vary in the number of prejudices that they hold, everyone holds some prejudices against some groups.
   a. True.
   b. False.
6. People cannot be prejudiced against people or groups that they have never met.
   a. True.
   b. False.
7. Governments and organizations often attempt to inspire prejudices against other groups.
   a. True.
   b. False.
8. Once a prejudice is created in a person, it cannot be changed.
   a. True.
   b. False.
9. Two methods for reducing prejudices among people are:
   a. _____
   b. _____
10. Inequality among groups is the major cause of prejudices.
    a. True.
    b. False.

CHAPTER 8

1. Describe Myrdal's concept of "the vicious circle of discrimination."
   _____
   _____
2. Stereotypes usually tell more about the class standing of the ascribers, than the class of the group being stereotyped.
   a. True.
   b. False.
3. Middle-class blacks are likely to hold considerably different attitudes than middle-class whites.
   a. True.
   b. False.

138   Examination 3—chapters 7–9

4. Deferred gratification means:
   a. To plan toward retirement.
   b. To invest in education.
   c. To compile savings and investments.
   d. All of the above.
   e. None of the above.

5. Which of the following modes of adaptation is characteristic of acculturation:
   a. The minority group accepts and adjusts to a subservient status.
   b. The minority group adopts and internalizes the new culture.
   c. Both minority and majority groups are merged into a new culture.
   d. Minority and majority groups coexist side-by-side with equal power.

6. Which of the above modes of adaptation is characteristic of pluralism?
   _____

7. Which of the above modes of adaptation is characteristic of integration?
   _____

8. Which of the following groups is least likely to be assimilated into a dominant culture?
   a. Racial groups.
   b. Religious groups.
   c. Ethnic groups.
   d. Nationalist groups.

9. According to the theory on structural and attitudinal change presented, would it be true or false to make the following statement: "You can tell me what to do, but you can't make me change my attitude!"
   a. True.
   b. False.

10. The goal of most blacks in America is to be integrated.
    a. True.
    b. False.

CHAPTER 9

1. The two definitions of poverty are based upon:
   a. _____
   b. _____

2. The poor are easily ignored because:
   a. They are largely invisible.
   b. Definitions of poverty vary, creating uncertainty as to the number of poor.
   c. What is judged an adequate income in one region, may not be in another region.
   d. All of the above.

3. The sociological perspective would suggest that poverty is the poor people's own creation.
   a. True.
   b. False.

4. For the most part, the government spends more on technological and physical development than on aid to the poor.
   a. True.
   b. False.

5. Systemic factors that enhance poverty in America are:
   a. _____
   b. _____
   c. _____

6. Basic causes of poverty are:
   a. Unemployment.
   b. People refusing to work.
   c. Racial minorities.
   d. All of the above.
   e. None of the above.

7. Once a person starts on welfare, they are unlikely to ever get off it voluntarily.
   a. True.
   b. False.

8. The state of poverty in America cannot be changed without widespread institutional and structural change.
   a. True.
   b. False.

9. Most poverty-stricken people have learned to adjust to their station in life and do not aspire to achieve middle class standing.
   a. True.
   b. False.

10. The theory of the culture of poverty was proposed by _____.

Now check your answers with those on page 147.

Examination 4—Chapters 10–12

CHAPTER 10

1. The definition of deviance is: _____

2. People commit deviant acts because:
   a. They lack self-control.
   b. Some people are basically immoral.
   c. The deviant persons have come to view the behavior as desirable.
   d. None of the above.

3. Widespread deviance tends to produce social disorganization in society.
   a. True.
   b. False.

4. The sociological perspective of deviance would suggest that the major cause of deviance in society is:
   a. A lack of religious commitment among the population.
   b. The degeneration of society itself.
   c. Psychological abnormalities.
   d. Social change.

5. Anomie is defined as: _____

6. The processes involved in learning to commit a deviant act are:
   a. _____
   b. _____
   c. _____

7. It is drinking that produces alcoholism, and cultural values have little influence.
   a. True.
   b. False.

8. The sexual revolution of the 1970s is destroying the marriage and family institutions.
   a. True.
   b. False.

9. Given the right situation, such as long term deprivation of heterosexual opportunity, a major portion of people will try a homosexual experience.
   a. True.
   b. False.

10. Research shows that pornography causes moral degeneration of the person.
    a. True.
    b. False.

CHAPTER 11

1. Is it true or false to assert that "the more laws a society has, the more crime it will have."
   a. True.
   b. False.

2. Laws are based upon absolute principles and do not change with time and situation.
   a. True.
   b. False.

3. Cheating on income tax and "liberating" office supplies is known as:
   a. Situational crime.
   b. White collar crime.
   c. Organized crime.
   d. Psychopathic crime.

4. Psychopathic criminals are the major threat to law and order in society.
   a. True.
   b. False.

5. Organized crime in America is purely an Italian or Sicilian invention.

140 Examination 4—chapters 10–12

    a. True.
    b. False.
6. Organized crime could not function if "honest and proper" people did not patronize its services.
    a. True.
    b. False.
7. Criminal arrest rates provide a good indication of the amount of crime in society.
    a. True.
    b. False.
8. Rural areas show less crime than urban areas, because of:
    a. The high anonymity of rural people.
    b. The high observability of rural people.
    c. The high heterogeneity of rural people.
    d. Actually, rural crime rates are higher than urban rates.
9. The lower class in America show higher arrest rates than the middle class because:
    a. The lower class is more criminal.
    b. The lower class commits the crimes that are most likely to result in arrest.
    c. The lower class are more visible.
    d. The lower class are less capable of defending themselves once they are apprehended.
    e. All of the above except a.
10. People of all social classes have approximately the same criminal potential.
    a. True.
    b. False.

CHAPTER 12

1. Research indicates that criminal tendency is produced by an extra Y chromosome.
    a. True.
    b. False.
2. Which of the following theories would suggest that persons learn criminal patterns in the same way that they learn proper behavior?
    a. Merton's goals-means theory.
    b. Sutherland's theory of differential association.
    c. Delinquent subcultures.
    d. Control theory.
3. Which of the above theories would suggest that persons commit criminal acts because they are denied legitimate opportunities to achieve success and wealth in society?
    a. b. c. d.
4. Which of the above theories would suggest that persons become criminal because they are born and live in a crime-ridden community?
    a. b. c. d.
5. Sutherland would suggest that most hardened criminals have rejected the middle class values for wealth, comfort, and pleasure in life.
    a. True.
    b. False.
6. The more highly integrated a person is into the social order, the less likelihood of criminal conduct.
    a. True.
    b. False.
7. Membership in a delinquent subculture can be rewarding as it provides an alternate status system and reward structure for youth that are not accepted into the larger society.
    a. True.
    b. False.
8. The effectiveness of punishment in determining criminal conduct is dependent upon:
    a. _____
    b. _____
9. As the American society becomes more industrialized and urbanized, the rate of criminality is likely to:
    a. Increase.
    b. Decrease.
10. The current system of imprisonment and punishment in America is based upon philosophy established in England and Europe in the 17th century.
    a. True.
    b. False.

Now check your answers with those on page 148.

Examination 5—Chapters 13–15

CHAPTER 13

1. List the three major functions that religion serves for people (according to Malinowski):
   a. _____
   b. _____
   c. _____
2. The social function of religion in America has:
   a. Increased.
   b. Decreased.
3. The educational function of religion in America has:
   a. Increased.
   b. Decreased.
4. The major sources of change in the institution of religion in America was caused by:
   a. Industrialization.
   b. Urbanization.
   c. Modernization.
   d. All of the above.
   e. None of the above—people just have less need for religion today.
5. What is meant by "situational ethics"? _____
6. Protestant churches in America are more (church-centered; individual-centered) _____ _____, while Catholic and Jewish churches are more _____ centered.
7. What is the "protestant ethic"? _____
8. Fundamentalist religions today support scientism, while modernist religions prefer a literal interpretation of the Bible.
   a. True.
   b. False.
9. Youthful charismatics appear to be returning to fundamentalistic or pentacostalistic tenents of religion.
   a. True.
   b. False.
10. Most religions appear to be constantly evolving. List the three stages of the process.
    a. _____
    b. _____
    c. _____

CHAPTER 14

1. The three major philosophies of education in America are:
   a. _____
   b. _____
   c. _____
2. Which of the educational philosophies emphasized the social and mental development of the whole person for a successful career in life?
   _____
3. Which educational philosophy would allow free personal choice of curriculum and substantive content in courses?
   _____
4. The system of education in America has been quite effective in removing inequality among groups.
   a. True.
   b. False.

5. To "deschool" society means to:
   a. _____
   b. _____
6. The free school movement is becoming so popular that your author would predict that it will soon replace the conventional educational system.
   a. True.
   b. False.
7. Aside from a few discontents, people basically agree upon the preferred philosophy of education for American schools.
   a. True.
   b. False.
8. List the major problems in the administration and operation of the schools as described in the text.
   a. _____
   b. _____
   c. _____
9. Most small communities desire local control and decentralization of the schools, but wish the advantages of state and federal financing and the economies of centralization.
   a. True.
   b. False.
10. Your author would predict that the public schools will return to local financing.
    a. True.
    b. False.

CHAPTER 15

1. List the three major factors in the world's population problem:
   a. _____
   b. _____
   c. _____
2. Fertility refers to the total number of children a woman is capable of producing in her lifetime.
   a. True.
   b. False.
3. The sex ratio is fixed by nature and not subject to change with different age groups.
   a. True.
   b. False.
4. Whereas in agrarian societies the total population of a society is primarily determined by the amount of farmable land, in technological societies the total population is mostly dependent upon _____ _____.
5. Currently the United States has a smooth pyramidal age structure while undeveloped nations have an unbalanced age pyramid.
   a. True.
   b. False.
6. Although land and resources are important, the population growth is primarily determined by cultural values.
   a. True.
   b. False.
7. Name the theory that suggests that "in industrialized nations, a change in cultural values eventually cause a reduction in the birthrate."
   _____
8. Large families are necessary in agrarian societies, but are less necessary in industrialized societies.
   a. True.
   b. False.
9. In modern America, which of the following factors is applying the greatest pressure for population control?
   a. Food production.
   b. Living space.
   c. National income.
   d. Pollution and ecological pressures.
10. Your author predicts that the women's liberation movement will cause an immediate drop in the birthrate of America.
    a. True.
    b. False.

Now check your answers with the correct one on page 148.

Examination 6—Chapters 16–19

CHAPTER 16

1. Most early communities in America were carefully planned and designed by their founding fathers.
   a. True.
   b. False.
2. The small community with close intimate interpersonal relations that were based upon trust is known as the _____ _____ community, while the large community with secondary and formal relationships is known as the _____ _____ community.
3. Rural communities have high anonymity, which encourages a high degree of social control over people.
   a. True.
   b. False.
4. Urban communities are more:
   a. Homogeneous than rural communities.
   b. Heterogeneous than rural communities.
5. The major opponents of planning and zoning improvements are:
   a. Private homeowners.
   b. Small businessmen.
   c. Government officials.
   d. Vested interest groups.
6. A century of experience has proven that people are rational and self-restrained in planning and zoning if given the opportunity.
   a. True.
   b. False.
7. Which form of interpersonal relationships provide the greatest social control over people?
   a. Primary group relationships.
   b. Secondary group relationships.
8. As anonymity increases, observability:
   a. Increases.
   b. Decreases.
9. Personal deviation is greatest in:
   a. Rural areas.
   b. Urban areas.
10. Actions that increase the spirit of _____ _____ in urban communities would increase citizen involvement and create a greater degree of social control.

CHAPTER 17

1. The science of human ecology is _____ _____.
2. Two ecological impacts of forests and vegetation are:
   a. _____
   b. _____
3. Cities tend to improve the efficiency of nature in the use of its natural resources.
   a. True.
   b. False.
4. Monoculture is _____ _____.
5. Barry Commoner postulates four laws of nature, which are:
   a. _____
   b. _____

144   Examination 6—chapters 16–19

      c. _____
      d. _____
6. List four natural chemical cycles in nature.
    a. _____
    b. _____
    c. _____
    d. _____
7. Most of the earth's oxygen comes from algae in the _____.
8. Increased consumption of products today is largely a result of:
    a. Increased actual need.
    b. Changing levels of expectations.
    c. Gluttonous consumption.
9. Conspicuous consumption is _____.
10. It is the use of technology that has created all of the modern problems of ecology.
    a. True.
    b. False.

CHAPTER 18

1. Most social problems can also be analyzed from the perspective of interest groups in conflict.
    a. True.
    b. False.
2. The different types of interest groups are known as:
    a. _____
    b. _____
    c. _____
3. Vested interest groups are always organized to serve the public's interest.
    a. True.
    b. False.
4. Most legislators are opposed and leery of lobbyists.
    a. True.
    b. False.
5. List some of the functions (desirable services) served by interest groups in society.
    a. _____
    b. _____
    c. _____
    d. _____

6. List some of the dysfunctions (disorganizing services) served by interest groups in society.
    a. _____
    b. _____
    c. _____
    d. _____
7. Power and authority by fiat means: _____ _____.
8. The two major models of power are:
    a. _____
    b. _____
9. The concept which states that opposing power groups emerge to challenge existing power groups is known as _____ _____.
10. The elitist conception of power holds that the people decide the basic issues in government and society.
    a. True.
    b. False.

CHAPTER 19

1. Jefferson believed that if the government remained strong, it would protect the rights of the people.
    a. True.
    b. False.
2. According to the Constitution of the United States, the right of the minority is: _____ _____.
3. Preventive detention is a reliable rational approach to protecting the rights of citizens in America.
    a. True.
    b. False.
4. Since the press provides information to the public, governmental leaders genuinely support the free press.
    a. True.
    b. False.
5. Political extremism is as much a threat to the civil liberties of the people as governmental oppression.
    a. True.
    b. False.

6. Rightist political groups are more oppressive to individual civil liberties than leftist political groups.
   a. True.
   b. False.
7. The goal of most political liberals is to maintain the status quo in society.
   a. True.
   b. False.
8. Once a civil right is defined by the courts, it stands with little threat of change.
   a. True.
   b. False.
9. From the civil libertarian point of view, the government itself is one of the people's greatest threats to personal civil liberties.
   a. True.
   b. False.
10. Jefferson believed that if the issues were left to the people, they possessed the rationality to decide in their own best interest.
    a. True.
    b. False.

Now check your answers with the correct one on page 149.

Answers to Examinations

Examination 1 (Chapters 1–3)

Chapter 1

1. c.
2. False.
3. e.
4. False. Social problems are now viewed as normal and expected products of industrialized-complex societies.
5. False. Values change in society, and what is viewed as a social problem this year may not be next year.
6. c.
7. a. The development of awareness.
   b. The determination of policy.
   c. A period of reform.
8. a. Social change.
   b. Cultural change.
   c. Technological change.
9. a. Subjective.
   b. Objective.
10. a. Specify the problem.
    b. Plan the research design.
    c. Collect relevant data and information.
    d. Analyze the data.
    e. Draw conclusions that represent the data.

Chapter 2

1. c.
2. c.
3. False. Cultural lag refers to the inability of society to adapt to technological changes.
4. The complex whole of knowledge, beliefs, morals, norms, laws, customs, and values acquired by the people of a society.
5. All people who share a common culture.
6. A cluster of related norms and values centering around a major social concern. The most prominent social institutions are family, education, religion, government, and economy.
7. a. Folkways.
   b. Mores.
   c. Laws.
8. a. Achieved.
   b. Ascribed.
9. Decreases.
10. Increase.

Chapter 3

1. True.
2. True.
3. a.
4. False.
5. b.
6. False. Conflict is a source of social change and enhances group unity.
7. d.
8. d.
9. d.
10. a. What was the prior state of organization?
    b. What are the forces of change that created the conflict?
    c. How were the rules affected?
    d. What new norms need to be established to rectify the conflict?
    e. What will be the nature of the new state of organization?
11. a. What are the values in conflict?
    b. What groups are involved in the conflict?
    c. What value sacrifices are necessary to resolve the conflict?
    d. What group actions are necessary to resolve the conflict?
12. a. What are the groups in conflict?
    b. What are the differences in their goals?
    c. What actions are the groups taking?

Answers to examinations

      d. What will be the effect of the new power balance upon society?
13. a. What are the characteristics of the deviant behavior?
      b. How did the person come to be labeled as deviant?
      c. What is the reaction of the group to the deviant behavior?
      d. What are the alternatives available for dealing with the problem?

Examination 2 (Chapters 4–6)

Chapter 4

1. Responses 2, 3, 5, 7, 10.
2. Responses 1, 4, 6, 8, 9.
3. e.
4. e.
5. d.
6. False.
7. b.
8. False. In the traditional marriage, economic necessity encouraged people to marry.
9. e.
10. c.

Chapter 5

1. Instrumental.
   Expressive.
2. True.
3. True.
4. False. Expressive roles are very necessary in society, however, either sex can perform the role.
5. b.
6. a. Increased wealth and independence.
   b. Increased education for women.
   c. The assumption of more instrumental roles.
7. d.
8. False.

Chapter 6

1. a. Age-related.
   b. A product of status position and role expectations.
2. True.
3. False.
4. d.
5. False. Parents serve as role models for youth.
6. True.
7. b.
8. True.

9. a. Increased youth population.
   b. The concentration of youth into college campuses, the military, and communes.
10. False. The age of revolt produced a new youth intelligentsia.

Examination 3 (Chapters 7–9)

Chapter 7

1. False.
2. d.
3. False.
4. a. Prejudices are learned.
   b. Prejudices are learned from other people, not the groups who are the subject of the prejudice.
   c. Prejudices are assigned to groups, not individuals.
   d. Prejudices are unconscious and exist because they are satisfying.
   e. Prejudices can be created or dissolved.
5. True.
6. False.
7. True.
8. False.
9. a. Increase equal-status contact between the groups.
   b. Create superordinate goals to unify the groups.
10. False.

Chapter 8

1. Discrimination in employment creates discrimination in housing, which creates discrimination in education, which finally increases discrimination in employment. (Responses may be in any order.)
2. True.
3. False.
4. d.
5. b.
6. e.
7. c.
8. a.
9. False.
10. False. Most would prefer pluralism.

Chapter 9

1. a. Fixed income.
   b. Relative need.
2. d.
3. False.

148 Answers to examinations

4. True.
5. a. Technological unemployment.
   b. Inflation.
   c. Social inequality.
6. e.
7. False.
8. True.
9. False.
10. Oscar Lewis.

Examination 4 (Chapters 10–12)

Chapter 10

1. Behavior that does not conform with conventional norms.
2. c.
3. True.
4. d.
5. Feelings of alienation, estrangement, and uncertainty.
6. a. Learning the technique and acquiring the skill.
   b. Learning the attitudes which support the act.
   c. Defining the result as desirable and worth repeating.
7. False.
8. False.
9. True.
10. False.

Chapter 11

1. True.
2. False.
3. b.
4. False.
5. False.
6. True.
7. False.
8. b.
9. e.
10. True.

Chapter 12

1. False.
2. b.
3. a.
4. c.
5. False.
6. True.
7. True.
8. a. The degree of commitment to the criminal pattern.
   b. The likelihood of arrest for the crime.
9. a.
10. True.

Examination 5 (Chapters 13–15)

Chapter 13

1. a. Contingency.
   b. Powerlessness.
   c. Scarcity.
2. b.
3. b.
4. d.
5. That the right or wrong of a particular act should be determined by the nature of the situation.
6. Individual-centered.
   Church-centered.
7. A set of agrarian-based values emphasizing hard work, thrift, clean living, achievement, and personal responsibility for one's own conduct.
8. False.
9. True.
10. a. Fragmentation.
    b. Decentralization into cults.
    c. Recentralization into a new religious ideology.

Chapter 14

1. a. Elitism.
   b. Pragmatism.
   c. Eclecticism.
2. Pragmatism.
3. Eclecticism.
4. False.
5. a. Remove the formal system of education.
   b. Replace it with personalized instruction in a free school setting.
6. False.
7. False.
8. a. Financing.
   b. Local control versus state and federal financing.
   c. Centralization versus decentralization.
9. True.
10. False.

Chapter 15

1. a. Size and rate of growth.
   b. Age and sex composition.
   c. Distribution of population.
2. False. It is fecundity.
3. False.
4. The level of industrial production.
5. False.
6. True.
7. Demographic transition.
8. True.
9. d.
10. False.

Examination 6 (Chapters 16–19)

Chapter 16

1. False.
2. Gemeinschaft.
   Gesellschaft.
3. False. It is observability.
4. b.
5. d.
6. False.
7. a.
8. b.
9. b.
10. Neighborhood, or Community.

Chapter 17

1. The study of how people interact with and adapt to their environment.
2. a. Maintain rainfall.
   b. Provide a huge reservoir for water.
3. False.
4. The large-scale cultivation of a single specie of vegetation.
5. a. Everything in nature is connected to everything else.
   b. All chemical or natural elements in nature enter into the system somewhere.
   c. The forces of nature act to maintain a dynamic equilibrium.
   d. Nature is an intricate web of organization.
6. a. Water cycle.
   b. Carbon cycle.
   c. Nitrogen cycle.
   d. Carbon dioxide-oxygen cycle.
7. Ocean.
8. b.
9. Conspicuously displaying or consuming goods to enhance one's status.
10. False. It is the misuse of technology.

Chapter 18

1. True.
2. a. Special interest groups.
   b. Vested interest groups.
   c. Pressure groups.
3. False.
4. False.
5. a. Interest groups provide a focus for group interest and involvement.
   b. Interest groups unify people and create a sense of belongingness.
   c. Interest groups serve to focus public attention upon social issues.
   d. Interest groups may promote reform and social change.
6. a. Interest groups may seek their own interest over the public's interest.
   b. Interest groups may exploit their position of power.
   c. Interest groups often oppose constructive change in society.
   d. Interest groups may ignore the rights of others.
7. Power and authority is granted only by tacit approval of the majority of the people.
8. a. Elitism.
   b. Pluralism.
9. Countervailing power.
10. False.

Chapter 19

1. False.
2. To protest against the majority as long as the minority does not practice revolution or overthrow of the government.
3. False.
4. False.
5. True.
6. False.
7. False.
8. False.
9. True.
10. True.

Glossary/Index

A

Abortion, 26–27
Accelerative thrust of change, 12
Accommodation, defined, 49
Acculturation, defined, 49
Alcoholism, 63
American Dilemma (The), 47
Anatomical specialization—bodily changes in persons caused by environmental adaptation, 41
Androgynous sex roles—neuter roles that may be performed by either sex, 30
Anomie—widespread collective feelings of disorganization in society, 61
Anonymity—being anonymous, where few people know of your activities, 61, 72, 107
Antisemitism, 43
Assimilation—the process whereby persons or groups become culturally similar, 49–51
Authoritarianism—beliefs that favor complete subjection to authority.

B

Bandura, Albert, and Walters, Richard, 78
Becker, Howard, 19, 61
Bell, Daniel, 70
Blacks, 47–52
Blauner, Robert, 46
Bogardus, Emory, 42
Brown, Claude, 20, 77

C

Calvinist doctrine, 83
Calvinist movement, 83
Caudill, Harry, 53
Centralization of school administration, 93
Chauvinism—fervent, blind devotion to a belief or point of view, 28
Chicana women, 33
Chicano, 41
Child-centered values, 24

Church-centered approach to religion, 83, 85
Churches
    and government, 87
    tax-free status, 87
Civil Rights Act, 91
Class-conflict theory of racism, 46
Cloward, Richard S., 78
Cohen, Albert, 78
Common school, 90
Commoner, Barry, 111
Communist Party of the United States, 127
Complex societies—highly industrialized and urbanized societies.
Conflict, functions of, 17
Consciousness levels, 37
Conservatives, 126
Conspicuous consumption—consuming products for the purpose of gaining status, 113
Contact, role in reducing prejudice, 45
Control theory of delinquency, 78
Cooley, Charles Horton, 107
Coser, Lewis, 17
Countercultures, defined, 9
Countervailing power, defined, 121
Crime
    biological theories, 74
    chromosomal theory, 75
    civil disobedience, 69
    constitutional inferiority, 74
    felonies, 68
    Judeo-Christian law, 68
    misdemeanors, 68
    organized crime, 69–70
    personality traits, 75
    against persons, 67
    premeditated crime, 68
    against property, 67
    psychological theories, 75
    psychopathic crime, 69
    rural-urban rates, 72
    situational crime, 69
    sociological theories, 76
    white-collar crime, 69

Glossary/Index

Cultural integration—the extent that values, norms, and roles are integrated in the social organization of society, 9
Cultural lag—the tendency for social change to lag behind technological change in a society, 11
Cultural pluralism, defined, 50
Culture, defined, 8
Culture of poverty, 59

D

Deferred gratification, defined, 49, 59
Delinquent subcultures, 78
Demographic transition, defined, 98–99
Deschooling society, 91
Deviance, defined, 19, 60
    learning deviance, 61
    situational deviance, 19
    structural deviance, 19
Deviant careers, 62
Deviation
    primary, 61–62
    secondary, 61–62
Dewey, John, 90
Differential association, defined, 60, 76
Disorganization (described), 11
Division of labor—the separation of tasks into several different parts, whereby people specialize in the performance of each task, 10
Divorce, 25–26
Durkheim, Émile, 76

E

Ecological laws of nature, 111
Educational opportunity, 91
Educational philosophy
    early American, 89
    eclecticism, 90
    elitism, 89
    pragmatism, 89
Equalitarian—the belief in equality among persons, 45
Equalitarian rule—rule by parties of equal power, 29
Ethical neutrality—seeking scientific truth regardless of whom it pleases or what values it serves, 6–7
Expectations—basic comforts and standards for behavior that people expect to have, 113
Expressive roles, defined, 29

F

Familism, defined, 23
Family
    extended, 22
    frontier family, 22
    modern family, 23–24
    traditional family, 22–23
Family-centered values, 22–24
Fecundity, defined, 95
Fertility, defined, 95
Flacks, Richard, 38
Folkways, defined, 9
Freud, Sigmund, 30, 75
Fuller, Richard C., and Myers, Richard R., 5
Future Shock, 12

G

Galbraith, John Kenneth, 54
Gemeinschaft, defined, 104
Generation gap between youth and adults, 35
Gesellschaft, defined, 104
Goals-means theory of crime, 76

H

Harrington, Michael, 53
Heterogeneous—possessing a wide variety of characteristics, diverse.
Holtzman, Abraham, 118
Homogeneous—possessing similar characteristics, all alike.
Homosexuality, 65
Hypothesis, defined, 6

I

Illich, Ivan, 91
Indian, 48, 51
    women, 33
Individual-centered approach to religion, 83
Individualism—the beliefs that stress personal autonomy and freedom, 4
Industrialization—the process of an agricultural society becoming industrialized, 10
Inflation, 57
In-group—the group of which the person is a member, as opposed to out-groups, which are all groups of which the person is not a member, 43

Glossary/Index 153

Institutions, defined, 9
Instrumental roles, 29
Integration (societal or cultural)–the way norms, values, and roles of a culture are organized and interrelated, 11
    racial, defined, 50, 52
Invisible poor, 54
IQ and crime, 75
Isolationism, defined, 50

J

Jeffersonian doctrine, 124
Jesus cults, 85
John Birch Society, 127
Juvenile delinquency, 78

K–L

King, Martin Luther, 52
Labeling–the process through which characteristics are assigned to a person. They may be correctly or incorrectly assigned, 20, 43, 61–62
Laws, defined, 9, 67
Lazarsfeld, Paul, 45
Learning theory, 60
    and deviance, 61–62
Leftist groups, 127
    New Left, 127
    Old Left, 127
Lemert, Edwin M., 61
Lerner and Lowe, 28
Lewis, Oscar, 59
Liberals, 127
Lombroso, Cesare, 74
Luther, Martin, 83
Lutheran doctrine, 83
Lutheran movement, 83

M

Mafia, 70
Magic, defined, 81
Majority groups–a category of people who possess an advantaged position of power or size, 41
Malinowski, Bronislaw, 85
Malthus, Sir Thomas, 97
Marx, Karl, 10, 17
Mead, Margaret, 35

Merton, Robert K., 76
Militant nationalism, defined, 51
Mills, C. Wright, 2, 19, 121
Minority group–a category of people who are in a disadvantaged position of power, wealth, or size in society, 41
Minutemen, 127
Modernization–the process of adopting new ideas and technology; the values which support their adoption, 10–11
Monoculture, 110
Monogamy–marriage to one spouse only, as opposed to polygamy, which is marriage to several spouses at the same time.
Mores, defined, 9
Mormon Church, 87
Moynihan, Daniel P., 38
Myrdal, Gunnar, 47

N

Norms–expected standards for behavior, 8
    behavioral norms, the actual norms people follow, 8
    ideal norms, idealized standards that are not always followed, 8
    and social problems, 9

O

Objectivity–a realistic and unbiased view of reality, 5, 7
Observability–the extent to which one's behavior is observable to others, 72, 107
Ogburn, William F., 11
Organized crime, 69–70
Out-group–all groups of which the person is not a member.

P

Park, Robert, 17
Patriarchal authority, defined, 22
Patriarchal rule, 29
Permissiveness–to tolerate a wide range of behavior and beliefs without imposing negative sanctions, 11
Personal deviation (conceptual approach to social problems), 19

Personal disorganization—when a person possesses conflicting purposes and goals; a state of confusion and uncertainty, 11–12

Planned obsolescence—designing products to have a limited life, rather than being repairable and durable, 11, 113

Pluralism, defined, 50, 52
    cultural pluralism, 50
    religious pluralism, 84
    structural pluralism, 50

Political groups, 126
    conservative, 126
    leftist groups, 126
    liberals, 127
    rightist groups, 126

Population pyramids, 96–97

Pornography, 66

Positive checks on population growth, 97

Poverty lifestyles, 59

Power, defined, 17

Power group—a group of people who possess superior economic or political power, or social prestige, 41

Power groups, 120
    countervailing power groups, 121
    elitist power groups, 121
    pluralist power groups, 121

Prejudice—a judgment of a person according to some presumed group characteristic, 42–46

Prejudiced personality, 44

Pressure groups, defined, 118
    functions of, 118–19

Preventive checks on population growth, 98

Preventive detention, 125

Primary groups, defined, 107

Protestant ethic, 77, 83

Protestant values, 83

Psychoanalytic theories of crime, 75

Punishment, effectiveness of, 79

R

Racial groups, defined, 41

Radial sociologists, 7

Reformation, 83

Reich, Charles, 36–39

Reiss, Ira L., 26, 36, 101

Religion
    charismatics, 85
    church and state, 86–87
    contingency, defined, 81
    cults, 85
    educational function, 82
    fragmentation of, 85
    functions of, 81–82
    fundamentalists, 84–85
    and government, 87
    modernists, 84–85
    political and moral leadership, 82
    powerlessness, defined, 81
    scarcity function, defined, 81
    secularism, 86
    social functions, 81
    social gospel, 85

Retreatism, defined, 50

Rogers, Will, 42

Role—the expected behavior for a person who holds a particular status, 9

Roman Catholic Church, 83–84

S

Schlesinger, Arthur, 121

Schur, Alan, 19

Scientific method, defined, 6

Scopes Trial, 86

Sexual deviation, 64

Sheldon, William, 74

Sherif, Muzafer, 46

Situational ethics—the view that the proper ethics are dependent upon the nature of the situation, as opposed to absolute standards of propriety, 82

Small, Albion, 17

Social change, defined, 4, 9–11
    cultural change, 4
    processes of change, 10
    technological change, 4

Social class, defined, 10

Social conflict (conceptual approach for social problems), 17

Social control, defined, 14

Social Darwinism, defined, 56

Social disorganization—when the different elements of society do not function properly; when people are uncertain as to what is occurring in society, 11–13

Social distance, defined, 42, 45

Social organization, defined, 13, 60

Social pathology, 6, 13

Social problems
    defined, 2
    permanency of, 2

public awareness of, 2
science of, 6
selection of, 4
social aspects of, 2
and social change, 4
stages of, 5

Society, defined, 8

Special interest groups, defined, 117

Specialization—the exclusive performance of a single task, 10

Status, defined, 9
achieved, 9
ascribed, 9

Stereotype, defined, 42–43

Stratification—a ranking of people into status levels according to some criteria of superiority or inferiority.

Strip-cities, 105

Structural pluralism, defined, 50

Students For A Democratic Society (SDS), 127

Subcultural deviance, defined, 20, 77

Subcultural theories of crime, 77

Subculture, defined, 9

Subjectivity—a view of reality that is biased toward personal preferences and interests, 5

Sumner, William Graham, 3, 9, 67

Superordinate goals—all encompassing or major goals held by people collectively, 46

Sutherland, Edwin, 76

T–U

Technological unemployment, 56

Technology—the use of technical or scientific knowledge, 10

Theory, defined, 6

Tocqueville, Alexis de, 116

Toffler, Alvin, 12

Trobriand Islanders, 81

Urbanization—the process of development of large urban communities, 10–11, 103

V–W

Value—a cherished belief or principle.

Value commitment, 7

Value-conflict (conceptual approach for social problems), 15, 17

Value-free—to not advocate any particular value position, 6–7, 13

Value judgment—a judgment that favors a particular value position, 15

Veblen, Thorstein, 113

Vested interest groups, 118–19
functions of, 118–19

Vested interests, defined, 117

Victimless crime, 70

Weber, Max, 84

Women's liberation movement, 28–33